D1535059

The Crisis of Growth Politics:

Cleveland,
Kucinich,
and the
Challenge of
Urban
Populism

The Crisis of Growth Politics:

Cleveland, Kucinich, and the Challenge of Urban Populism

Todd Swanstrom

Temple University Press
PHILADELPHIA

Temple University Press, Philadelphia 19122
© 1985 by Temple University. All rights reserved
Published 1985
Printed in the United States of America

Library of Congress Cataloging in Publication Data

Swanstrom, Todd.
  The crisis of growth politics.

  Revision of thesis (Ph.D.)—Princeton University, 1981.
  Includes index.
  1. Cleveland (Ohio)—Politics and government.
2. Cleveland (Ohio)—Economic policy.   3. Kucinich,
Dennis J., 1946–   .   4. Business and politics—Ohio—
Cleveland.   I. Title.
JS768.S95   1985   320.8′09771′32   84-16369
ISBN 0-87722-366-1

This is the first great thing to be kept in mind—that the battle is not against persons, but against unnatural conditions, against a wrong social order!

Tom Johnson
Mayor of Cleveland (1901–1909)

To Jessica
For a Better Future

Contents

Tables, Figures, and Illustrations

Tables

Figures

Illustrations

Preface

Scholarly works are rarely written because some disinterested academic decides that a topic requires analysis. The reasons are usually much more pragmatic, more pressing.

In winter 1978–1979, I was living in New York City. My status was, as they say, ABD (All But Dissertation). Having passed the qualifying exams to write a Ph.D. dissertation in politics at Princeton University in 1975, I had been groping about ever since to find a suitable topic. Beginning to despair of ever getting my degree, one day I ran into an old friend from Princeton, who suggested that we collaborate on an article about urban politics. I agreed. It soon became clear that we were both intrigued by a young politician from Cleveland who was just beginning to get national media attention. At that time, Dennis Kucinich (pronounced Koo-SIN-itch) had been mayor for only a year, but he had already survived a narrow recall election and engaged in a noisy confrontation with Cleveland banks over the city's default. *Enfant terrible*, the media labeled him, Dennis the Menace, scourge of the Establishment and ruin of Cleveland. My friend and I were skeptical. Some of the sins Kucinich was charged with—killing special tax subsidies for big business and fighting to keep the city-owned electrical utility—seemed more like virtues to us. We decided to look into the matter.

The resulting article, "A Tale of Two Cities" (*Nation*, March 24, 1979), compared Kucinich to New York's Mayor Koch—to the detriment of the latter. I look back on the article now with mixed feelings. Never having visited Cleveland, our treatment of Kucinich's political movement was necessarily shallow. We painted him in rosy colors as an unambiguous defender of democracy. Later, close-up, I saw that his commitment to democratic values was far more spotted than it appeared from afar. Nevertheless, I remain convinced that our positive assessment of Kucinich's economic stands, in contrast to Koch's, was fundamentally correct. Unlike Koch, Kucinich opposed using special tax subsidies to attract corporate investment in downtown office buildings and fought to prevent Cleveland's public sector, albeit much smaller than New York's, from shrinking further by refusing to sell the municipal light plant to the area's private utility.

It soon dawned on me that here was a suitable topic for my dissertation. I rushed off a letter to Mayor Kucinich in May 1979 asking for a job in his administration so that I could see things firsthand. A few days later I got a phone call from Bob Weissman, Kucinich's right-hand man, offering me a position. My wife's jaw dropped as I immediately accepted. (Lesson 1: always tell your wife when you apply for a job in Cleveland, especially if you don't live there at the time.)

When I arrived in Cleveland in May 1979, the Kucinich administration was in a state of seige. Public opinion was polarized to a degree rarely seen in American politics. I did not consider myself naïve, yet I remained shocked for months by the local media's biased attacks on Kucinich. The two daily newspapers painted the administration, inaccurately, as in a state of utter chaos and collapse. Every calamity that befell Cleveland was blamed on Kucinich. Strangely enough, Kucinich and his top aides seemed to thrive on this seige atmosphere. The second day I was in Cleveland, Weissman tossed a copy of the evening paper across his city hall desk at me. "Read this," he said, pointing to one article. The headlines read: "Least popular of politicians is Weissman." I was nonplussed. Weissman only smiled. In fact, the Kucinich administration contributed to the polarization of opinion by treating anyone who wasn't 100 percent with them as an enemy. "Confrontation politics," Weissman called it, and it was the key to their electoral success, he said.

A few months after arriving in Cleveland, I began working in the Kucinich campaign organization in the evenings and on weekends. It was an extraordinary operation, part machine, part crusade. Composed almost entirely of patronage city workers, it was small, with only 150 out of about 10,000 city employees participating. There were no geographically based ward leaders or precinct captains. Everybody did the same thing: door-to-door canvassing with leaflets. It was less a machine and more an alternative media, a direct and personal means of communication between Kucinich and the voters. While remarkably efficient, the Kucinich organization was hardly democratic; it was run in a top-down fashion with almost no effort to discuss issues. Countless hours spent walking through Cleveland's neighborhoods and knocking on doors, however, gave me invaluable insight into Kucinich's grassroots support—and opposition.

My first job in city government was with the CETA federal jobs training and employment program. After a few months, I transferred to the Department of Community Development, the city's most political department, which administered the federal Community Development Block Grant. I worked there as a program evaluator through the last few months of the Kucinich administration and stayed on through most of the first term of Kucinich's successor, George Voinovich, as a neighborhood planner and policy analyst. My work did not let me observe the inner sanctums of the mayor's office, but it did allow me to view firsthand the effect of Kucinich's urban populism on the employees and programs of city government.

I was impressed with the efficiency of the Kucinich campaign, but I was not impressed with the efficiency of city government. So much energy was focused on the reelection effort that some of us jokingly referred to the administration as a campaign organization that, unfortunately, had to run a government in its spare time. I was also disappointed to learn that few Kucinich activists had anything in the way of political ideology. Their attachment was not to urban populism but to "Dennis." (Everyone in Cleveland called the mayor by his first name; for supporters it was a term of endearment, for opponents a term of derision.) Most Kucinich appointees were young, intelligent, well-intentioned, scrupulously honest, and utterly without experience or expertise in government.

There was little positive policy direction during Kucinich's hectic two-year term. The most visible issues were negative: stop the sale of Muny Light, end tax abatements for downtown. The day-to-day operations of city government remained pretty much the same as they had been before. The main difference was a sincere effort to stop corruption and a "get tough" management style that attempted to cut costs at every corner. Notwithstanding the inertia of city government, the hostility of the economic dominants—the large banks and corporations—was unremitting. It reached the point, according to Kucinich, that the banks pushed the city into default for "political" reasons—to punish Kucinich for attacking big business and refusing to sell Muny Light to the private utility. (The question of whether default was political is taken up in Chapter 7.)

The central issue raised by Kucinich's experiment in urban populism, I soon realized, was the extent of power exerted by large corporations, not through traditional lobbying techniques but through their control over investment. Many of us began to wonder: what would happen if a populist government actually went on the offensive, expanding Muny Light and buying up its private competitor or imposing steep taxes on speculative gains in downtown real estate? How much room is there for reform? We soon saw that this question could not be separated from an analysis of internal political factors—the electoral system, the structure of city government, and the role of interest groups. It was on this set of issues, what I call "growth politics," that I wrote my Ph.D. dissertation, finally completed in May 1981. This book is a revised version.

I would like to acknowledge the help of two friends, Bob Kerstein and Steve Esquith, who read and criticized early drafts, only dimly related to this manuscript. Without their encouragement the entire project might never have gotten off the ground. Ron Berkman also gave me a crucial early push. Little did we know where our modest effort would lead. Members of a study group in New York City (Audrey, Mary Jo, Bob, Neil, Marc, John, Karen, Fran, and Sarah) motivated me to study things political at an otherwise discouraging time.

I would like to thank the Kucinich administration for giving me the chance to experience a great, if flawed, adventure. I would like to thank the Voinovich administration for not firing me because I was a Kucinich appointee. Two distinguished professors at Princeton, Sheldon Wolin and Duane Lockard, showed unusual forbearance in taking on a long-lost graduate student. Their wise criticisms and encouragement were invaluable. The following individuals read all or parts of the manuscript and provided valuable responses: Dick Butsch, Sandy Buchanan, Michael Danielson, Susan Fainstein, Craig Glazer, Ed Kelly, John Logan, Bruce Miroff, Harvey Molotch, Paul Ryder, Bill Tabb, Bill Whitney, John Wilbur, Jerry Webman, Jay Westbrook, and Sharon Zukin. Jennifer French, my production editor at Temple, worked tirelessly to deal with the myriad details of bringing the project to completion. Finally, Murdoch Matthew, my copyeditor, deserves thanks for mercilessly eliminating the academic pretensions in my writing style.

Many people in Cleveland, too many to mention, have my gratitude for guiding me through the labyrinthine pathways of Cleveland politics. Two, however, deserve special recognition. Everyone reads, but few acknowledge, Roldo Bartimole's *Point of View*, a one man muckraking operation that has a virtual monopoly on tweaking the noses of Cleveland's establishment. Past issues, going all the way back to 1968, gave me a rare glimpse into the hidden history of Cleveland politics. Norm

Krumholz, former director of Cleveland's City Planning Commission, is better known nationwide, as a founder of equity planning, than he is in his hometown. Nevertheless, Krumholz, and his protégés at the City Planning Commission, produced a series of reports on Cleveland as notable for their clarity and forthrightness as for their unswerving advocacy of neighborhood interests. They were a prime source of analysis and information for me.

I would also like to thank John Cosari for generously allowing me to use his considerable collection of clippings on Kucinich and Cleveland politics. A number of people agreed to be interviewed or supplied clippings and documents. I cannot thank them all here, but I greatly appreciate their efforts.

Thanks, as well, to Ruth Harris, Addie Napolitano, Maxine Morman, and Suzanne Hagen, for fairly flawless typing.

Last, but not least, I wish to thank Mary Jo Long, without whose help the whole project would have been impossible.

The Crisis of Growth Politics:

Cleveland,
Kucinich,
and the
Challenge of
Urban
Populism

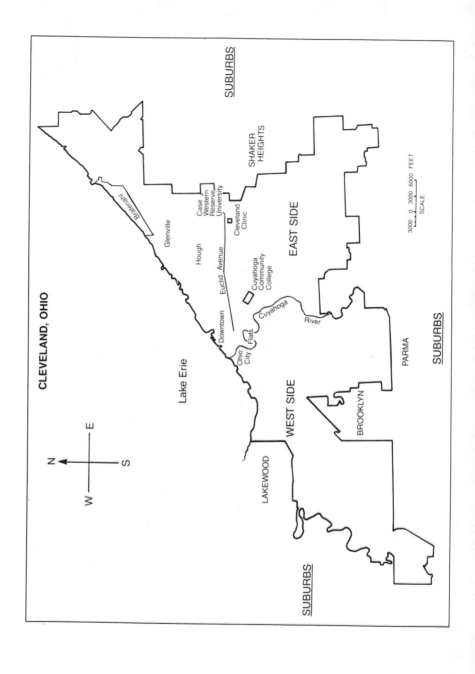

CLEVELAND, OHIO

Introduction

Those are the rules and I'm going by the goddamn rules.
This suicidal outthrust competition among the states has got
to stop but until it does, I mean to compete. It's too bad we
have a system where dog eats dog and the devil takes the
hindmost. But I'm tired of taking the hindmost.[1]

Coleman Young
Mayor of Detroit

In his younger days Coleman Young, Detroit's first black mayor,
was a labor organizer and Marxist radical, blacklisted by the auto
companies and the United Automobile Workers (UAW) union for his
communist leanings. After he was elected mayor in 1973, however,
Young became better known for giving generous incentives to large
corporations to invest in Detroit. Young has supported extensive tax
abatements for downtown development, including his pride and joy:
the $350 million Renaissance Center. Recently, Detroit used its powers
of eminent domain to clear 465 acres of a working class neighborhood,
Poletown, to make way for a new General Motors Cadillac plant. When
all is finished, the loans, grants, federal monies, and tax incentives that
the city will pour into this project will total about $300 million. As the
quotation above illustrates, Young justifies these subsidies to big business on the ground that mayors simply have no choice but to enter the
investment competition between cities and states; it's compete or die.
This "logic" of growth politics is what I propose to examine in this
book.

Varieties of Growth Politics

Growth politics can be defined, simply, as the effort by governments
to enhance the economic attractiveness of their locality, to increase
the intensity of land use by enticing mobile wealth to enter their

3

boundaries.² Growth politics varies according to the type of mobile wealth pursued. In the nineteenth century, railroads were the key to economic expansion, and cities competed viciously for rail connections. Next came highways, which radically decentralized economic activity, contributing to rapid growth in suburbia and the Sunbelt, with older central cities wracked by debilitating disinvestment and middle-class flight.

Today, however, central cities are benefiting from a new centralization of economic activity: segments of the burgeoning service sector, knowledge intensive services associated with high level corporate management and control functions, are concentrating in central business districts—largely because of the economies of agglomeration associated with the availability of specialized business services, such as accounting and advertising, in downtowns. This book is a case study of one city, Cleveland, Ohio, and the stresses and strains associated with the transition from an industrial to a service sector growth strategy. I begin by examining some varieties of growth politics in transitional cities. These practical manifestations of growth politics have their counterparts in theories of urban politics, theories that I critically examine in Chapter 1.

Growth politics varies not only by the type of growth but also by the role assigned to government. In the United States, there are basically two varieties of growth politics: conservative and liberal. In the conservative varient, the planning and execution of growth are left primarily to the private sector; the main function of government is to stand out of the way of private accumulation by keeping taxes low and, if necessary, enacting special incentives for investors. In the liberal varient of growth politics, the public sector is given a more active role, both in planning economic development and in ameliorating the condition of those left behind by growth. In a sense, liberal politics play both sides of the street: growth policies, which have a regressive effect on income distribution, provide special incentives for wealthy investors to expand the economy, while redistributive policies siphon off a portion of the growth dividend through taxes to pay for social welfare programs benefiting the less fortunate.

In the 1960s and early 1970s, liberal activist mayors, like Cavanagh of Detroit, Lindsay of New York, and Stokes of Cleveland, prevailed. Aided by massive infusions of federal funds, liberal mayors held out the hope, in classic pluralist fashion, that all major groups in the city could get a piece of the action. Federal programs, like urban renewal, provided mayors with the resources to subsidize service sector expansion, especially hospitals, universities, and corporate offices. At the same time, with the help of Johnson's War on Poverty, liberal mayors were determined advocates of a more interventionist government role in attacking the problems of urban poverty and blight.

Not surprisingly, liberal growth politics reached its fullest potential in New York City. From LaGuardia to Lindsay, New York City built a local welfare state unsurpassed in the United States: the excellent City University, tuition-free; an extensive municipal hospital system, providing free care for those who could not afford to pay; welfare and medicaid payments richly supplemented by the city; pension and retirement benefits for city workers well beyond those of most municipal employees; and the largest system of mass transit in the country.

Just as it led the way in liberal growth politics (some would argue, precisely because it led the way), New York City has also led the recent trend toward conservative growth politics. The 1975 fiscal crisis woke New Yorkers suddenly, like a bucket of cold water in the face, from their dream of a local redistributive welfare state. There simply was not enough money to pay for the dream anymore. Cutbacks became the order of the day. New York City, as Ken Auletta once put it, was liberalism's Vietnam.[3]

In retrospect, it can be seen that the path of retrenchment trod by New York City was the harbinger of a national trend toward Reagan's supply side politics (although, it should be pointed out, the movement to the supply side really began during the administration of "liberal" Jimmy Carter). The logic of conservative growth politics at the local level is the same as supply side economics at the national level: greater inequalities must be tolerated, in the short run, in order to provide incentives for discretionary wealth to invest and expand the economic pie, with the benefits trickling down to help everyone in the long run. A kind of local Laffer Curve is postulated: by lowering taxes on mobile wealth, cities will eventually increase tax revenues through an expanding tax base. The main difference between local growth politics and supply side economics is that the former is not designed to draw wealth out of consumption and unproductive sumps but to entice economic activity to enter a city's boundaries. Interestingly, the movement to the supply side took place first at the local level, where aging northeastern cities suffered economic stagnation, severe balance of payments deficits, and fiscal crisis long before the federal government did.

New York's Ed Koch is a bold representative of this neo-conservative shift in urban governance. As mayor, Koch has devised a two-pronged strategy for urban revival that can be described very succinctly: incentives for the rich and disincentives for the poor. The former was announced in 1978 as the city's "New Urban Partnership" with business in a forty-six page spread in *Business Week*.[4] Designed by New York's business community, the package of incentives included reduction of the corporate tax rate and commercial rent tax, lowering and capping of real property taxes, tax credits for the purchase of machinery, tax exempt industrial bonds, and a generous program of tax abatements to stimulate construction. The program has, indeed, delivered generous benefits to business. Looking only at tax abatement for commercial and industrial developers, as of 1981, New York City had already committed more than one half billion dollars of past and future property tax revenues.[5]

There is another side, however, to Koch's strategy. Along with incentives for those with money have come disincentives for those without. For decades New York City, with the highest welfare payments in the nation, was a haven for the poor. No more. Koch tells why: "Under Lindsay, they brought us to bankruptcy by going out and telling people to come in—'C'mon, get on the welfare rolls, you don't even have to file an affidavit.' No, I don't do that."[6] "Aggressive" enforcement of rules trimmed more than 160,000 off the city's welfare rolls (from a peak of 894,000 in 1972); at the same time, welfare payments have lagged far behind the cost of living.[7] Koch's efforts to balance the budget have forced sacrifices on many people, especially those dependent on public services. The city's workforce has been cut by more than 60,000; tuition has been imposed at the City University (itself the victim of many cuts); a number of municipal hospitals have been closed; the subway fare has skyrocketed. For many New Yorkers, especially minorities and the poor, the quality of life has declined.

Koch, however, does not see his policies as anti-poor—or even a matter of political choice. To him, they are nothing but "common sense" (which was his reelection campaign slogan in 1981). "Anybody who's mayor today," Koch asserts, "must be a fiscal conservative."[8] Indeed, the logic of conservative growth politics seems ineluctable: without a healthy tax base, cities cannot fund social services (whether for the poor or anybody else) and they will be denied access to badly needed credit on the national bond market; the local tax base will never revive without private investment; the private sector will not invest in cities without a balanced budget and special incentives. Q.E.D.: cities must pare social services in order to balance the budget and provide special incentives to private investors. Mayors who conform to this logic illustrate Irving Kristol's end-of-ideology definition of a neo-conservative: "a liberal who has been mugged by reality."

Pragmatic Illusions and the Uses of Urban Populism

The goal of this book is to dispel the pragmatic illusion of growth politics: that its policies are nothing but a rational technocratic response to economic imperatives.[9] There is a great deal more politics hidden at the core of these economic growth issues than is commonly believed. Cleveland, where the costs of economic transition have been about as great as anywhere in the nation, is a city where the political issues have been pushed painfully to the surface. Dennis Kucinich, and his peculiar brand of urban populism (which defies labeling as either liberal or conservative), grew up on the soil of this growth crisis. Incomplete as it is, urban populism, by challenging conventional wisdom, makes us more aware of the value laden issues, the political choices, at the heart of the urban development process.

Growing up in the ethnic ghettos on the edges of the steel mills in Cleveland's "flats," Kucinich knew real poverty. A skilled rhetorician, Kucinich gave political expression to the class resentments and frustrations felt by inner-city ethnics stuck in a declining industrial economy, where they were excluded from the benefits of both suburbanization and the growth of white-collar employment downtown. To them, the growing collaboration between the public and private sectors, brought on by the economic crisis, smacked of political corruption. Kucinich took advantage of these feelings with a confrontational political style, resembling, in the words of one historian describing Huey Long, a political buzz saw, ripping into everyone and everything in his path.[10]

Kucinich's urban populism can be thought of as growth politics turned inside out. Growth politics always involves, as we have noted, some sort of trade-off between equity and efficiency, equality and growth. More inequality, it is maintained, is necessary to create more growth through incentives for those who control discretionary wealth. According to Kucinich, the politics of growth no longer works: the cost of enticing corporations to invest downtown through tax abatement, for example, is greater than the benefits that finally "trickle down" to residents of inner city neighborhoods. The limited resources of city government, he maintained, should be distributed to the people in the neighborhoods in the form of public works and basic services. Equality should be stressed over growth.

As mayor, Kucinich went beyond populist rhetoric, engaging in a series of confrontations with Cleveland's corporate community that demonstrated his belief that what was good for business was not necessarily good for the city. In one controversial move, Kucinich returned $41 million to the federal government that had been granted Cleveland for a downtown People Mover (a 2.2-mile elevated mass transit loop around downtown) calling it a "contemptuous substitute" for the real transit needs of Clevelanders. Later, Kucinich killed a deal with Republic Steel to build a $20 million dock to handle 1,000-foot ore boats, charging the company with seeking to gain a gigantic public subsidy, totaling $153.5 million over the life of the agreement, that would create few jobs. Over the opposition of City Council, Kucinich also succeeded in killing the burgeoning tax abatement program in Cleveland. His argument that tax abatement did not promote growth but only distributed windfall profits to downtown developers is examined in Chapter 6.

Kucinich's most celebrated corporate confrontation, however, occurred over Cleveland's default, the first default by a major city since the Depression.[11] Default was the culmination of a year of conflict with local banks and the Cleveland Electric Illuminating Company (CEI), the area's private utility. Nine days after Kucinich took office, CEI filed liens on city land and property to recover a disputed $30 million debt from Muny Light, Cleveland's public utility. Meanwhile, the city was pursuing a massive $150 million antitrust suit against CEI for damages to Muny. In subsequent months, local banks, with close ties to CEI, repeatedly refused to rollover short term notes, forcing Kucinich to dip into scarce cash reserves. Tension with the banks mounted. At one point, Kucinich vowed to lead "a movement to severely hamper normal business operations of area banks if they do not begin to respond to the needs of city residents."[12] Forced to pay the CEI debt to keep the antitrust suit alive, Kucinich had no cash to pay the $14 million in notes that came due on December 15, 1978. Kucinich claims that Brock Weir of Cleveland Trust offered to rollover the notes and raise an additional $50 million for the city if only Kucinich would sell Muny Light to CEI. The pragmatic thing to do would have been to sell a money losing city operation; for Kucinich, however, Muny Light was not a technical matter of profit and loss but a political issue. With investment being withheld for political reasons, according to Kucinich, selling Muny

Light would have been giving in to a form of municipal blackmail. (The claims and counterclaims in default are examined in Chapter 7.)

Does Kucinich's urban populism represent a viable alternative to conservative growth politics? Certainly the impression given in the mass media is that Kucinich almost ruined Cleveland and that under his successor Cleveland has become "Comeback City." In my view, this is largely political puffery, and I say why in the Afterword. Reports of Cleveland's demise under Kucinich were greatly exaggerated; and, media boosterism to the contrary notwithstanding, Cleveland's economic decline, despite the best efforts of the new mayor, continues. While Kucinich's opposition to certain policies, such as selling valuable city assets and bidding away the tax base to lure investors, does represent a stinging critique of conservative growth politics, it does not constitute an alternative program for combatting Cleveland's economic dependency. Vague talk about "economic democracy" was never translated into a positive program. (Kucinich's inability to develop a positive program is exemplified in his handling of the federal Community Development Block Grant, discussed in Chapter 8.)

Just as important as Kucinich's lack of an economic program, however, was his lack of a political program. Kucinich rose to political power by making a complete end run around the established political parties and interest groups, appealing directly to the voters on the basis of their economic deprivation and political alienation. Kucinich's go-it-alone approach brought him to power with few political debts, free to pursue his populist instincts. At the same time, it isolated him from the established interests inside and outside government. Kucinich put together an effective campaign organization, outside the political parties, but it had little effect on other elected officials. As a result, Kucinich could count on few votes in City Council. He was relatively powerless, even in his own bureaucracy. When Kucinich ordered the police to conduct special foot patrols in the public housing estates, they refused, precipitating the first police strike in the city's history. His inability to play coalition politics even resulted in conflict with neighborhood groups, his natural allies. Kucinich's confrontational political style was a formula for political paralysis. In short, even if Kucinich had developed an economic program, his political isolation would have prevented him from enacting it.

Dennis Kucinich, in my view, was not the doctor coming to save a troubled city as his fervent supporters believed; nor was he the illness itself as many of his opponents maintained. He represented, rather, the thermometer, a gauge of the fever of frustration, both economic and political, gripping many older American cities. In chemistry, the presence of certain elements can be verified only by heating the solution and observing the reaction; it may be the same in politics. With the dominant forces in New York City coalescing around a public-private partnership to "Save the City," conservative growth politics appeared to be the only possible course, a pragmatic response to economic imperatives. In Cleveland, on the other hand, the public and private sectors split apart in noisy confrontation during the fiscal crisis of 1978–79. Kucinich's "irrational" actions forced key economic actors, accustomed to operating behind the scenes, to take visible public stands. The heated opposition to the consensus politics of growth in Cleveland, in short, provides a rare opportunity to observe, flushed into public view, the political conflicts inherent in growth politics.

1

The Political Economy of Urban Growth

If a man's major life work is banking, the pluralist presumes he will spend his time at the bank, and not in manipulating community decisions.[1]

Nelson Polsby

The distinction between power and exchange, between politics and markets, is decisive in modern social science. Around this distinction have grown the academic disciplines of political science and economics—power, of course, being the object of political science, exchange the object of economic science. While in logic the distinction is clear and unambiguous, in reality, power relations and exchange relations intermingle in all sorts of curious ways. This creates problems for any method of inquiry that assumes a neat and clean separation between the two.

Milton Friedman has written a lucid account of the conceptual distinction between politics and markets. According to Friedman, since the outputs of government are relatively indivisible "public goods," power must, by necessity, be exercised. Citizens cannot get precisely the amount they want in highways or national defense; some are forced to conform to the will of others. "The characteristic feature or action through political channels," writes Friedman, "is that it tends to require or enforce substantial conformity."[2] This is true even in a democracy, where the minority is forced to conform to the will of the majority.

11

Market exchange, at least in theory, coordinates economic activity without requiring individuals to conform to the will of others. Owing to the divisible nature of private goods (commodities), consumers can vote for, and get, the type and amount they want, without conforming to a group decision. The result, in Friedman's words, is "unanimity without conformity."[3] This holds, however, only if the exchanges are "bilaterally voluntary and informed." Consumers must know what they want and be able to pursue those wants rationally in the marketplace. Individuals do not enter into an exchange unless they benefit from it; or, to say the same thing, everyone has an absolute veto over each exchange.

At one time, during the age of *laissez faire* in the nineteenth century, perhaps a hard and fast distinction between politics and markets made some sense; today it only makes nonsense. Market behavior is saturated by the actions of government; the actions of government are conditioned, at every step, by market pressures. My claim, however, is not just that the two spheres are related, but that, at root, they cannot even be understood apart from each other. The intention is to transcend the arid separation of economic and political science and revive, at least for urban politics, the classical discipline of political economy: the study of the systematic interaction between economic and political processes. The abstract methods of economic and political science, rooted in a neat conceptual separation between their objects of inquiry, must be replaced by a concrete method appropriate to the real object of inquiry, as messy and contradictory as it is. Before developing my positive approach, however, I want to examine how separating our thinking about power and exchange has limited our understanding of urban politics.

Pluralist and Market Theories of Urban Politics

Beginning in the 1950s, a spirited debate erupted over the nature of power in urban communities. Both sides agreed on the definition of power. Power was defined simply as "the achievement of intended effects," or "the ability to get other people to do something, even against their will." The goal of inquiry, then, was to discover the true distribution of power in a community. At the same time, there was widespread disagreement on how best to approach that goal and what the real distribution of power was. Led by Robert Dahl and his justly famous study of New Haven, *Who Governs?*, political scientists challenged the view, held by many sociologists, that power in urban communities is concentrated in the hands of a single socioeconomic elite.[4] Pluralists, as they came to be known, viewed power in local politics as dispersed and fluid: many different elites share in decision making; power relationships vary from one issue arena to the next; sources of power are many and varied, including wealth, prestige, organization, and skill. With its implication that every major interest group could get a piece of the pie, pluralism corresponded ideologically, and historically, to what I described in the Introduction as liberal growth politics.

In the 1970s, interest in pluralist studies, indeed in the entire community power debate, waned. It was not so much that the pluralists were proved wrong; in fact, most agreed that they had largely won the debate. In the process, however, the debate had been so narrowed that crucial issues of community power were excluded. Even if the pluralists were right, many scholars reasoned, so what? Repeatedly, pluralists were criticized for ignoring key issues. E. E. Schattschneider, for example, faulted interest group theorists for failing to examine the power involved in setting the agenda of politics, instead of studying who prevails on particular issues.[5] Thomas Anton censured pluralists for defining power narrowly as the actions of government.[6] A Polish Marxist even contended that pluralists could be right about power over government decision in the "particular" sense, but this did not necessarily affect the "sufficient condition" for "class domination" in general.[7] Finally, Bachrach and Baratz, perhaps the most influential critics of the scope of community power research, charged that pluralists ignored the "other" face of power, nondecision making: how the political process is limited to issues relatively unthreatening to dominant interests.[8]

The growing dissatisfaction with the scope of community power research arises particularly from its ignoring the effects of private economic decision making.[9] Clearly, economic decisions, such as whether to move a factory, have as much or more impact on a city than the decisions of government. From the moment in 1958, however, that Dahl defined the pluralist project as the study of "important political decisions," pluralists ignored private decision making.[10] Of course, pluralists studied with great care the influence of business interests on government through overt political pressure, such as lobbying techniques and campaign contributions. The effect of economic decisions on political power, however, was completely ignored. Focusing on proximate political relations, pluralists never critically examined the broader economic factors that shape these power relations, factors like economic growth and contraction, investment flows, changes in technology, and the availability of credit.[11]

Behind the pluralists ignoring of economic decision making lay the assumption (rarely made explicit and never examined critically) that the conceptual distinction between power and exchange was a reasonable approximation of the real world.[12] Power, the pluralists argued implicitly, does not exist in the private market. As the quote that leads off this chapter shows, pluralists assumed that bankers, as bankers, were not political actors. Private decision making, by its very nature, was not political; power relations could be understood apart from exchange relations.

It is not that pluralists saw economic factors as having no influence. They understood well the importance of the economic environment of cities; they simply did not see it as in the purview of political (power) analysis. The upshot was that, for the pluralists, the economic environment of cities became a kind of natural environment. The private market indeed constrains the actions of city government, but these constraints are impersonal, or objective, in nature—the result of changing tastes and technologies, not anyone's conscious decision. Just as we do not think of gravity as taking away our freedom because it keeps us from flying, pluralists did not view the economic environment of cities as a political constraint on action. Besides, pluralists essentially were saying, the economic pressures on cities still left plenty of space for the tug and pull of internal interest groups.

If the economic environment of cities can be seen as a natural environment, however, in the 1970s storms began to appear on the horizon. Compared with the halcyon days of the 1960s, the stagnation of the national economy and cutbacks in federal funding in the 1970s put greatly increased economic pressures on city governments. Fiscal crisis became the order of the day, at least for older central cities. The space for pluralist bargaining between interest groups seemed to shrink considerably as economic imperatives forced city governments into a period of austerity. Interest group bargaining gave way, as with New York City's Emergency Financial Control Board (EFCB), to rule by a financial elite in the name of fiscal responsibility. Economic conditions, it was felt, mandated cutbacks in redistributive social spending and increases in incentives for mobile wealth to expand the tax base. And, in the process, liberal growth mayors were replaced by neo-conservatives.

Not surprisingly, the changing economic environment of cities brought about a corresponding change in the way that academic researchers studied urban politics—part of a general shift in the intellectual climate due to the economic crisis. Whereas earlier, pluralism had been praised for allowing democratic access, now there was talk of "ungovernability," "overload," and the "democratic distemper"—and it was openly suggested that these problems stemmed from an "excess of democracy."[13] Increased interest in rational choice theories of politics went along with an increasingly common argument that governments, like private corporations, were subject to the strict discipline of the marketplace, which they ignored at their peril.[14] In national urban policymaking, this trend of thought was summed up by President Jimmy Carter's Commission for a National Agenda for the Eighties, known as the McGill Commission. Their final report, *Urban America in the Eighties*, argued that the decline of many American cities was the necessary byproduct of the transition from an industrial to a post-industrial economy. The federal government, therefore, should stop trying to stem urban decline, for this only has the effect of rooting individuals and businesses in inefficient locations. Policy should adapt to market imperatives, not *vice versa*.[15]

The trend toward market models of politics in the study of community power was brilliantly summed up in Paul Peterson's *City Limits*, winner of the 1982 Woodrow Wilson Foundation Award as the best book published in the United States on government, politics, or international affairs.[16] *Contra* the pluralists, Peterson argues that each city has an overall public interest that is more than the sum of the competing interests within its borders. The city's interest, according to Peterson, corresponds to the economic viability or attractiveness of the local economy, for in the long run all other values (art, leisure, government services) depend on the surpluses generated by the local economy.

More specifically, cities can be thought of as having a kind of exchange relation with mobile wealth (capital and labor, or residents). Public policies tend either to repel or to attract different kinds of mobile wealth. Simplifying Peterson's theory greatly, policies that make a city more attractive for residents or investors who generate more in local taxes than they take back in city services, are in the city's interest; conversely, policies that make a city less attractive for such residents, or which attract residents who absorb more in city services than they pay back in taxes, are against the city's interest.[17] Necessarily, this means that cities, insofar as they are acting in their own best interest, will not enact redistributive policies, for redistributive policies benefit precisely those residents, the poor, who do not enhance the local economy, who receive more in government benefits than they pay out in taxes.

One of the intriguing aspects of Peterson's theory is that, while it shifts attention to economic factors previously ignored by pluralists, the theory itself is perfectly consistent with pluralism. Peterson leaves room for pluralism by arguing that certain policy issues, such as whether to hire Italians, Irish, or blacks for patronage jobs, have little effect one way or the other on the attractiveness of the local economy. Hence, these "allocational" issues, as Peterson calls them, leave room for political discretion, the traditional arena of pluralist bargaining. On the other hand, policies that enhance the local economy, "developmental" policies, Peterson calls them, tend to be decided by a small business elite reflecting the natural tendency of citizens to defer to business expertise in promoting economic growth. The community power debate, then, boils down to the empirical question of which sphere is larger. Peterson argues, reflecting the temper of the times, that most policy questions in local government do, indeed, affect the economy; in the long run, therefore, elitism is the rule, pluralism the exception. While the book makes it clear that Peterson himself values redistributive policies, he believes those policies can be carried out only at the federal level; at the local level, his theory has undeniable neo-conservative implications.

Both pluralism and Peterson's market theory of urban politics are consistent with, indeed, they are premised on, a strict separation between power and exchange. Pluralism examines cities as arenas for the exercise of power, with autonomous interest groups vying for influence over policy.[18] Peterson's market theory deliberately ignores those internal power struggles, viewing cities, like private corporations, as essentially market entities, with rational policies dictated by market pressures. What Peterson has produced is not a theory of political economy but an economic theory of politics—what I call a "market theory" of urban politics.

Pluralism and market theory divide the world of urban politics essentially into two spheres. In the allocative sphere, where market pressures ease off, policy is governed relatively democratically by the jockeying of plural interest groups. In the developmental sphere, market pressures allow little political discretion and policy is governed by a small business elite, whose rule is legitimated by their technical expertise in promoting growth. (A third possible sphere, redistribution, is forced off the political agenda by the harm it would do to the local economy.) In short, pluralism and market theory are two sides of the same coin: one side marked power, the other marked exchange.

Urban politics, however, is not two sided; it is many sided. Peterson requires, for example, that the elite deciding developmental issues be, like Plato's philosopher king, totally disinterested, concerned only with the well-being of the city as a whole. (Curiously, for a rational choice theorist, Peterson can give no consistent account of their motivations, except under the highly improbable premise that the private interests of big business correspond to the interests of the city as a whole.) But what if selfish interest groups were involved in developmental issues, steering development to benefit themselves and not the city as a whole? On the other hand, what if business elites used their claim of technical expertise in economic growth to decide on issues that were essentially allocative in nature? What if the exchanges between mobile wealth and cities were not, in Friedman's words, "bilaterally voluntary and informed?" In short, what if the spheres of power and exchange intermingled in many curious ways? In that case, we would need not a political science or a science of economics but a theory of political economy—or what I call a theory of growth politics.

Growth Politics: Power in the Governmental Marketplace

At the same time as economic theories of politics have sprung up, there has also been a revival of interest in urban political economy. Work in this exciting new area stretches all the way from a critique of suburban fragmentation to a class theory of place to a neo-Marxist interpretation of urban political economy.[19] There is even a textbook now that takes the perspective of what I call "growth politics."[20] While this is not the place to lay out a full analysis of this burgeoning subfield, a few general comments are in order. The main thrust of much of the work, influenced by French structural Marxism, has been to understand particular urban political systems as the expressions of the deep underlying logic of international capitalist accumulation. Although I have learned much from this literature, it has serious flaws. Theoretical claims are pitched at such a high level of abstraction that it is often hard to imagine any empirical evidence to refute them. There is a tendency toward economic or technological determinism that devalues human agency or political action. Structural theory has little power to explain the obvious differences between political systems based on ethnicity, race, and culture. And, above all, peculiarly political factors, such as the structure of the political system, are given little theoretical weight.[21]

In this chapter, I want to draw some of the emerging understandings of urban political economy into a general approach that can validate the role of economic factors without falling into economic reductionism. In particular, I attempt to leaven the new urban political economy with the contributions of recent literature in political science. What results is not a full blown theory of urban political economy or a scientific methodology but a loose framework, or approach, for asking the right questions about any particular political system.

Ironically, the place to begin is with a pure market model of urban politics à la Peterson. Local governments can be viewed as being in an exchange relationship with mobile wealth. Each acts to protect its own selfish interests: mobile wealth seeks to find the most profitable location for investment; cities seek to maximize revenues over expenditures, to attract "profitable" investment that provides more in additional tax revenues than it takes back in added city services. In a pure market model, where wealth was perfectly mobile and governments made policy completely independently of each other, the result would be thoroughgoing: like corporations, governments would pursue wealth at the expense of other values, redistributive welfare policies would be suppressed, and the tax load would be shifted away from mobile wealth.

Let us pause, however, before jumping to any vulgar Marxist conclusions. The market model is only the starting point for analysis, not its conclusion. The approach here begins with the pure market model of local politics but then looks at deviations from it. Concepts of political economy, taken largely from welfare economics, are introduced and then applied to the governmental marketplace. Deviations from the market model come essentially in two forms. Most important is the extent to which power permeates the exchange, violating the presuppositions of a free market. When the exchanges between city governments and mobile wealth are not "bilaterally voluntary and informed," we enter the realm of growth politics. The mechanistic conception of power, however, with its view that proximate relations between individual and groups "cause" the behavior of others, is too narrow. It ignores the possibility that a system of rules could benefit an elite without requiring its day-to-day intervention. Power would be exercised, in that case, even though the effects could not be traced to the identifiable actions of an elite. Looking at who benefits and who loses can, indeed, tell us something about power. If outcomes can be attributed to bias in the rules of political economy, the establishment and reinforcement of those rules is a factor in political power.

What follows is a set of concepts for uncovering specific kinds of power or bias in the marketplace of governments. They are not intended to be mutually exclusive or exhaustive of growth politics. Also, no claim is made here that all market relations are political. Like any tools, these concepts must be used with care. In each case, it is an empirical question whether political power is at work.

Political Discretion

According to the market model, consumers vote with their dollars on what commodities they want produced and in what quantities. All other decisions—the production decisions delegated to corporations—are, in theory, open to little discretion. Corporations have no choice but to satisfy consumer demand in the most efficient manner possible; otherwise, they will be wiped out by their competition. In *Politics and Markets*, Charles Lindblom, a scholar of theretofore impeccable pluralist credentials, argues that the decisions delegated to corporate managers by consumers—"decisions instrumental to production: among others, on technology, organization of the work force, plant location, and executive prerogatives"—are, *contra* the market model, open to a great deal of discretion.[22] This is because there is often not one "least-cost" solution to the complex problems of production. There may be many least-cost solutions to choose from; executives may simply have to exercise judgment because certain factors are impossible to quantify; or the decision may depend on how factors are looked at, how they are weighted, and over what time period costs and revenues are estimated.[23] The result is that corporate decision makers exercise discretion in technological matters. Essentially, this is a form of political power, political power not held in check by consumer choice or the technical demands of efficiency.

This has some bearing on the study of urban politics. Traditional accounts of the decline of the older industrial cities of the Northeast rely heavily on technological change, especially the development of automobile and truck transportation.[24] David Gordon maintains, however, that the flight of industry from central cities was motivated as much by a desire to control labor as by the need to take advantage of more efficient technologies and locations for production. Citing testimony before the

U.S. Industrial Commission at the turn of the century, Gordon argues that employers moved out of cities because they were hotbeds of union organizing and radical agitation.[25] Whether or not Gordon is right, the point is that researchers cannot *assume* that the movement of investment is based solely on technical considerations of profit and efficiency. Where suspicions exist, researchers should examine the possibility that political motivations played a role in investment decisions. For example, in the case of Cleveland's default, we will look at the decision of bankers to call in city loans, to see whether it was based on purely technical considerations of creditworthiness or whether political factors entered the decision.

City governments, of course, may also be able to exercise political discretion in the governmental marketplace. Different taxing and spending policies, for example, may all have the same effect on mobile wealth. Wealth is never perfectly mobile; there is a great deal of friction or inertia. Within a certain range, investors may not be sensitive to variations in taxing and spending policies. Within this range, government policies would not be determined by the need to attract mobile wealth but would be subject to political choice; distribution of the pie would not affect growth of the pie. This, of course, is the traditional space of pluralism: policy issues are decided not by external growth forces but by the internal jockeying of interest groups. To determine the degree of political discretion open to city governments is a prime goal of this study.

On the face of it, then, where economic pressures leave off seems to be where growth politics ends and pluralist interest group politics begins. It is not so simple as that, however, because the lack of hard evidence means that the demarcation line itself is subject to continuous political controversy. Politics is not just about who prevails on particular issues but how those issues are seen in the first place. What matters is *perceptions* of growth pressures, not their reality. Consider the tax load on business. Should it be set by the democratic process in the name of distributive justice, or must local governments reduce business' tax load in the name of growth? Where to draw the line between allocative and growth issues is the heart of the controversy over local tax abatements, discussed in Chapter 6.

Monopolies

Monopolies, or more frequently, oligopolies are clear examples of market power. While unable to force consumers to buy products they do not want, monopolies can, depending on the elasticity of demand

and the ability to find substitutes, force consumers to pay more than the competitive price. This skews the allocation of resources toward that industry. This is political power, a kind of monopoly tax. Antitrust laws have been enacted in the United States to restore competition and stop this exercise of political power in the market.

In the governmental marketplace, monopolies both create the conditions for the exercise of political discretion and give it a power or leverage it would not otherwise have. A city would be subject to monopoly power in the governmental marketplace if its tax base depended on investment in only one industry (and the town could not easily substitute investment in other industries) and that industry was controlled by one or a few firms. For example, a city that, for whatever reasons, was a profitable location only for automobile production could be forced to pay a higher "price" for that investment if the automobile industry itself were an oligopoly. Cities with a diverse economic base will be less subject to monopoly power, because they can substitute other kinds of investment when the price gets too high. It should be noted that labor unions, like business, can exert a kind of monopoly over city governments. In Cleveland, however, the weakness of the labor unions, with the exception of the police, prohibited the exercise of this power. Particularly, in the case of Cleveland, I examine whether CEI, the area's private utility, obtained a monopoly in the production of power and used that power to exert political leverage over Muny Light and the city.

On the other hand, governments can exercise monopoly power over mobile wealth as well. If a certain product can be produced only within one political jurisdiction, that government could force the industry to pay a kind of monopoly tax. Depending on a number of variables, this tax either eats into corporate profits or is passed on to consumers. The latter is what happens with severance taxes imposed by state governments on oil and coal production.

Nonrational Choice

The free market assumes that each individual is the best judge of his or her interests and can pursue them rationally in the marketplace. This assumption is violated by the manipulation of consumer demand through advertising. Consumers are hardly sovereign if Madison Avenue creates demand for a new product or if consumers buy a product because of false or misleading information. For this reason, the federal government has regulated false or manipulatory advertising, such as commercials for presweetened cereals aimed at young children.

In the governmental marketplace, market theory assumes that both governments and mobile investors are unitary actors, with decisions made rationally in the interest of the city or corporate entity as a whole. In the case of cities, at least, this is clearly not the case.[26] City governments are not just economic entities; they are also political entities. The rules for forming a government are based on the principle of one person, one vote; votes are not weighted according to the possession of economic resources. Local policymakers must please two constituencies—mobile wealth and the voters who put them in office. Either constituency can withdraw support with devastating effect. Local government policy, then, is essentially a compromise between two competing functions of government—in the words of James O'Connor, accumulation and legitimacy.[27] Or, to say much the same thing, local governments must be concerned not just with economic growth but with the distribution of that growth.

In the final analysis, local government policies are never "determined" by economic pressures. No one puts a gun to the heads of local policymakers; there is not simply one "rational" policy to follow. Policies are always a choice between competing values. At one extreme, the claim of market theorists (and the conservative growth politicians associated with them) is that cities approach what economists call a condition of Pareto optimality, which means simply that after a series of exchanges no one is worse off than before and the level of satisfaction in the system as a whole is higher due to the exchanges. Here, the claim is that due to the exchanges in growth politics between cities and mobile wealth, no one is worse off and the city as a whole is better off because of the economic growth created by the new investment. Even in this extreme case, however, it is still essentially a value choice; citizens of a democratic polity could choose to reject this highly advantageous exchange because it created an unacceptable degree of inequality. More importantly, in the vast majority of growth policies, some people must lose. In any case, there is always a choice to be made, a tension between competing values.

In short, with regard to city governments, it is difficult to define "rational" behavior in any precise way. Presumably, rational choice would mean choosing the course of action that was most beneficial to the city as a whole. The public interest, however, is not easy to discern. In politics, everything depends on perceptions of costs and benefits, not the reality. Rational decision making is distorted not only by different values and perceptions but also by how complex political forces are aggregated by the political rules into policy decisions. Political structure has its own effect. Pluralist political institutions, for example, have a tendency to spread out the benefits in order to cement a minimum winning coalition. In order to attract investment, however, incentives must be concentrated. Political institutions have imperatives that often cut against the grain of growth pressures. How these conflicting pressures are reconciled is at the heart of growth politics.

Contrary to the technocratic model of corporate decision making, corporations are also subject to internal interest group pressures on distributive issues and clashes of values. The decision of where to locate a corporate headquarters, for example, could be influenced by the interests of one division of the company over the others or the residential preferences of top executives as opposed to the economic interests of the firm as a whole. In analyzing Cleveland's default, a central question is whether the decision not to rollover the city's loans was made by an objective assessment of the city's creditworthiness by the key bank's commercial loan department or whether the decision was unduly influenced by trust department holdings of CEI stock, as well as the political animosities of top executives. In short, we should not be oblivious to the political structure and process *within* corporations.

Political Manipulation of Externalities

Decisions on where to invest (when not based on some political animus) are based on a corporate concept of efficiency: calculation of the comparative internal costs and benefits to the firm (profit maximization) of alternative courses of action. The corporate concept of efficiency is often faulted for being too narrow, for ignoring important neighborhood effects or externalities. Externalities are the costs or benefits of an exchange borne by persons who did not take part in the exchange. People suffer air pollution, for example, who neither buy the product nor work at the factory. Government intervention in the marketplace is justified as necessary to regulate external costs or to establish a method of compensation. The decision to move a factory, for example, is based on a calculation of internal profit and loss, ignoring external costs such as workers' relocation expenses, loss of community ties, social pathologies, or mental illness.[28] Plant closing legislation has been proposed in the U.S. Congress, and passed in some state legislatures and city councils, to force corporations to compensate communities for the costs of capital flight.

Externalities are not randomly distributed across the population;

they can be manipulated by public and private interests. For this reason, externalities have always played a key role in growth politics. The manipulation of externalities has been used to cement the broad growth coalitions that have often dominated city politics. The key externality of urban growth is rising land values. For this reason, landowners have always played a central role in city politics. Essentially, growth coalitions are alliances of immobile wealth (in particular real estate interests, but also banks, utilities, and newspapers) with particular kinds of mobile wealth that can advance these interests, especially land prices.[29]

In the nineteenth century, railroads were the King Midas of growth coalitions, the key to all forms of economic expansion. City governments dug deep into their treasuries for various subsidies, including the direct purchase of railroad stock, in order to attract railroad connections. These subsidies were supported by growth coalitions centered on landowners who stood to gain from rising land values, joined by commercial and industrial interests that would benefit from cheaper transportation. Since local governments depended on property taxes for revenues, their interests were easily aligned, the argument being that rising land values would generate increased tax receipts to pay off the railroad bonds. Even the lowliest workers were drawn into the net of railroad growth coalitions with the promise that the prosperity brought by the railroad would benefit all. While railroad connections generally did bring advantages, there were costs. The costs of railroad growth politics, however, were usually drowned in the celebration of American industrial expansion.[30]

Robert Caro's monumental biography of Robert Moses analyzes growth politics in the age when highways, not railroads, were the key to economic expansion. According to Caro, Moses manipulated the externalities of massive public works projects, especially highways, to put together a growth machine that dominated New York politics for a generation. Moses used the location of his highways to punish enemies (in crowded urban areas where highways meant dislocation and blight) and reward his friends (in undeveloped areas where highways meant burgeoning land values and growth). In Long Island, opposition to Moses' parkways melted as key politicians, forewarned, bought up land around parkway exits and realized huge profits.

> Moreover, in terms of development, the impact of a parkway
> spread in ever-widening ripples: stores and laundries and gas sta-
> tions and insurance brokerage firms for the residents of the houses,

subcontractors and material-supply houses for the factories. This meant a burgeoning in land sales, insurance premiums, legal fees—in all the areas in which politicians grow fat.[31]

Moses' political organization of the externalities of his projects did not stop there; it included fees for lawyers, real estate brokers, insurance brokers, public relations firms—what Caro called the Retainer Regiment. Finally, of course, there were huge profits for the bondholders.

The key point about the political manipulation of externalities is that it is, for the most part, a way of putting together a political machine, a growth machine, while avoiding legal prosecution for corruption. If private interests pay a government official in order to influence the actions of government, the traditional definition of corruption is fulfilled. There is an identifiable corrupt transaction that could possibly be taken to court. On the other hand, if those same private interests are tipped off on the location of a highway exit and just happen to purchase the land for miles around, giving their tipsters a piece of the action, the collusion is obvious but much more difficult to prove in court. Even less culpable are those who benefit more indirectly, such as real estate agents who make money on the land sales. The payoff is indirect—well "laundered," so to speak.

Back in 1905, George Washington Plunkitt of New York City perceptively pointed out the difference between "honest graft" and "dishonest graft." After all, Plunkitt observed, he did not steal a single dollar from the city treasury and if he had not made money on rising land values, somebody else would have.[32] The political manipulation of externalities is the key to a type of machine politics, the growth machine, that has been largely overlooked by reformers. For the most part, its corruption cannot be treated by traditional legal methods or by reforms that focus on the structure of city government.

Cumulative Inequalities

One problem with the doctrine of consumer sovereignty is that some consumers have more dollars to vote on what society will produce than do others. Free market theory completely ignores the question of the proper distribution of income. It does not take a Marxist to see that tendencies exist within markets for inequalities to widen, for the rich to get richer and the poor to get poorer.[33] As the saying goes, "It takes money to make money." Government intervention to redistribute income through various transfer mechanisms, such as welfare payments or steep inheritance taxes, can be defended as making market competition fairer, as well as consumer sovereignty more democratic.

Cumulative inequalities also exist in the governmental marketplace. Conventional market models posit a system in equilibrium: obeying the law of diminishing returns, investment in prosperous sectors pulls back after a time, to be invested in backward areas. The investment competition between cities, however, has a built-in cycle of cumulative growth and decay. Jurisdictions with a large tax base relative to demand for services (as in many Sunbelt cities) can afford to keep taxes low and offer large special incentives for industry to invest. The rich get richer. On the other hand, jurisdictions that find themselves in a tax squeeze because of a declining economy (older cities of the Northeast and Midwest) need to raise tax rates to meet service demands and thus other things being equal, repel investment and high income residents as well.[34] Class stratification manifests itself geographically as well as socially.[35]

These cumulative inequalities generate different kinds of growth politics in different cities. Having a tax base more than ample to meet the service demands of a largely middle class population, many suburban governments practice the politics of exclusion, not the politics of growth.[36] They are more concerned with excluding the poor and minorities, as well as dirty industry, than with attracting new investment and residents. Ironically, it is precisely in those cities where growth is least possible that growth politics, as it is defined here, has its most tenacious hold. Local governments undergoing disinvestment, with a low tax base relative to service demands, must do everything in their power to entice mobile wealth and jobs back into the city. The politics of exclusion and the politics of inclusion (growth) are two sides of the same coin: suburbs are simply trying to protect advantages derived from earlier successes in growth politics, while inner cities, losers in the growth competition partly because of suburban success, must scramble to regain an advantage.

By favoring mobile interests over immobile interests, growth politics also exacerbates inequalities within the private sector. Immobile sectors of capital, tied to declining jurisdictions, will have relatively higher tax burdens and lower levels of service delivery. Small businesses, especially those in the service sector, will suffer more than large businesses that have national and international mobility. The mobile middle class, likewise, will be able to escape the costs of urban decline by moving to the suburbs, while poorer inner city residents, unable to afford expensive suburban housing, will be forced to bear the costs of urban decline. Involving as it does a trade-off between equality and growth, growth politics by its very nature exacerbates inequalities. A central question regarding the trickle down theory is whether those at the bottom benefit from the resultant growth. In "loser" cities, the trade-off between equality and growth becomes steeper: deeper and deeper subsidies are needed to attract mobile wealth and overcome the forces of disinvestment. If enough people feel left out of the benefits of growth politics, this can lead to political instability and loss of legitimacy.

Summary

There are five factors that can distort the operation of the governmental marketplace—political discretion, monopolies, nonrational choice, political manipulation of externalities, and cumulative inequalities. All involve the exercise of power over the market or structural features in the market that systematically favor certain interests over other interests. These five concepts will be used to plumb the "politics" of urban growth. The point is not that malevolent monopolists move wealth about in order to subject city governments to their political will. Rather, the point is that previous approaches to community power, both pluralist and market, *assumed* the opposite; they did not see the market context of cities as part of the problem to be analyzed, but as the result of inevitable economic and technological forces. This assumption was unwarranted. Any urban power study worthy of the name must critically examine the market environment of cities and determine the extent to which power, or systematic bias, is involved.

Rationalizing the Growth Competition:
The Role of the Federal Government

The growth competition between governments in the United States is basically constituted by two sets of rules:

1. Capitalism: wealth is mobile, with the location of investment decided by competing investors;
2. Federalism: local governments have considerable autonomy in setting taxing and spending priorities independently of each other.

Correspondingly, two distinct remedies are available to counteract the ill-effects—the assertions of power and the uneven development—of growth politics. Governments could either intervene directly in the private market to limit the mobility of wealth, or they could alter the fragmentation of policymaking by moving decision-making authority up the federal ladder to larger and larger political units. In the United States, the latter strategy has overwhelmingly been favored.

Given the extreme economic, social, and political problems generated by mobile wealth, there has been surprisingly little effort by the public sector to plan private investment flows in the United States. There is no national effort to plan the geographical distribution of jobs and population to counteract uneven development, as in the European social democracies.[37] In the United States, control over investment decisions has been left largely in the hands of the owners and managers of private corporations.[38]

While federal government plays little direct role in allocating profitable investment, it does play a major indirect role in shaping investment flows. Basically it does so by altering the costs and benefits of market decisions through taxing and spending policies. Far from ameliorating the costs of growth politics, these policies have tended to accelerate the mobility of wealth, intensifying the growth competition and increasing uneven development. Federal tax policy, for example, in both liberal and conservative administrations, has largely been formulated under the supply side goal of achieving the textbook ideal of perfect capital mobility. Eliminating "friction" in capital investment, it is thought, will increase the efficiency of capital markets and stimulate growth. A good example is the accelerated depreciation for new commercial and industrial property first enacted in the 1954 revision of the Internal Revenue Code and increased several times since then.[39] Presumably, such a policy does not mandate any particular use or location for capital but simply stimulates new investment. But it has had the effect of rendering older buildings in central cities relatively less attractive for investment and accelerating the decentralization of jobs and the flight of industry out of central cities.[40]

The same thing can be said of many federal spending policies. The federal interstate highway system subsidized the development of transportation in the Sunbelt and contributed to the obsolescence of the rail network in the Northeast. FHA and VA mortgage insurance programs went primarily for new homes in the suburbs and not for rehabilitating older homes in central cities. By now, there is a mountain of evidence documenting the role of the federal government in the economic decline of the older cities.[41]

Since the public sector has been reluctant to directly plan the geographical distribution of wealth and has tended to exacerbate the problems of growth politics through the indirect effect of its taxing and spending policies, the main way that government in the United States has dealt with the costs of growth politics has been to move policymaking authority up the federal ladder to larger and larger jurisdictions. The larger the jurisdiction, the more leverage governments have over mobile wealth. While city governments must compete with one another in dealing with most sectors of wealth, the federal government is, relatively speaking, close to a monopoly. The federal government can exercise more discretion in its taxing and spending policies with less fear of disinvestment. Taking advantage of its superior tax-raising ability, the federal government has set itself up as a kind of sovereign over the competing state and local governments, attempting to rationalize the internecine competition.

There are two main rationales for this federal intervention, both closely related to failures in the governmental marketplace. Private markets, everyone agrees, are capable only of serving selective interests, not collective, or shared, interests. Collective interests, such as clean air or national defense, must be provided for by government. Likewise, the governmental marketplace cannot provide for the shared interests of city governments or mobile investors. Since many of the benefits of economic development or education spill over state and local boundaries, there will be a tendency for these levels of government to invest less than some ideal. For this reason, the federal government has intervened to stimulate such expenditures and to provide for collective goods, such as an interstate highway system. The second main rationale for federal intervention has been to counteract the inequalities, both within and between cities, that, as we discussed earlier, are exacerbated by the governmental marketplace. Federal intervention has been aimed at moderating inequalities between classes (people-oriented programs), and, more recently, at reducing inequalities between places (intergovernmental grants).

The development of this federal sovereign over the past fifty years has dramatically changed the nature of urban growth politics. Before the New Deal, the growth competition between states and municipalities was, in most areas, unhindered by a federal sovereign. The prevailing interpretation of the Constitution, relying on the Tenth Amendment, reserved most important domestic welfare and economic functions for the states and, hence, also for municipalities. The result was that, while these lower levels of government had certain formal powers, they were not able to exercise them fully for fear of disinvestment. What we think of as welfare, poor relief, was overwhelmingly funded by local governments with the help of charities, at an extremely low level by today's standards.[42] Regulation of business was left to the states, which did little for fear of disinvestment.[43]

This system reached a crisis during the depression of the 1930s. In the first years of the Depression, public relief for the unemployed was the responsibility of city governments. It was a makeshift effort: cities were not prepared for the large numbers of unemployed; emergency programs were slapped together, only to run out of funds every few months; relief payments were abysmally low. Nationwide, only about one-fourth of the unemployed were able to get help.[44] Armies of unemployed marched on city halls demanding relief. But city tax revenues could not meet the need. And welfare demands were going up just at a time when many cities could not even collect property taxes. On top of it all, demands for relief were greatest in those cities that had suffered the largest shrinkage of their tax base.

The New Deal responded to this crisis by bringing the federal government into areas previously reserved for states and localities. These initiatives were approved in a series of Supreme Court decisions that gave the federal government concurrent spending authority, alongside the states and localities, to legislate for a whole range of domestic functions. The federal government, for the most part, did not directly administer these new programs. Rather, it used its superior taxing powers, based in large part on its greater ability to outflank mobile wealth, to set up an intergovernmental investment market that stimulated state and local governments to establish programs that fear of disinvestment would otherwise have discouraged their funding.[45]

The new federalism has developed, since the New Deal, into an extensive network of grants-in-aid to states and cities constituting approximately 25 percent of domestic federal outlays. The system varies from close federal supervision (categorical grants) to almost no federal strings (revenue sharing). Federal welfare programs, as well as many grant-in-aid programs, distribute federal funds in a pattern directly counter to private investment flows: poor cities get the most. Urban renewal, for example, first enacted in 1949, was consciously designed to counteract disinvestment in inner cities. The Community Development Block Grant, enacted in 1974, distributes funds to cities based on a formula that rewards cities with higher levels of poverty and greater growth lags relative to their suburbs.

In short, the policies of the federal government are profoundly contradictory. On the one hand, many taxation and spending policies increase the mobility of wealth, further restrict the options of local governments, and reinforce the flow of investment out of central cities. On the other hand, programs have been set up specifically to counter this uneven development and to enable cities to do things they would otherwise be dissuaded from doing by the pressures of growth politics. In the study of growth politics today, the intergovernmental marketplace of federal grants must be analyzed and its relationship to the private market fathomed. Too often, this has been overlooked in studies in community power.[46] In the case of Cleveland, the effect of the Community Development Block Grant program is studied in detail in Chapter 8. The central question is whether these intergovernmental transfers give freedom to local governments to act counter to the pressures of growth politics.

Conclusion: Civil Free Will and Necessity

Figure 1 presents an overall view of the process of growth politics. The *mobility of wealth* and the relative *independence of local governments* in the American economic and political system brings into being a *governmental marketplace*: local governments compete to attract mobile wealth in order to keep their tax base up and service demands down. Neither of these factors is absolute, however. In each case, the degree to which wealth is mobile and the extent to which local governments make policy independently of each other must be investigated. Specifically, *intergovernmental grants* may exert pressures on local policymakers directly counter to those of the private market. The extent to which local governments succumb to *growth pressures* will vary with their dependence on mobile wealth to perform essential functions (in turn a function of tax base, service demands, and political organization). I do not contend here that these external pressures of growth politics constitute all of local politics, merely that they supply the dynamic factor in local politics, a dynamic factor heretofore overlooked by community power studies.

Growth politics should not be seen as a form of economic determinism. The growth pressures themselves are permeated by political factors arising from market failures or power assertions (political discretion, monopolies, nonrational choice, political manipulation of externalities, and cumulative inequalities). City governments may have the discretion to set policies without any effect on mobile wealth, or they

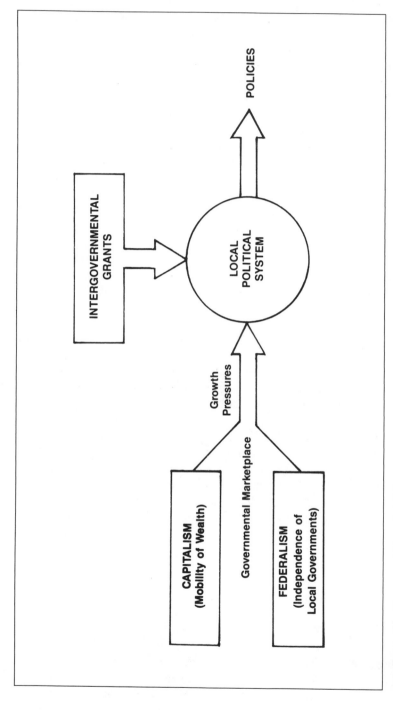

FIGURE 1. The Elements of Growth Politics.

may be tightly constrained by economic pressures, which may themselves result from an anonymous market or elite manipulations. In any case, city governments do not simply respond, in knee jerk fashion, to the pressures of growth; growth pressures must be filtered through *local political systems* with particular rules, power arrangements, and perceptions of the governmental marketplace. The needs of the political system may clash with the need for economic growth. Moreover, while the economic environment largely determines the size and shape of the public sector, the economic environment is in turn shaped by the *policies* of government. Feedback loops could be added to the diagram.

In short, growth politics is a complex interplay between determinism and free will, economics and politics, structure and agency.[47] At the center of American urban politics is a profound tension between a political system based on democratic participation and an economic system based on the unfettered mobility of wealth and the inviolable rights of private property. Cities in the United States are free to choose their own policies according to the rules of democratic politics but they are not free to choose the economic conditions under which they make those choices. The exercise of civic free will takes place within the structural constraints of modern political economy. This tension between democracy and capitalism, equality and growth, animates the urban political system. Any theory of urban politics worth its salt must give play to both forces, as well as their dynamic interaction.

2

Conservative Growth Politics: The Age of Steel

> GAIN! Gain! Gain! is the beginning, the middle and the
> end, the *alpha* and *omega* of the founders of the American
> towns.[1]
>
> *Morris Birkbeck*

American urban history is the history of growth, phenomenal growth. From the founding of the first colony, town promotion—or "civic boosterism"—was a way of life in the New World. Indeed, civic boosterism was one of the peculiar forms that the dominance of business values took in American public life. The famed entrepreneurial spirit of American capitalism was expressed as much in founding cities as it was in founding fortunes (although, in truth, it was often hard to separate the two). In the New World wealth and population were mobile to an incredible degree. Freed from a rigid feudal social structure and attracted by a vast expanse of cheap and productive land, European migrants flooded across the North American continent, leaving towns and cities in their wake. Cities competed vigorously for the new settlers and investment that were essential to economic, social, and political success. Cities rose, and sometimes fell, with stunning speed. One thing was certain: to stand still was to fall behind, to be assured of oblivion in the race of growth politics.

There are many varieties of growth politics. The kind of growth politics pursued depends on the place of each city within the economic division of labor. Specialization of economic function along product lines, such as lumber, automobiles, or steel, manifests itself geographically as well as socially. Each city pursues a *growth strategy*, a particular mix of public and private programs designed to exploit its advantages for capital accumulation and growth. Much depends on available natural resources. Asheville, North Carolina, for instance, with its beautiful mountain setting, has long pursued the mobile tourist trade and the town fathers have done everything in their power to keep industry out. Other cities, such as Pittsburgh and Detroit, pursued industrial growth with a vengeance, to the exclusion of other forms of growth such as office development or tourism. Within the same city, political conflict often arises over competing growth strategies.

Each growth strategy is supported by a *growth coalition*. Growth coalitions are alliances of different interests that work together to implement a growth strategy. Some interests are more central to a growth coalition than others. Immobile interests, such as real estate, banks, utilities, and newspapers, usually play a central role in any growth coalition since they benefit indirectly from all kinds of growth. They ally with mobile investors to push a strategy for growth. In democracies, workers play an important role in growth coalitions by providing the mass electoral base for political power.

Each growth coalition disseminates a *growth ideology*. Growth ideologies paper over the conflicts within growth coalitions by hiding the costs of growth and emphasizing how the entire community will benefit from the particular type of growth envisioned. Civic boosters spread the growth ideology in speeches before the Chamber of Commerce, in the editorial pages of local newspapers, and even at meetings of local labor leaders. Growth ideologies can be divided, as described in the Introduction, into liberal and conservative varieties. Liberal growth politics emphasizes a central role for government, both in guiding private sector expansion and in creating an expanded welfare state to help those left behind by growth. Conservative growth politics advocates a passive role for government—with taxes kept to a minimum and planning left entirely to the private sector.

While Cleveland began as a commercial center, it really took off only during its industrial period. For almost a century, from the 1850s to the 1950s, Cleveland pursued an industrial growth strategy, becoming one of the premier industrial cities in the world. The growth coalition behind this industrial growth strategy was very broad, held together by the glue of economic growth. While industrial growth generated tremendous inequalities between classes, the constantly rising standard of living, and the chance for a few to make tremendous fortunes, siphoned off class resentments and unrest. Phenomenal opportunities in the private economy sustained a conservative growth ideology that prescribed a minimal role for government, and low taxes, presumably to avoid choking off the private sources of investment that were booming the economy.

Cleveland's period of industrial growth politics was not static, however. For long periods the conservative industrial elite, absorbed in entrepreneurial activity, ignored local government, which took a passive attitude toward the problems of industrialism. When the problems accumulated to the point that they threatened profitability or political legitimacy, a reform movement would arise, often led by the economic dominants, to deal with the problems. The literature on urban reform stresses the "progressive" phase, with its focus on structural reform of city government in the name of economy and efficiency. There was an earlier "populist" phase, however, led by men such as Samuel "Golden Rule" Jones of Toledo and Hazen Pingree of Detroit, which combined structural reform with a positive program for curing the ills of industrial capitalism. How the radical roots of reform were killed off, leaving a spineless plant clinging congenially to big business, is a fascinating story.[2]

In Cleveland, populist Mayor Tom Johnson led a working class rebellion at the turn of the century that expanded local government, even to the point of threatening the prerogatives of private capital. The economic elite responded with a sustained push for structural reforms, designed to both insulate city government from ethnic working class majorities and make it a more efficient instrument for economic growth. The final result, in Cleveland, was a stand-off, with working class ethnics controlling city government (the spoils being handed out in classic pluralist fashion) but with the scope of public control greatly restricted (threats to the prerogatives of corporate capital were withdrawn).

Cities are branded forever by their period of greatest growth, their period of greatest dynamism. This is especially true of Cleveland. Quintessentially, Cleveland is a city of the industrial period. This is vividly reflected in its physical layout (designed to facilitate industrial production, its ingress and egress, not the quality of residential life) and its political structure (designed to accommodate a polyglot ethnic working class, not to engage in sophisticated economic planning). As Cleveland enters the post-industrial economy of the future, it is still mired in the industrial patterns of the past, still hoping that by repeating the old formulas, like some cargo cult, the god of economic growth, which bestowed such munificence upon the city, will return.

The Politics of Steel: Private Prosperity, Public Squander

Cleveland was originally part of the Western Reserve, a land grant to Connecticut stretching back to a proclamation by King Charles II in 1662. In 1795, the State of Connecticut sold the Western Reserve lands to the Connecticut Land Company, a group of investors. General Moses Cleaveland, a shareholder, led the first expedition to the new land and founded the town that bears his name. The early settlers were enterprising New England Yankees and the city, conveniently located where the Cuyahoga River flows into Lake Erie, prospered as a commercial center. The Erie Canal, completed in 1825, provided uninterrupted water transit through Lake Erie to the Hudson River and the Atlantic. A few years later Cleveland became the northern terminus of the Ohio Canal, which linked it to the Ohio River and the Gulf of Mexico. As the editor of the *Daily Gazette* wrote in 1837: "The plodding methods of the farmer is [sic] not our way, but rather that of a maritime port in a growing country."[3] By 1850, Cleveland was a bustling town of 17,034 residents. But with its location at the northern edge of a vast agricultural land, Cleveland faced a limited future as a trans-Appalachian distribution center.

A discovery had been made a few years earlier, however, that would transform this bustling town into a booming metropolis.[4] In 1845 a Chippewa chief named Marji Gesick led Philip Everett of Jackson, Michigan, to a strange mountain near Lake Superior in Michigan's Upper Peninsula. Everett reported to the world "a mountain of solid iron ore, 150 feet high." When word of the discovery reached Ohio, Cleveland entrepreneurs quickly organized an expedition to explore the region, now known as Cleveland Mountain. Industry began to be pushed over commerce. In 1856 the Cleveland *Leader* opined, "No thinking man with capital will stop here when we have only commerce to sustain us. A manufacturing town gives a man full scope for his ambitions."[5] Mass meetings were held in the 1850s to boost Cleveland as an iron center. A civic committee, formed to boost the town, reported in 1856 that iron was the destined industry for Cleveland owing to its fortuitous location as an economical meeting place for iron ore and coal. Rich iron ore could be shipped from Lake Superior through the locks at Sault St. Marie, first completed in 1885, down past Detroit into Lake Erie, where the boats could unload the ore directly at steel plants on the Cuyahoga River in Cleveland. Railroads, however, were necessary to bring coal from abundant fields in the Mahoning and Hocking valleys. Like many cities, Cleveland city government subscribed to stock in railroad companies to entice them to town.[6] Cleveland's industrial greatness was assured by the arrival of the railroads in the 1850s. The burgeoning steel industry concentrated in cities like Cleveland in order to take advantage of the water and rail connections, avoid government taxes on separate processes, and profit from the cheap immigrant labor that converged there.

Cleveland soon became one of the fastest growing industrial cities in the world. Apart from attracting the railroads, city government played a very minimal role in the process of industrialization; it was a time of wild and wooly capitalism, remarkably free of social and political restraints. The industrial elite, largely self-made men unmindful of social interdependencies, saw little positive function for government. Their conservative growth ideology left city government little political discretion for expansion: higher taxes, it was thought, would only choke off the industrial boom. Private growth would cure all of society's ills. Indeed, it was hard to argue with success. The economy did expand at a frightening pace, providing unheard of opportunities for those with energy and ambition. Henry Chisolm, for example, arrived from Scotland in 1842, a nearly penniless young man of twenty. In the 1850s, he began making iron rails for railroads. Chisolm's Cleveland Rolling Mill Company became one of the great steelmaking enterprises in the country, eventually forming a basis of United States Steel. John D. Rockefeller began as a produce and grain merchant, branching out into the nascent oil business in 1863. By the mid-1870s Cleveland was the world's leading oil refiner and Rockefeller's Standard Oil Company was well on its way to dominating the world market. (When the Supreme Court of Ohio found the company guilty of antitrust violations in the 1890s, Rockefeller simply transferred control to more lenient states, eventually consolidating power in Standard Oil of New Jersey.)

As in war, so in growth politics: history is usually written by the winners, not the losers. Most histories of Cleveland are paeans to the joys of economic growth.[7] Cleveland's past becomes the history of a succession of daring enterpreneurs, succeeding almost beyond belief. The public sector, at best, is a sideshow. What life was like for the immigrant workers is ignored. And the considerable costs of growth are hidden.

Beneath the gaudy exterior of what Mark Twain called the Gilded Age, however, lurked a grim reality of festering problems engendered by an urban industrial civilization. Foremost among these was poverty. The immigrants formed a vast army of unskilled labor forced to work sixty hours a week at subsistence wages. Unions existed only for a handful of skilled workers, and welfare benefits, by present-day standards, were pitiful. At a time when welfare, limited to those unable to work, was almost entirely the responsibility of local government, Cleveland city government did very little. For the period 1851–1855, the city contributed an average of $.61 per city resident for all forms of charity and relief; in 1891–1895 the figure was exactly the same. This was the only major item in the city budget not to increase more rapidly than population.[8]

Poverty was made harder to bear by extreme inequalities in wealth, inequalities exacerbated by the loading of the external costs of industrialization on the lower classes while the more mobile upper classes were able to escape the costs of growth. Industry in Cleveland concentrated along the Cuyahoga River. The Flats, as it was called, took on an almost hellish cast: blast furnaces lit up the sky, blackened by coal smoke and oil fumes, with a fiery orange glow. The captains of industry attempted to escape the noise, smoke, and confusion of the Flats by building homes on a ridge jutting east from the river overlooking Lake Erie. Euclid Avenue became a showcase of the wealth and power of the industrialists. "Clevelanders boasted of Euclid Avenue, comparing it with Unter den Linden of Berlin and the Champs Elysées of Paris."[9] A list of the families on Euclid Avenue is a veritable *Who's Who* of Cleveland's industrial elite, many descending from early Protestant Yankee settlers: Rockefeller, Chisholm, Hanna, Mather, Otis, Bradley, Andrews, Severance.

Lacking adequate public transportation, the workers were unable to escape the foul industrial district. They crowded into wooden shanties built on the slopes and plateaus bordering the industrial Flats. A report by the Cleveland *Leader* in 1873 described conditions:

> The houses are small, dirty and wretched. Most of them are mere
> sheds boarded up and provided with a floor. The woodwork is rot-

> ten, the real estate lies thick on the floor and the windows are
> stuffed with rags. The houses are ranged so that the floor of one on
> the hill-side is on a level with the roof of another and so the refuse
> water and filth from those above finds its way upon the tables and
> into the beds of those beneath . . . In these old shanties there ranges
> from one to three families each, and to each one is accorded space
> sufficient only for a bed. There is no ventilation, the stench is only
> what might be expected, and all the habits of the inmates are
> directly opposed to the rules of cleanliness and health.[10]

During the early industrial period, Cleveland's population grew
phenomenally, from 17,034 in 1850 to 381,768 in 1900. The effect of
throwing all these people together with little planning was to create all
the problems of a boomtown: congestion, pollution, crime, disorderli-
ness, and disease. During the early period of rapid industrialization, the
local public sector, for the most part, abdicated its responsibility for
dealing with these problems. "Sanitarily, Cleveland remained medieval
almost up to the middle of the Nineteenth century."[11] Until 1875, there
was no garbage collection at all, and after that only an inadequate
system of private contracts, labeled, in 1884, a "failure and a
swindle."[12] Work was not begun on a sewer system until 1860. Progress
was slow. People continued to throw their garbage into the streets
where raw sewage flowed down open gutters. Contaminated wells
prompted the city to begin supplying water from Lake Erie in 1856, but
the dumping of raw sewage into the Cuyahoga, along with industrial
waste, soon threatened the city's new water supply. No serious effort
was made to curb water pollution. In 1881, the mayor called the
Cuyahoga "an open sewer running through the center of the city."[13] To
avoid contamination, the city was forced to build a new water intake
further out into Lake Erie.[14] The air fared no better than the water.
Notwithstanding Cleveland's sobriquet, the Forest City, by the late
nineteenth century what original forest had not been cleared had died
from air pollution.[15]

Why did the city allow such conditions to exist? Part of the reason
was a deficiency in political leadership. In the earlier commercial
period, Cleveland's economic elite, following the New England town
meeting tradition, had participated actively in civic affairs. With the
advent of industrialism, however, the economic dominants increasingly
withdrew from public responsibilities to pursue private gain.[16] At
Cleveland's centennial in 1896, the Cleveland *World* compiled a

celebration of the City's economic progress that, nonetheless, put its finger on the trouble spot:

> Although peopled and controlled commercially and industrially by some of the most highly endorsed, successful and commanding executive minds in the country, ward politicians—products of the caucus and the saloon—made its laws and forcibly executed them. . . . Its [Cleveland's] commercial and private magnificence was equalled only by its municipal squalor.[17]

After the Civil War, most of Cleveland's mayors were distinctly second rate. It is not surprising. In 1875, when millions could be made in the private sector, the mayor of Cleveland was paid only $3,000. There simply was not enough at stake to induce substantial men of iron and steel to run for mayor or council. Of course, some businessmen became involved in local politics because of particular business connections, such as railway franchises. But for the most part the industrialists were not interested in government. They were content to let professional politicians, primarily of small business origins, manage the local public sector. As long as taxes were kept low, they were satisfied.

More important than the lack of political leadership, however, was the hold that conservative growth politics had on the system at the time. Private initiative and private growth would take care of society's problems, it was believed, even though it was uncontrolled private sector growth that had created the problems in the first place.[18] An editorial in 1861, supporting a petition to repeal an ordinance against water pollution, revealed the attitudes of the city fathers: "This petition should be granted. To refuse to do it, is to pursue the same policy toward manufactures that has diverted trade and business to other more favorable points, and has greatly retarded the legitimate growth of the City. Our prosperity hereafter will be measured by our manufactures."[19] Working class voters, unable to escape the effluents of industrialism by moving to "the heights," frequently petitioned their councilmen to do something about the obnoxious fumes from the steel factories, oil refineries, and railroads. Many times council passed ordinances to control air pollution, but they were never effectively enforced.[20] The reason was obvious: fears that curbs on industry would "kill the goose that laid the golden eggs." Prosperity was more important than livability.

One of the few areas where industrialists demanded, and got, positive results from city government was police. The city needed a professional police force. Older forms of social control, which relied on personal face-to-face relationships in the community, broke down in the anonymous urban environment. The industrialists needed professional police to protect their property and to defeat unionization.[21] A good example is the strike at the Cleveland Rolling Mill Company in 1882. Henry Chisolm, founder of the company, had established close, if paternalistic, relations with his skilled workers. After his death in 1881, his son, William, took over and instituted a hardline policy of replacing skilled workers with unskilled operatives. When skilled workers struck, young Chisolm decided to speed up the process of technological change, even knowing "this would mean inefficiency and temporarily operating at a loss."[22] (Forms of technology are not, indeed, always chosen on the basis of efficiency; political motives, including the motive of social control, enter in.) Chisolm succeeded in exploiting the social and cultural divisions between the British skilled workers and the unskilled, mostly Catholic, Bohemian and Polish workers. City police escorted the "scabs," some specially imported by Chisolm, into the plant and the union was defeated. The support provided the industrialists by city police played a key role in defeating a number of strikes.[23] The bias of city government was clearly shown in 1895 when six policemen who expressed sympathy for the workers were dismissed.[24]

Cleveland was founded by land speculators. This had a profound effect on its physical development. Public Square (ten acres) was reserved as open space, but everything else was sold as private plots to maximize profits, including almost the entire lakefront and riverfront. In order to facilitate sales, the city was laid out in uniform lots. Under the pressure of rising land values, lots were crowded together on a multiplicity of narrow streets, contributing to congestion. Despite a crying need for greenery and open space, Cleveland did not make a significant expansion of its park system until 1873. As late as 1890, Cleveland had less than one hundred acres of parks. "No city in the land," declared the park commissioners, "is so poorly equipped and in none is the appropriation for park purposes so meagre."[25]

Cleveland developed at a time when city planning was almost nonexistent. Zoning laws were a thing of the future. One scholar described the result in Cleveland this way:

> With no tradition of long-range planning as a guide and ill-served by the motive of economic expediency, the design of the town was year by year more completely dissolved in formlessness. Space was

not properly allocated to the several functions of the town and both
the definition of areas and integration of operations gradually broke
down. By a cumulative process a chaotic result was ultimately
produced.[26]

The "several functions of the town"—industrial, commercial, residential—competed anarchically for space. Pushed out of the Flats by
industry, commercial establishments spread out from downtown along
the main thoroughfares, disturbing quiet residential neighborhoods. In
the rush to attract railroads, the city permitted them great latitude in
choosing rights of way. Rail lines preempted almost the entire lake
frontage from West 65th to East 105th and were allowed to cut swaths
of destruction through neighborhoods.[27] It was not just that railroads
brought noise and smoke; they also brought warehouses and factories
that competed for sites along the rights of way, threatening the viability
of neighborhoods. Everywhere residential values were sacrificed to
industrial expansion.

Even the rich were not exempt. Euclid Avenue gradually declined
because of traffic, encroaching retail establishments, and the blighting
influence of the railroad, which crossed Euclid at Willson Avenue (now
East 55th). As early as the 1880s, Euclid millionaires began beating a
tactical retreat to country estates.

The realization that the costs of growth could also impinge on them
may have played a role in a gradual change in attitude of the elite
toward city government in the late nineteenth century. More important, however, was the realization that city government provided essential services (streets, bridges, sewers, sanitation, water, police, fire) and
that if they were not provided efficiently, business growth would, in the
long run, be hampered. In the 1890s, a minor civic revival emerged. The
Parks Movement expanded the city's park system from 100 acres in
1890 to 1,000 acres in 1895. In 1893, the Cleveland Board of Trade, a
narrow trade organization, changed its name to the Chamber of Commerce and became active in citywide issues. (In 1967, it became known
as the Growth Association.) In 1896, the Municipal Association, pre-
cursor of the Citizens League, was founded, part of the good government reform movement that was stirring the country.

The most significant development, however, was the reform of city
government. After 1852 city government had been hamstrung by a
board system of government that fragmented policymaking and dif-
fused responsibility. As early as 1876, the economy and efficiency of the

board system was called into question. Fears were expressed that the autonomous boards would drift the city into bankruptcy. In 1891, Cleveland became a model for the rest of the nation when it adopted the Federal Plan, modeled after the federal government. The executive function was separated from the legislative and centralized under the mayor, who appointed the heads of six executive departments. Great hopes were placed in the new structure. Soon after it was enacted, the Cleveland *Leader* proclaimed it a success: "The success of the Federal Plan is due in the main to the substitution of strict business methods for the often corrupt jobbery that characterized the conduct of municipal affairs under the old board system."[28]

The political reformers were soon disappointed. In 1895, Robert McKisson, an aggressive young anti-Hanna Republican, was elected mayor. (Mark Hanna was the epitome of the conservative Cleveland industrialists, who, after making a fortune in iron, coal, and lake shipping, went on to become a dominant force in the Ohio Republican party, engineering William McKinley's defeat of William Jennings Bryan in 1896). McKisson used the new powers of the mayor to construct a powerful political machine, probably the most centralized machine in Cleveland's history. He padded the payroll with his political hacks, expanded the activities of government, and called for municipal ownership of the utilities. McKisson was defeated in 1899 by an unlikely alliance of Democrats, Hanna Republicans, and reformers.[29] His administration, however, turned out to be the harbinger of the most controversial and progressive mayor in Cleveland's history.[30]

Tom Johnson: Populist Growth Politics

Tom L. Johnson was a self-made millionaire, inventor, and, by his own admission, monopolist. According to his autobiography, he learned his first lesson in monopoly at age eleven when a train conductor gave him a corner on the sale of newspapers. Johnson made his original capital by inventing a farebox for counting coins on street railways. Most of his fortune was accumulated by investing in municipal railway franchises in Indianapolis, St. Louis, Brooklyn, and, of course, Cleveland, where he engaged in a titanic battle with Mark Hanna for control of street railways.

In 1883, a train boy sold Johnson a book by the American political economist Henry George that transformed his life. Best known for *Progress and Poverty* (1880), George examined why a society characterized by tremendous material wealth and technical progress could have within its midst such poverty and deprivation. His answer was that the just rewards of labor were confiscated by various forms of monopoly. By far the most important monopoly, George said, was in land. Private monopoly in land forced producers to pay landowners a monopoly rent that drove down wages and enriched an idle class of speculators. The increasing value of land (in contrast to the improvements upon it) was due to the increase in population, George said; being socially derived, it rightfully belonged to the entire community. Since confiscating all private property in land "would involve a needless shock to present customs and habits of thought," George proposed a simpler solution: "abolish all taxation save that upon land values."[31] George and his followers became known as "single taxers."

Convinced that George's theory was true, Johnson resolved to commit himself to the struggle against monopoly and apply George's political economy to the myriad problems of municipal government. The source of political corruption, Johnson contended, was monopolies upheld by government—what he called Privilege: "the advantage conferred on one by law of denying the competition of others."[32] Johnson essentially argued, to use the terms introduced earlier, that certain capitalists were able to exert *power over the market*. By denying competition, they were able to monopolize the *positive externalities* of urban growth. The greatest unearned profits, George maintained, came from increasing land values. Railroads had also been able to achieve a monopoly in transportation. But "the chief source of corruption in municipal life," according to Johnson, was exclusive franchises granted street railway, water, gas, electric light, and telephone companies. Land values, railroads, and streetcar lines increased tremendously in value not because of the productive efforts of the owners but because of general growth in the population and the economy. Privileged capitalists then used this speculative booty to corrupt the political system.

Johnson's analysis of the corruption of municipal government can be understood as a critique of conservative growth politics. The claim that taxes must be kept low and the public sector small in order to attract investment was false, Johnson argued. This was nothing but a growth ideology designed to protect the unearned profits of monopolists from the claims of the public. This nonrational growth policy was held in place by the corruption of the democratic process. Monopolists used their unearned profits as boodle to bribe machine politicians, who organized the ignorant foreign voters into the mass base of a conservative growth coalition. Machine politics, the target of good government reformers, was more the effect of corruption than its cause.

Johnson suggested that cities had much greater political discretion than they were led to believe to raise taxes and increase the size of government without hurting economic growth. In fact, Johnson argued, the right kind of taxes and public expansion would not only not choke off growth but would accelerate it. The method for funding this expanded public domain was simple: since the positive externalities of growth had been produced by the community, they should go back to the community. They then could be used to finance a civic revival that would compensate the many victims of industrialism and create a City Beautiful. One way to do this was for the public to own all technical monopolies, such as railways and utilities. This way services could be provided to working people at cost and a source of municipal corruption dried up. Another method was to impose a confiscatory tax on increasing land values (as opposed to the improvements on land). Far from shutting off growth, this would spur investment, Johnson believed, by forcing speculators to make productive improvements on their land. This was populist growth politics.

After serving two terms in Congress, where he attacked tariffs as an unfair tax on consumers and an anticompetitive advantage for domestic manufacturers, Johnson was elected mayor of Cleveland in 1901. He took the oath of office minutes after the official vote count in order to prevent railroads from grabbing a final strip of land on the lakefront worth $15–20 million. Johnson's greatest struggle during his four terms as mayor (1901–1909), however, was with the private streetcar companies to fulfill his promise to deliver a three-cent fare. Since state law prohibited public ownership of railways, Johnson helped form a private railway corporation, that would be run in the public interest and force down fares by competing with the other railways. Johnson sank a great deal of his own fortune into this venture. Rotund, optimistic, indefatigable, Johnson's considerable energies were sorely taxed by the protracted streetcar battle that lasted throughout his administration. The final result was a qualified victory: the streetcars remained in private hands but under close regulation by the city, which limited profits to 6 percent on stock.[33]

Johnson's administration brought about an unprecedented expansion in the scope and functions of city government. He succeeded in establishing a municipal light plant (more on that later), and garbage collection and street cleaning were taken out of private hands and made municipal services. He also established a model building code, built numerous public bathhouses and parks, and adopted the largest venture in city planning since L'Enfant in 1791—over 100 acres of public buildings downtown. To pay for all this, Johnson carried out extensive tax reform that equalized assessments and increased taxes on land over improvements. The business class cried that he would bankrupt the city and drive out business. Lincoln Steffens, on the other hand, was moved to call Johnson "the best mayor of the best-governed city in the United States."[34]

Johnson was different, it is important to understand, from the typical good government reformers of his day. For middle class reformers, the solution to municipal problems was to put the "right men" into office. Johnson attacked unjust institutions, economic privilege, not men. The petty corruption of the ward heelers, the lower class immigrants, was not the main problem in city politics, he maintained. "I agree with those who say that it is big business and the kind of big business that deals in and profits from public service grants and taxation injustices—that is the real evil in our cities and country today."[35] For this reason, nearly all the "right men" in Cleveland opposed Johnson. The Municipal Association, that bastion of good government reformers, attacked him. Johnson was considered a traitor to his class.[36]

The attacks came even though Johnson supported large parts of the reform agenda. He threw out the spoilsmen, hired experts from around the country, and used business methods in government. But this was not efficiency for efficiency's sake. The goal was to expand the public domain, even at the expense of the private sector. While not a socialist, Johnson believed in the public ownership of all monopolies. A revitalized public sector, he felt, had a key role to play in humanizing cities.

Tom Johnson had what the good government reformers lacked: a *political* vision. He wanted to make Cleveland, as he called it, "A City on the Hill." He had an architectonic vision of the city as a community enterprise that could reconcile beauty, efficiency, and opportunity. Johnson attempted nothing less than a revival of political community:

> Of course, what I wanted to convey to the people in my platform was what I have been trying to make them understand ever since, that the city with its privileges and responsibilities is *their city*, that it is as much their home in the collective sense as the houses in which they live are their individual homes.[37]

For Johnson, the problem was not too much democracy but too little. Johnson's electoral support came from the "wrong people," working

class immigrants, precisely those people whose baneful influence reformers warned against.[38] His exciting tent meetings created a new form
of communication between voters and politicians, lifting immigrant
voters out from under the control of petty bosses. Like Jefferson,
Johnson believed in decentralized government. But unlike Jefferson, he
saw cities as the hope of democracy.[39]

Political Impasse: Conservative Growth Politics Restored

By the end of Johnson's fourth two-year term, the citizens of Cleveland had grown conflict weary. In 1909, Republican boss Maurice
Maschke shrewdly ran a German, Herman Baehr, against Johnson and
the German vote, which had been a pillar of Johnson's success, ousted
him from office. Two years later, Johnson died. Newton D. Baker,
Johnson's law director, served two terms as mayor (1912–1915), but he
lacked Johnson's charismatic appeal. He was more the able technocrat,
someone to consolidate earlier gains. (Baker later served as secretary of
war under President Wilson and became a wealthy corporate lawyer.)

The fact is, after Tom Johnson, the reform movement in Cleveland
took a decidedly conservative turn. Part of the explanation is the First
World War. Cleveland's factories hummed day and night to meet the
increased wartime demand. People seemed to turn away from public
commitments, distracted by the chase for private gain. More important,
however, was the way in which the reform movement, itself, was used
by the industrial elite for conservative purposes. Ironically, it was the
very economic success of Cleveland's industrialists that brought about
their political weakness and need to support reforms. In search of
profits, they had massed hundreds of thousands of working class immigrants in the city who suffered nearly all the costs of industrialism. At
the same time, in order to escape these costs, the elite moved rapidly out
of the city, diluting their own political influence. With substantial
investments still in the city and local government playing a larger role in
the economy, the business elite feared what the working class immigrants could do with their electoral majority. The experience of McKisson and Johnson confirmed their worst fears. In the 1911 mayoral
election, the Socialists got 10 percent of the vote. Something had to be
done.

The reform movement, stripped of its excess Johnsonian baggage of
grassroots democracy and economic justice, provided the instrument.
The conservative side of reform has been largely overlooked by political

scientists who, too often, portray city politics as a struggle between "good guys" (reformers) who attempt to solve the problems of the city and "bad guys" (party politicians and ethnic voters) who stand in the way of progress. Banfield and Wilson, for example, postulate the existence of two contrasting orientations toward politics in the American cities: the public-regarding ethos of middle class WASPs and the private-regarding ethos of working class immigrants:

> The Anglo-Saxon Protestant middle-class style of politics, with its emphasis upon the obligation of the individual to participate in public affairs and to seek the good of the community "as a whole" (which implies, among other things, the necessity of honesty, impartiality, and efficiency) was fundamentally incompatible with the immigrant's style of politics, which took no account of the community.[40]

The existence of two different orientations toward city politics, and their correlation with certain income and ethnic groups, is confirmed by the Cleveland example.[41] To equate one with "public values" and the other with "private values" does not accord with the facts. In fact, it is patently absurd.

Good government reforms primarily served the needs of one class. In the twentieth century, Cleveland's industrial elite found itself faced with a dilemma. On the one hand, city government clearly needed to be strengthened and made more efficient in order to provide the infrastructure needed for economic growth; on the other hand, given the democratic rules of the game, this threatened to give working class majorities a more powerful instrument for invading the prerogatives of private capital. The reform agenda provided a way of slipping between the horns of the dilemma. Power could be centralized in city government at the same time that it was insulated from democratic pressures. Weakening political parties meant that wealth would replace party organization as the pathway to public office; and separating politics from administration, if carried far enough, would place more decisions in the hands of "neutral" experts who would be more responsive to the imperatives of growth than ward-based political interests.[42]

By now, considerable evidence demonstrates that good government reforms are not public-regarding but rather have favored certain private interests over others in a decidedly undemocratic fashion.[43] Nonpartisan elections, for example, give an advantage to Republicans, favor middle class white Protestants over working class, minority, and Roman Catholic candidates, suppress divisive issues, and frustrate protest voting. In general, nonpartisan elections make policy less responsive to socio-economic factors, such as class, and make politicians less accountable to the electorate.[44] Many of these effects are heightened when elections are at-large rather than by district. At a general level, studies have shown that cities with reformed governments tend to tax and spend less than their unreformed counterparts.[45] Reform seems designed to limit both the cost and the scope of city government. Examined carefully, reform seems less a public-regarding ethos and more a private-regarding ideology.[46]

Tom Johnson had adopted parts of the reform agenda, certain business-like reforms in administration, in order to expand the scope of government and make it a more efficient instrument of social justice. To him, the problem was not too much democracy but too little. Johnson's followers, however, lost his democratic vision of "A City on the Hill." "The watch-word of the Johnson remnant upon re-entry was 'efficiency,' the more readily attainable and more generally acceptable portion of the Johnson reform."[47] The deradicalization of reform is not surprising when one considers who backed it in the post-Johnson era. In Cleveland, it was overwhelmingly financed and staffed by the business elite.[48]

After Tom Johnson, the reformers became isolated from the mass of working class voters. Even under cover of the public interest, it would be very difficult to enact their reform agenda. As a result, reformers were forced to compromise with ward-based politicians, an essential compromise that characterizes Cleveland politics to this day. This is exemplified by the controversy surrounding Cleveland's first home rule charter, voted on the year after the State of Ohio finally approved home rule for cities in 1912. The most controversial issue was the composition of City Council.[49] One group advocated a five-man council elected at-large. A large council, they argued, was inefficient and promoted machine politics. Opponents charged that this was an effort to disenfranchise foreign-born voters, especially Roman Catholics. Heated opposition came from party politicians and councilmen, who saw it as an effort to destroy their ward organizations. A second group, including Baker, advocated a twenty-six member council elected by wards. Most supported this on pragmatic grounds—that it was necessary to attract the political support necessary to pass the new charter, which contained important advances, including a strong executive and nonpartisan elections. The charter passed in 1913 with a twenty-six member council, but it showed the necessity of compromise between reformers and ward-based politicians.

Cleveland's experience with the city manager system also showed that business was not able to completely control city government. In 1921, reformers, exploiting the ineffectiveness of mayors after Baker, persuaded the electorate to vote in a city manager form of government. Cleveland was the largest city in the country to do so. Modeled on the private corporation, the city manager plan was designed to make government more responsive to hierarchically organized administrative systems, like big business, and less responsive to local subcommunities, like ethnic neighborhoods. As William Hopkins, Cleveland's first city manager, put it: "It is undoubtedly easier for a city manager to insist upon acting in accordance with the business interests of the city than it is for the mayor to do the same thing."[50]

The new charter, however, did not work as intended. Theoretically, the council would select a city manager according to professional standards. Instead, Maschke and Burr Gongwer, the Democratic boss, chose Hopkins, a well-known Cleveland businessman and real estate promoter. Maschke and Gongwer agreed to split the patronage on a 60/40 basis. Refusing to play the role of low-key administrator, Hopkins vigorously promoted new development projects like a publicity seeking politician. According to Section 34 of the new charter, "The council and its members shall deal with the administrative service solely through the city manager." But council members continued to act as before, asserting patronage rights and exacting special favors for their constituents from the bureaucracy.

In the late 1920s, a series of councilmanic scandals reflected poorly on the entire system. Hopkins attempted to free himself from Maschke, resulting in a legislative-executive deadlock. Maschke replaced Hopkins in 1930. Four times an issue was put on the ballot to dump the city manager plan. Finally, in 1931, the voters, sensing the hypocrisy of the system and desiring to elect their chief executive directly, replaced it with a strong-mayor system that is still in effect today.

The reform impulse was blunted in Cleveland more than in most cities. Cleveland's large foreign born, working class population did not buy the reform agenda. The result was a curious political compromise between businesslike government reforms and traditional pluralism. Part of the reform agenda was enacted—nonpartisan elections and the strong-mayor system, for example. But government still responded primarily to the pull and haul of ethnic and racial subcommunities in almost classic pluralist fashion.

The entire period of Cleveland politics from the fall of Tom Johnson to the recent crisis of growth politics can be characterized as an uneasy compromise between the Protestant industrial capitalists and the ethnic, largely Roman Catholic, workers and small businessmen. More than a compromise, it was really a kind of division of turf, with separate spheres of influence. The economic elite, unable to gain control of city government through good government reforms, was content, for the most part, to let professional politicians, primarily of working class origin, manage local government. As long as taxes were kept low, public order preserved, and the basic services necessary for industry maintained, they were satisfied. The ethnic working class, for their part, withdrew from any challenge to private control over basic economic decisions, such as investment. In return, they controlled the prestige and patronage of city government, limited as it was.

The implicit compromise, or division of turf, between ethnics and industrialists raises puzzling questions. Why did the economic elite withdraw from city politics and allow it to be controlled by working class politicians? Why did working class ethnic, and later black, voters ignore issues of economic distribution and put up with a fragmented political system that was often corrupt and inefficient?

Cleveland's economic dominants, the old wealth based on iron and steel, have always been close-knit and conservative. Stretching back to the early stage of American industrial capitalism, Cleveland's big businesses were able to maintain financial independence from the Eastern financial establishment. In a well-known study in the 1930s, Paul Sweezy named the "Cleveland Group," alongside the Mellon and Rockefeller groups, as one of the big eight interest groups in the American economy. The group was centered on the Mather interests in iron ore and steel, Goodyear Tire, and Cleveland Trust.[51] Whereas the Rockefeller interests became bastions of liberal Republicanism, Cleveland industrialists, who relied primarily on domestic markets, were bulwarks of the far right of the Republican party, supporting conservative and isolationist candidates. In 1964, Cleveland was one of the few cities where big business did not switch to Lyndon Johnson and strongly supported Barry Goldwater to the end.[52] George M. Humphrey, who led the expansion of the Hanna industrial empire in the twentieth century, organized a business committee of 450 for Goldwater.[53]

In short, Cleveland's conservative business elite was not ideologically inclined to use government to further its long term interests. On the whole, their ideology corresponded to their material interests. Some businessmen, of course, benefited from the prevailing pluralist system through contracts and franchises. But the big iron and steel interests did not need any new initiatives from local government. The basic infrastructural investments necessary for heavy industry had already been made. Local politics was kept within safe and narrow confines—not, primarily, by direct elite manipulation but by indirect fiscal pressures and control over credit. Muny Light, for example, was allowed to survive, but through lack of aggressive management and access to credit, ceased to be a threat to the private utility, which, by the 1960s, was scheming to take over its public competitor.

The elite also lost interest in city government simply because they were leaving the city at a rapid rate. This was true of both their investments and their residences. Industrial investment began to decentralize around 1900 with the trend accelerating in Cleveland after the Second World War. The business elite in Cleveland moved their homes early to the suburbs to escape the pollution, congestion, noise, and traffic of the industrialized city. Wealthy suburbs, such as Shaker Heights, formed in the early twentieth century, even before the automobile. Today there is almost no upper class and remarkably little middle class left within the city. It is not surprising that the reform impulse was blunted in Cleveland.

There were only two exceptions to the withdrawal of the business elite from Cleveland. One was the continued strength of white collar and service investments downtown. The other was the strong investment of the economic elite in Cleveland's charities and cultural institutions. Following its political ideology, the elite criticized the welfare state while funding a large philanthropic sector that, unlike city government, was safely under its control. In 1913, Cleveland originated the idea of a United Fund and even today has the largest per capita contributions of any major city.[54] In 1914, Frederick Goff, chairman of Cleveland Trust, led in the formation of the nation's first community foundation, the Cleveland Foundation.[55] Recently, Cleveland ranked sixth in the nation in the number of foundations.[56] Among other activities, private charities ameliorated the condition of those left behind by industrial growth. Industrial philanthropists also invested heavily in an impressive cultural complex on Cleveland's East Side, called University Circle, that included Case Western Reserve University, the Museum of

Art ($100 million endowment), Severance Hall (home of Cleveland's world famous orchestra), Western Reserve Historical Society, the Natural History Museum, and the Botanical Gardens. While located in Cleveland, these institutions, for the most part, serve suburbanites and do not pay city taxes.

While distant from the business elite in class and culture, the ethnics had a similar conservative political orientation. On economic decision making, they deferred to the business elite. Ethnics benefited, after all, from private sector growth. As time went on, relatively high-paying industrial jobs were increasingly available, especially after the success of industrial unions in the 1930s. This conservative approach was buttressed by acceptance of a diffuse ideology that stressed upward mobility out of one's class rather than solidarity with one's class. The ideal was individual advancement in the private economy rather than community advancement through the public sector. As long as the private economy kept expanding, there would always be upward social mobility, and perhaps a plot of land in the suburbs, to siphon off discontent. Generally satisfied with the *status quo*, the ethnics did not expect any new initiatives from local government.

Although firmly entrenched in ward politics, the ethnics did not control the mayor's office until 1941, when they elected Frank Lausche, a Slovenian Democrat, as mayor. Since then, the ethnics have had a virtual stranglehold on City Hall, electing one of their own as mayor every time, with the single exception of the two terms of Carl Stokes.[57] While FDR brought the ethnics into the Democratic fold for national elections, their political philosophy was closer to the Dixiecrats than the New Dealers. Lausche is the archetype of this strange bird: the fighting, conservative, ethnic Democrat. Lausche was a phenomenally successful vote getter, elected twice mayor of Cleveland, five times governor of Ohio, and twice senator from Ohio. He ran as a Democrat but, in office, acted more like a Republican.[58] Lausche portrayed himself, however, as the independent champion of the little people, fighting to save the taxpayers' money.

While the fragmented pluralist system in city government was often inefficient and sometimes corrupt, it represented well the immediate interests of the balkanized racial and ethnic minorities in Cleveland. Politics was the exchange of petty favors (patronage, city contracts, special services) for votes, the classic pluralist politics of exchange, devoid of ideology. The fragmented system prevented any broad class interests from being realized through government; opposition was brought off rather than confronted.[59] Cleveland's large City Council, elected for almost its entire history from single member districts, gave relatively easy access to minorities. Blacks, for example, elected their first councilman, Thomas Fleming, in 1909, even though they represented less than 2 percent of the population. Fleming delivered the black vote for the Maschke machine and in return got a small amount of patronage and favors from the government.[60] While blacks were clearly shortchanged by city government, they did get a piece of the pie in exchange for their votes. Every ethnic group that elected a member of council could get a piece of the pie.

What reformers could not understand was that pluralist machine politics met the needs of poor immigrants in the city the way reform politics never could. The ward leader, who spoke the mother tongue, would meet the new arrivals at the railway station, find them a place to stay, help them get a job, and perhaps provide them bail money or a small loan. Newcomers needed the face-to-face contacts of the ward organizations, someone to help them find their way through a foreign, often bureaucratic, system. And, of course, as election day neared, the boss would make sure the immigrant had naturalization papers and was registered to vote in order to repay the favors.[61] Even after the institution of the welfare state, the ward organizations performed important "latent functions" that social workers and bureaucrats could not perform.[62] "They [reformers] asked the ward heeler to withdraw, but made no effort to satisfy the human wants of the immigrant, such as advice, aid, encouragement, or friendship, which were important functions of the machine."[63] City government provided an escalator of upward mobility for each new immigrant group. Eventually different groups became entrenched in different sections of city government: blacks got a corner on laboring jobs in sanitation, Italians became inspectors, Irish dominated the courts. It was not hard to see that if civil service had controlled city hiring, middle class suburbanites, who were good at taking tests, would have had a better shot at these jobs than poor inner city residents.[64]

Conclusion: The Impasse of Conservative Growth Politics

In short, the conflict between ethnics and industrialists, between pluralism and reform, was not a conflict between private-regardingness and public-regardingness, but between two conceptions of self-interest. In Cleveland, the conflict resulted in a kind of truce, a retreat into

separate spheres of influence. The movement to reform city government
was stopped, even rolled back, and pluralism remained the norm in city
politics.

The result was classic conservative growth politics. The growth
process was led and financed by the private sector, with local government acting mainly to keep taxes low to attract industrial investment.
The Tom Johnson era, to be sure, had greatly expanded the functions of
city government, in some cases even invading the prerogatives of private capital.[65] The economic elite, however, did not attempt to roll back
these advances as it became clear that a larger public sector would not
impede industrial growth and that better services would, in many ways,
make Cleveland a more attractive city for investors. After Johnson, the
government continued to grow and reforms were enacted, but they did
not fundamentally alter the parameters of city government. A City
Planning Commission was created in 1913, but it had, at best, advisory
powers—and no real powers over private development. In 1929, the
city finally passed a zoning code. Cleveland was almost fully developed,
however, and the code could do little to roll back the destruction of
residential areas. In short, while city government was larger than it had
been before 1900, and this contributed to the well-being of the average
citizen, it still had very little power over development.

The capstone of conservative growth politics was the regime of
ethnic mayors. The era of ethnic mayors has been summed up in these
words:

> The regime of mayors beginning with Lausche produced a city
> administration that was characterized by party independence, hon-
> esty, low taxes, low service levels, and, in the words of a long-time
> observer, "a caretaker-type government that never really appreci-
> ated the tremendous changes taking place in the city and never
> moved to really respond to them."[66]

"Tremendous changes" were indeed brewing beneath the surface,
changes that would strain to the breaking point the peculiar compromise between ethnics and industrialists that had dominated Cleveland
politics for so long.

3

Growth Crisis

Cleveland—a city that has achieved pre-eminence in industry, commerce and culture through enterprise of men and women who exercise scientific knowledge, inventive genius, productive labor and wise management. Taking advantage of their favorable location on the greatest of all inland waterways and the proximity of rich mineral resources. Has brought into being in the finest tradition of local self-government, a community self-disciplined where those of every race, of all creeds and of whatsoever national origin, live and work in harmony so that they may transmit to posterity a city with an enlightened vision and a civic soul.

J. H. Crowley

Emblazoned in six-inch-high letters on the main wall of Cleveland's majestic city council chambers, on either side of a dramatic mural depicting Progress through the union of Science and Industry in the vortex of Cleveland's industrial flats, these words reflect an outlook deeply etched in the Cleveland psyche but one that is further and further removed from present-day reality.

Cleveland has changed. After almost a century of phenomenal economic expansion, Cleveland's industrial boom finally broke in the 1930s. The increased demand of the Second World War brought about a recovery, but in the 1950s Cleveland's industrial economy began a long slow slide that has continued to this day. As Figure 2 shows, Cleveland's population followed its industry. The city reached its population zenith—914,808—with the 1950 census. Since then it has been all downhill. From 1950 to 1980, Cleveland's population declined more than 340,000—an astounding 37 percent. A transition from continuous growth to sustained contraction is bound to have a profound impact on all aspects of society, including politics.

The words on the wall of the city council chamber now ring with

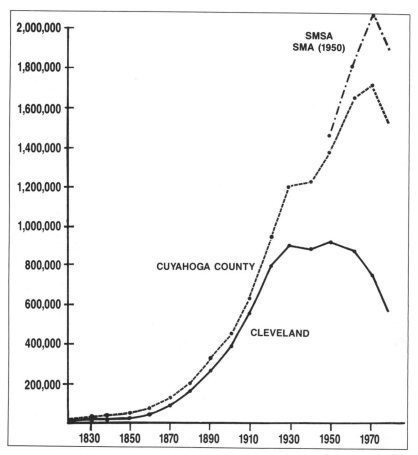

FIGURE 2. Population Trends; Cleveland, Cuyahoga County, and Standard Metropolitan Statistical Area, 1820–1980. **Source:** U.S. Bureau of the Census, *Census of Population*, 1820–1980.

irony. The almost Enlightenment faith in the union of science and technology to reconcile social contradictions and guarantee civic harmony clashes with the rancorous politics of recent years: shrinking economic resources and dwindling city services have heightened social conflict, especially around racial divisions, recently inflamed by court ordered busing; formerly distant but polite relations between the public and private sectors have given way to oscillations of close embrace and bitter separation, accompanied by heated debate over the proper relationship. Class conflict and class resentment, formerly covered over by waves of upward mobility, have come to the surface amid charges of "corporate corruption" and "populist demagoguery."

Uneven Development: Regional Decline

Cleveland has been on the short end of three major trends in the uneven development of the American economy:

1. The flow of capital, and along with it jobs and population, from the Northeast to the Sunbelt and overseas;
2. The decentralization of industry and jobs, as well as middle income taxpayers, from the central city to the suburbs;
3. The shift in the U.S. economy from heavy industry and manufacturing to white collar management and service functions.

Of these three trends, the weakest in its effect on Cleveland has been the regional shift from Northeast to Sunbelt. By now the nationwide trend is well documented. The effect of regional shifts on the Cleveland area economy is relatively recent. A glance at Figure 2 shows that the Cleveland area has, since 1970, begun to share in the central city's population decline.[1] Figure 3 shows that Cleveland's employment growth began to lag seriously behind the rest of the nation in the 1970s.

Part of the apparent regional decline of the Cleveland area is, in fact, an artifact of the transition of the entire economy from manufacturing to services, a transition discussed in detail later in this chapter.[2] Having traditionally relied heavily on manufacturing, Cleveland is naturally harder hit than most cities by the transition to services. In 1947, Cleveland, with 1.14 percent of the nation's total employment, had

1.88 percent of the nation's manufacturing employment. Figure 3 shows that manufacturing employment in Cleveland has stagnated. By 1977, Cleveland had dropped to 1.35 percent of the nation's total manufacturing employment.³ Increased employment in the Sunbelt has not been due so much to the migration of manufacturing jobs from cities like Cleveland but to the faster expansion of jobs in the service sector. Figure 3 shows that Cleveland has lagged further behind the nation in the growth of services than in manufacturing. Dun & Brad-

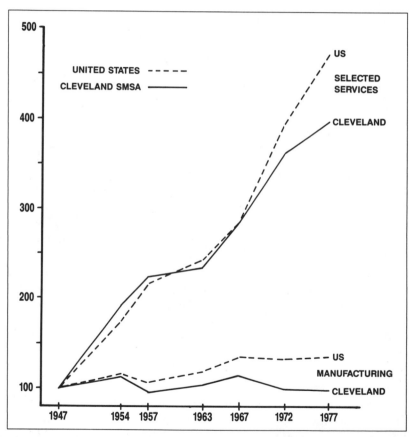

FIGURE 3. Relative Change in Employment: Selected Services and Manufacturing, 1947–1977.* **Source:** U.S. Bureau of the Census, *Census of Manufacturing and Selected Services,* 1947 through 1977 (Washington, D.C.: Government Printing Office).
*(1947 = 100)

street data has been used to examine Cleveland's job loss. From 1966 to 1971, more than half of Cleveland's manufacturing job loss was due to business terminations rather than relocations. And of those manufacturing jobs that left the inner city during that period, more than 90 percent moved to the surrounding suburbs, not to another region of the country.[4]

In other words, regional shifts are not nearly as important to the Cleveland area economy as some observers suggest. Moreover, the Cleveland area is not Appalachia. Northeast Ohio has been a relatively prosperous region with mean income above the national average and unemployment rates consistently below the national average until quite recently. Of course, the trend in regional underdevelopment is relatively recent; whether the trend will intensify or abate in the years to come remains to be seen. Chapter 1 argued that political factors played a much greater role in the regional shift of jobs and investment than is suggested by explanations that rely on changes in technology or consumer behavior. In a later chapter, I examine whether local property tax abatements can affect regional investment flows. It is clear, however, that both the political and market factors that shape regional investment flows are generally beyond the control of local government. Much closer to home, and a movement that has had a much greater impact on the inner city for a longer period of time, is the trend toward suburbanization.

Uneven Development: Suburbanization

Cleveland's economic problems can be summed up in one word: poverty. Many residents of the inner city lack sufficient income to maintain their health and homes, let alone to enjoy their American birthright, "the pursuit of happiness." In 1979, 124,860 Cleveland residents lived below the federal poverty level ($7,412 for a nonfarm family of four), an astonishing 21.8 percent of the total population. But to be poor is one thing. To be poor amidst a sea of riches is something else. The contrast between Cleveland and its suburbs is especially severe and this creates an even greater sense of deprivation, of the relative kind. Moreover, the presence of wealthy suburbs tends to suck money, brains, and talent out of the city like a sponge, creating a permanent condition of underdevelopment.

Richard Nathan and Charles Adams have constructed an index for measuring the contrast between central cities and their suburbs, using

1970 census data on percentage of dependent persons and levels of education, income, crowded housing, poverty, and unemployment.[5] Out of 55 Standard Metropolitan Statistical Areas (SMSAs) with a population of 500,000 or more, Cleveland ranked second from the bottom on "Central City Hardship Relative to Balance of SMSA." Only Newark was worse off.[6] The reason for Cleveland's extraordinarily low ranking was not so much that Clevelanders were extremely disadvantaged socioeconomically. When compared with other central cities, Cleveland ranked ninth from the bottom. Rather it was that Cleveland's suburbs were extremely advantaged. Cleveland's suburbs ranked number 1 out of 55 suburban areas on the hardship index. In the six factors examined, at least, Cleveland's suburbs were the most socially and economically well off in the nation.

On just about any measure of social and economic well-being, Clevelanders fare poorly compared with suburbanites. In 1979, average family income for Cleveland residents ($17,743) was only 61.5 percent of that for suburban residents.[7] The poverty rate in Cleveland (21.8 percent) is almost five times greater than the suburbs (4.6 percent). The crux of the problem is jobs. Cleveland's unemployment rate is consistently higher than the suburbs' or the nation's. In 1980, it was 13.8 percent overall, 18.6 percent among blacks and other minorities, and 26.1 percent for teenagers.[8] The problem is not just unemployment but underemployment. Many Clevelanders have jobs in the secondary labor market, where the pay is low and the chance of layoffs high.[9] Moreover, each employed city resident has to support, on the average, more people than workers elsewhere, as Table 1 shows.

The Cleveland workforce is also disproportionately made up of

TABLE 1.

Dependency Ratio: Number Not in the Civilian Labor Force per Employed Civilian (1960, 1970, and 1980)

Location	1960	1970	1980
City of Cleveland	1.59	1.62	1.56
Cleveland Suburbs	1.57	1.42	1.01
United States	1.50	1.38	1.21

Source: Cleveland City Planning Commission, *Jobs and Income*, vol. 1 (Cleveland: City Planning Commission, Dec. 1973); U.S. Bureau of the Census, *1980 Census of Population and Housing: Cleveland, Ohio, Standard Metropolitan Statistical Area* (Washington, D.C.: Government Printing Office).

women and blacks (Table 2). Women and blacks have historically been relegated to low paying occupations and, even in the same occupation, are consistently paid less. In 1979, black median family income was only 66.1 percent of the median income for all families in the SMSA; average income of female-headed households was only 52.0 percent of average family earnings that same year for the area.

A major cause of Cleveland's economic woes, simply put, is that jobs, investment, and the middle class have migrated beyond the political boundaries of the city. How did this tremendous disparity come about? Frequently, the movement to the suburbs has been interpreted as a value choice, as a preference, for example, for a combined city and country life-style. Political scientists have explained it as a search for a kind of Jeffersonian democracy in suburbia, a shunning of the corruption and inefficiency of big city governments.[10] In 1956 Charles Tiebout summed up this trend of thought by constructing an explicit market model of suburbanization.[11] Mobile citizens are seen as voting with their feet for different packages of public consumption goods. Some value high expenditures on education, others value parks and recreation, still others prefer low taxes even if that means fewer public services. Local governments are looked upon as firms, competing in the market for residential consumers. In order to compete effectively, they must produce their bundle of public consumption goods in the most efficient manner possible.

Tiebout's theory of suburbanization is very similar to Peterson's market theory of urban politics; in fact, Peterson acknowledges Tiebout as a prime source of his thinking.[12] Tiebout's market explanation of suburbanization, however, is flawed much as Peterson's theory is flawed—neither recognizes that relations of power penetrate the gov-

TABLE 2.
Women and Blacks as a Percentage of Total Resident Employed Workforce, Cleveland and Suburbs, 1980

Workforce	City of Cleveland	Cleveland Suburbs
Women	45.0	38.1
Blacks	39.3	6.3

Source: U.S. Bureau of the Census, *1980 Census of Population and Housing: Cleveland, Ohio, Standard Metropolitan Statistical Area* (Washington, D.C.: Government Printing Office).

ernmental marketplace. By now, the considerable power exerted by the federal government in promoting suburbanization, to the detriment of inner cities, is well documented.[13] Federal mortgage subsidy and guarantee programs (FHA and VA) helped build new homes in the suburbs, providing little to rehabilitate inner city housing; the federal government subsidized suburban sprawl by granting billions of dollars for new water and sewer systems, roads, and electrification; the huge interstate highway system subsidized the commuting needs of suburbanites.

In this study of Cleveland, however, our focus is on the role of local governments. Suburbanization in Cleveland is a fascinating story of power exerted over the market by suburban governments and real estate interests.

In the early period of industrialism (1850s to 1880s), Cleveland was remarkably integrated by race and class. Cleveland's small black community was not confined to a ghetto.[14] The lack of speedy transportation meant that both rich and poor had to live within walking distance of work. In Cleveland the upper and lower classes lived cheek by jowl, often with the wealthy on through streets and the poor on side streets. The invention of the streetcar, and later the automobile, made it possible for different races and classes to disperse and separate. It did not, however, make it necessary that there be separate suburban governments.

Until 1910, Cleveland grew along with the dispersing population by annexing contiguous municipalities. In that year, Cleveland contained 90 percent of the county's population, the highest figure it would ever achieve. According to Ohio law, annexation of an incorporated area required the approval of voters of both municipalities. Before 1910, Cleveland never lost a referendum on annexation. Suburbanites wanted Cleveland's superior public services; they realized it was more expensive to fund their own streets, street lights, police and fire departments. And Cleveland's heavy industry gave it a *per capita* tax base far exceeding that of most suburbs. Things changed, however, as suburban voters began to see the advantages of separating from the problems of the inner city. Between 1910 and 1940, Cleveland lost five out of nine annexation referenda.[15] West Park, in 1922, was the last major suburb to be annexed. While Cleveland's land area grew 600 percent from 1870 to 1930, since then it has grown less than 8 percent, and some of that is landfill along Lake Erie.

Suburbs separated from Cleveland for many different reasons.

North Randall, for example, was specially created to permit gambling and horseracing, which were prohibited in Cleveland. By 1930, it contained the two finest race tracks in the state but only 107 inhabitants.[16] Cuyahoga Heights became a tax haven; industry there was not burdened by the need to finance a large school system. Most surburbs, however, were formed to preserve and enhance residential values.

The motive for suburban class segregation can be discerned by looking at an early study of an inner city slum area. Commissioned by the Cleveland Metropolitan Housing Authority in 1934, the report concluded that the city, county, and Board of Education paid out much more than they got back in taxes from this poverty neighborhood in Cleveland: "In other words the City of Cleveland (taxpayers in the city, county, and School District) subsidized each man, woman and child in this area to an amount of $51.10 in 1932. This seems to be a rather large subsidy for the privilege of maintaining a slum area."[17] The report was used to argue for public housing. It could just as easily have been used to persuade middle class taxpayers to move to independent suburbs to avoid the fiscal burdens of inner city slums. For the mobile middle class, this seemed a more effective course of action than supporting public housing.

A whole range of devices were used to achieve suburban class segregation. Shaker Heights, formed in the early twentieth century, was one of the first exclusive suburbs. It was developed by the Van Sweringen brothers as a totally planned suburb for the rich. Advertising brochures stressed that, being 400 feet above Lake Erie on the "Heights," residents would avoid the noise and pollution of industrial Cleveland. The problem was how to prevent poor people from also moving out to enjoy the fresh air. The fabulously wealthy Van Sweringen brothers simply used their ownership of all the land to restrict it to the rich through contractual devices. Deed restrictions at the time the property was sold prohibited land uses deemed incompatible with residential districts, such as apartments, saloons, and commercial and industrial buildings. The design of each house had to be approved by the Van Sweringens, and each deed stipulated minimum setbacks and spacings.[18] No home was allowed to be built for less than $17,000 (the equivalent of over $150,000 today).[19] To enhance the land values, the Van Sweringen brothers built the Shaker Rapid, a streetcar line completed in 1920, which cut commuting time to downtown to fifteen minutes. By investing in a suburb accessible only to the rich, landowners in Shaker Heights captured the positive externalities of growth: phenomenally appreciating land values of 2851 percent between 1901 and 1920.[20]

Rarely, however, did real estate developers have the resources to exclude the poor by owning all the property in a suburb.[21] Other suburbs used the powers of local government to achieve the same result. The discrimination was aimed at lower income residents as well as racial minorities, especially blacks. The focus here is on class discrimination. Obviously, class discrimination and race discrimination are interrelated. Racism is buttressed by economic differences. Blacks are associated with poverty and, because of their skin color, are highly visible wherever they go. Lower middle class whites, especially, fear any threat to their precarious economic status by association with a group bearing the stigma of low status. This is not to imply that race discrimination can be reduced to class discrimination. Clearly, racism has a life of its own.[22]

While racial fears are buttressed by class differences, it is also true that class discrimination is intensified by racism. While courts have struck down laws that discriminate on the basis of race, they have generally upheld the right of governments to discriminate on the basis of income.[23] Consequently, suburban governments wanting to exclude racial minorities must employ laws designed to exclude low income residents. "Thus a *class* policy may be the only way to achieve *racial* goals."[24]

Cleveland's suburbs used a whole range of devices to exclude the poor and monopolize the positive externalities of residential housing markets. Ironically, many of these devices were originally developed in the early twentieth century by progressives to aid inner cities. Municipal home rule, enacted by the State of Ohio in 1912, gave the emerging suburbs powers denied to Cleveland during its crucial formative years. Home rule fueled the movement to the suburbs.

Zoning laws became the most important exclusionary device used by suburbs. Zoning laws were first enacted by municipalities around 1901. But it was not until 1926, in the landmark case of *Village of Euclid v. Ambler Realty Company*, that the U.S. Supreme Court upheld the right of a municipality to zone districts according to a comprehensive plan and prescribe the kinds of development permitted in each district. The village of Euclid, a suburb of Cleveland, zoned the area between the Nickel Plate and Lake Shore railroads, extending from Cleveland, for industrial use. In this way Euclid was able to enjoy the tax revenues from industry without the chaotic mixing of industrial and residential uses that had so damaged residential values in Cleveland.

Over the years zoning laws have become very sophisticated. The name of the game is to zone out urban costs and zone in urban resources.[25] In residential development, one of the main devices is restriction, or exclusion, of multifamily housing. A 1964 study in Cleveland's Cuyahoga County, for example, found that only 2.1 percent of undeveloped land was available for multifamily construction.[26] According to a 1974 survey, six suburbs do not permit any multifamily development at all and others limit such development by requiring extremely low densities or prohibiting buildings over a certain height, making development on expensive land economically unfeasible.[27] Another device used to keep lower income homeowners out is minimum lot zoning. During the 1960s, 67 percent of the available residential land in Cuyahoga County was zoned for lots of a half-acre or larger.[28] Other new forms of governmental power over the private market also were used to isolate the inner city. Strict building codes were used to prevent all but the most expensive new development and strict enforcement of housing codes, in essence, prevented poor families from moving into certain suburbs.

Why did the city of Cleveland not use these same devices to shape development to its advantage? The answer, for the most part, is timing. Cleveland was almost totally developed by the time the progressive movement overcame the resistance of *laissez faire* conservatives and made these instruments of power over the marketplace available to municipalities. At the same time that technological developments, such as advances in transportation, made it possible for population and industry to decentralize, new legal devices enabled suburbs to shape the decentralization of economic activity to their advantage. By excluding noxious industry and poor residents, suburbs could capture the positive externalities of urban growth, leaving the negative externalities behind in the inner city.

Cleveland's suburbs have also been extraordinarily successful at excluding low income public housing. Of the 12,200 units of conventional public housing in Cuyahoga County in 1973, 98.4 percent were located inside the city of Cleveland.[29] The most effective device for excluding public housing is for a suburb to simply refuse to sign a Cooperative Agreement with the local housing authority.[30] In 1973, a U.S. District Court, in a case involving Cleveland suburbs, held that the Cooperation Agreement requirement of the Federal Act "was constitutional both on its face and as applied, though suburbs may have used such requirement as a shield to protect their inhabitants from integration by low income Negroes."[31] In the Cleveland area, only four municipalities out of over fifty eligible have signed Cooperation Agreements.

In the case of subsidized low income housing that does not require a Cooperation Agreement, suburbs can use their control over building and zoning codes to exclude.[32] Parma, a suburb of Cleveland, was found guilty of excluding low income blacks by blocking privately sponsored low income housing using various devices, including: denying a building permit; requiring 2.5 parking spaces per dwelling unit; mandating voter approval of all zoning changes as well as of all subsidized housing projects; and limiting all future residential structures to 35 feet in height.[33]

"Beggar thy neighbor"—this has been the principle followed by suburban governments in Cleveland. They have used every power within their grasp to capture the positive externalities of metropolitan growth while foisting the negative externalities on the central city. This does not mean that inner city residents are somehow morally superior. Far from it. They, too, would do everything in their power to exclude the poor and protect their property values. Inner city residents continually discriminate on the basis of race and class. Cleveland has been ranked one of the most racially segregated cities in the nation.[34] In 1972, a federal judge found the city of Cleveland guilty of intentionally constructing nearly all of its public housing in low income black neighborhoods.[35] The difference between Cleveland and the suburbs, however, is that the inner city lacks the ability to use nice legal devices to exclude the poor completely from its jurisdiction. Also, being more dependent on federal funding, Cleveland is much more vulnerable to federal pressures to build low income housing within its boundaries. Since inner city residents have relatively little control over the changing racial and economic composition of their neighborhoods, it is not surprising that racial and class change are volatile issues in inner city politics.

The effect of suburban class segregation on the allocation of values has been overlooked by pluralist and market theories of community power. The well-known political scientist, Norton Long, who campaigned vigorously for metropolitan consolidation in Cleveland, identified the nature of the benefits reaped by suburbanites: "Unequal consumption of public goods among formally equal citizens by suburban segregation."[36] This is certainly true in Cleveland. In 1910, with its large industrial sector, Cleveland's *per capita* tax base far exceeded that of most of its suburbs. In 1977, its *per capita* tax base ranked in the bottom 17 percent of taxing jurisdictions in Cuyahoga County.[37] No matter where you look—schools, recreation, public safety, streets—services within Cleveland fall far short of those in the suburbs. And it is not just a matter of revenues. School children in Cleveland are harder to educate because many come from poverty-stricken, broken homes; police have a tougher job because the crime rate is much higher; the entire public infrastructure is harder to maintain because it is old and wornout. In other words, even if *per capita* expenditures were the same, which they are not, public services in Cleveland would compare unfavorably.

Suburban segregation does not lead only to the uneven provision of public services but also to the uneven distribution of the externalities of the metropolitan housing market, exacerbating income inequalities.[38] Roger Vaughan and Mary Vogel looked at the differences between central cities and suburbs involving environmental noise, aircraft noise, air pollution, open space, and crime. They calculated that, on the average, central city households bear external costs between $750 and $900 per year greater than the costs in a suburban location.[39] In Cleveland, undoubtedly, the cost difference would be greater. Other costs need to be taken into account, as well. Home insurance (if it can be obtained) and auto insurance are much costlier in the inner city than in the suburbs.[40] The decentralization of retail trade imposes a special burden on central city residents: "Suffering the most from changing retail patterns are lower income consumers who not only are likely to live in neighborhoods which have experienced the greatest commercial deterioration, but also most frequently lack the mobility to shop at distant stores where prices are lower and selection greater."[41] Also, many of the job opportunities for blue collar and unskilled city residents have migrated to the suburbs while their place of residence has been confined to the inner city.[42] Almost a third of city residents do not own a car and, since public transportation lines radiate from downtown, it is difficult for them to commute to dispersed jobs in the suburbs.[43]

Suburban class segregation also has a regressive effect through the uneven appreciation of home values. Suburban homeowners have been able to monopolize the positive externalities of the housing market so that suburban home values have soared while inner city values have stagnated. A representative sample of all single-family home sales by the Regional Planning Commission in 1969 found that the average selling price in the city of Cleveland ($15,777) was only 53 percent of the average sales price in the suburbs ($29,621).[44] The gap has widened. In 1979, according to sales records of the county auditor, the average sales price of all one- to four-family properties in the city of Cleveland ($28,445) was only 44 percent of the average sales price in the suburbs ($64,408).[45] This uneven development has been influenced not just by the exclusionary policies of suburban governments but by the unwillingness of private financial institutions to invest in minority inner city neighborhoods. A careful study of lending patterns in Cleveland by the Federal Reserve Bank concluded that redlining does, indeed, exist in Cleveland.[46]

It is crucial to understand that the uneven development between the suburbs and the central city was not due to the free workings of the private market.[47] The marketplace of metropolitan governments does not simply *allocate* public resources between different packages of public goods based on demand; it *redistributes* resources between classes based on power. Poor and minorities are excluded from suburban housing markets through minimum lot zoning, prohibitions on multifamily construction, maximum density limits, strict building codes, inadequate public transportation, discrimination by real estate agents, and refusal to accept public housing. There is no free market. The poor are left to shop for public goods in central cities where the costs are higher and the goods shoddier. The external costs of the housing market are loaded on immobile city residents while the external benefits are monopolized by suburbanites. The disparity sets in motion a vicious cycle of cumulative inequality: wealthy suburbs attract high income residents with low taxes and quality education, while inner cities repel them for the opposite reasons. While the benefits here do not accrue to some narrow corporate elite but to a broad spectrum of the middle class, this does not take away from the fact that suburban governments exercise market power. Politics takes place *between* cities, as well as *within* them. While often unnoticed, suburbs are "actors" on the stage of city politics, as surely as are inner city voters and politicians.

The chaotic and sprawling residential pattern in the Cleveland area and the anarchic proliferation of local governments did not arise because it was the most efficient pattern but because it represented the needs of the mobile middle and upper classes. Recognizing the inefficiency of this proliferation of governments and concerned that the "better people" might eventually lose all control over Cleveland City Hall, upper class reformers began working for metropolitan government in Cleveland as early as 1917. For the most part their goal was efficiency, not justice—streamlining government, not tax base sharing. Throughout the 1920s, efforts to get the state legislature to permit cities to institute metropolitan government were defeated by a coalition of suburban and rural interests. Finally, in 1933, the reformers were successful in getting the proposal on a statewide ballot and it won; but Cuyahoga County's new home rule charter failed to pass the necessary electoral hurdles. In 1950, the voters turned down a charter; in 1958 they rejected a new charter commission; and in 1959 again rejected charter reform. By 1959 the black electorate had turned against metropolitan reform, seeing it as an effort to take power away from the one government they were close to controlling.[48] The futile struggle continues: in 1981 voters again rejected county home rule.

Clearly, suburbanization is at the heart of Cleveland's economic crisis. Metropolitan government is no longer in the cards. The question raised here is whether there is anything that Cleveland, by itself, can do about it.

Uneven Development: The Growing Service Sector

While jobs have been moving out of Cleveland rapidly, different kinds of jobs have been moving at different rates. And some jobs have actually been moving into Cleveland. This is where the third factor comes in: the shift in the economy from manufacturing to white collar management and service functions. Behind the geographical shifts, qualitative changes are occurring in the function of Cleveland's economy—changes that could be the source of future growth.

The U.S. economy has moved through three basic phases. First there was a period of reliance on agriculture, then a period of industrialization, and, finally, the "post-industrial" period of the present in which the service sector leads the economy in jobs and investment. Cleveland is a city of the second, or "industrial," period; its economy grew to maturity in the soil of the industrial revolution. More specifically, Cleveland specialized in metal products manufacturing, taking the iron ore from the north and shaping and forging it into useful commodities. Cleveland always had a relatively diversified industrial base, compared with a city like Detroit, for example, with its heavier reliance on a single industry, automobiles. This has cushioned Cleveland somewhat from cyclical downturns in the economy. In the long run, however, Cleveland, with its emphasis on manufacturing, will inevitably suffer more job loss than most cities as the nation makes a gradual transition from an industrial to a more service-oriented economy.

The movement to a service-oriented economy is not due primarily to government intervention but to deepseated economic trends. The most important factor is differential rates of productivity. Productivity per worker has gone up tremendously in manufacturing as machines have replaced unskilled labor. Productivity in the service sector has lagged. This means that more and more workers must be employed in the service sector to produce the same amount of final product as is produced with fewer workers in manufacturing. It is not that consumer preferences are changing from durable goods to services, although important trends are at work there; rather, more and more people are employed in the service sector.[49] Just as increasing productivity in agriculture meant that many people had to leave the farm, today increasing productivity in manufacturing means that many workers will have to leave the factory.

The same thing is true of Cleveland proper, only more so. As Table 3 shows, Cleveland's manufacturing sector suffered the severe loss of over 100,000 jobs from 1947 to 1977. Cleveland also suffered from a painful hemorrhage of both wholesale trade and retail trade; most of the latter went to the suburban shopping malls. The only bright spot in Cleveland's employment picture was in the service industries, which increased 34 percent.

TABLE 3.
Employment by Sector in the City of Cleveland, 1948–1977
(in thousands)

Sector	1948	1958	1967	1977	%Change 1948–1977
Manufacturing	223.6*	174.6	171.3	121.4	−45.7
Wholesale Trade	36.8	38.2	32.6	25.8	−29.9
Retail Trade	68.9	61.9	47.2	36.1	−47.6
Selected Services†	24.9	30.9	32.1	33.4	+34.1

Source: U.S. Bureau of the Census, *Census of Manufacturing, Wholesale Trade, Retail Trade and Selected Services*, 1948, 1958, 1967, 1977 (Washington, D.C.: Government Printing Office).
*1947
†Selected services does not include health or government employment.

This increase needs to be looked at more closely. While employment in selected services increased 34 percent in Cleveland from 1948 to 1977, in suburban Cuyahoga County service employment increased 825 percent.[50] The city, however, did better in some areas than in others; Cleveland's growth in service employment was, itself, very uneven. The big increase between 1948 and 1977 was in business services (+228 percent), while other services in Cleveland such as personal services (−54 percent) and hotels, motels, etc. (−35 percent), declined. Cleveland gained more jobs in business services (+11,030) than suburban Cuyahoga County (+10,536). In certain business services Cleveland was especially strong: 72 percent of SMSA employees in advertising and 60 percent of employees in management, consulting, and public relations in 1977 were located in Cleveland. In another category, 72 percent of all practicing lawyers in Cuyahoga County were located downtown in 1980.[51]

Why, when goods production is dispersing to suburbs and small cities, are certain service activities concentrating in central cities? What do these activities have in common and what implications do they have for the future of central cities?

It is clear that many common services, such as drycleaning and barbershops, meet immediate needs of people and so follow the population as it disperses. However, there is another growing class of services, intermediate producer services, that serve the specialized needs of business. The same advances in transportation and communication that permit the dispersion of production also enable administrative and control functions to be physically separated from the sites of production. This does not necessarily mean, however, that they will congregate in the downtowns of large cities. In fact, many routinized producer services, such as data entry, tend to disperse to the lowest wage sites. "Other jobs demanding more specialized information and frequent decision making continue to function best in the CBD (Central Business District), since they require inputs of advice, data, and expertise from a variety of professions and other services that are relatively difficult to obtain in a suburban location."[52] These services are called "advanced services"—long range planning and coordination functions associated with corporate headquarters.[53]

The main reasons that advanced services tend to agglomerate in the downtowns of large cities can be summarized as follows:

1. *External economies of scale.* By concentrating, producer services can support an array of specialized business ser-

vices necessary for high level decision making such as financial analysts, stock brokers, accountants, engineers, management consultants, advertising agencies, and specialized law firms.

2. *Face-to-face-contacts.* Top decision makers and specialists need personal contact to exchange confidential information, partly to avoid its use by competitors or by the government in legal proceedings.

3. *Political access.* Corporate decision makers want to be close to centers of governmental power for maximum influence.

4. *Luxury tastes and culture.* Downtowns possess advantages for satisfying luxury tastes (hotels, restaurants, etc.) and access to culture (museums, theaters, etc.) that make it easier to attract high level managers and professionals.

These changes in the location of economic activity mark a historic break in the growth basis of central cities. As we saw earlier, cities have tended to specialize in different products according to the advantages of their locations for production. Now, cities specialize not only in specific useful products, such as lumber or automobiles, but also in specific management and control functions within the corporate hierarchy. Cities are becoming command and control centers for corporations that manufacture many different products all over the globe. Following the work of Alfred Chandler, Stephen Hymer has suggested that geographical specialization of cities according to economic function will come to reflect the hierarchy of corporate decision making within multinational corporations. This will produce three types of cities: *regional* cities, with corporate outposts managing the day-to-day operations of production and marketing; *national* cities, with corporate offices separate from the field offices, coordinating the managers in the regional cities; and *world* cities, with headquarters for top management who plan and set goals for all the other levels.[54]

Clearly, Cleveland is not a world city like New York; compared with other cities, corporations with headquarters in Cleveland have a relatively low ratio of foreign sales.[55] Cleveland lies somewhere between a national city and a world city. Nevertheless, Cleveland's central business district is clearly becoming a center for advanced services. Of the top 1,000 industrial corporations listed by *Fortune* magazine for

1979, 24 had headquarters in Cleveland. Cleveland ranked fifth in the nation, with one of the highest ratios of corporate headquarters to population among large cities. Business services abound: almost 400 CPAs work downtown and all of the national "Big Eight" accounting firms have offices there; over 100 advertising agencies are located downtown; and in 1973 Cleveland ranked fifth in the nation in the number of attorneys in large law firms (50 +).[56] Finally, with headquarters for the Federal Reserve Bank's Fourth District, Cleveland is becoming a regional banking center.

Cleveland's changing economic function has had a dramatic effect on its physical appearance. The growing service sector employment is concentrated in one area: downtown. Occupying only 3.5 percent of the city's land surface, downtown employed an estimated 150,000 persons in 1980, about 41 percent of the city's work force.[57] While the woodframe houses in the neighborhoods languish from neglect, downtown is booming with gleaming towers of glass and steel, rising with monotonous regularity, monuments to the emerging service economy.[58] The $80 million National City Center was recently completed, as well as a 31-story Medical Mutual Headquarters. The celebrated $200 million Sohio World Headquarters is nearing completion. Demand for downtown office space has been strong for over a decade. Office space increased 36 percent between 1970 and 1975, once of the largest increases in the nation.[59]

Traditionally, manufacturing has been regarded as the key to urban economic growth. By providing the export base of local economies, manufacturing brings money into the region to pay for necessary imports and to support local businesses. The service sector is generally thought to be dependent on a manufacturing base. Richard Knight, of Cleveland State University, argues that Cleveland's export base is shifting from manufacturing to advanced services. The cost of the advanced services needed to manage a modern corporation, Knight says, are included in the price of the final product. Through corporate headquarters, Cleveland has become an exporter of advanced services. Each corporate headquarters job (average salary $17,500 in 1972) generates another job in advanced services outside the firm (average salary $17,500), Knight says. This $35,000 in salaries, using the traditional one-to-three multiplier effect, generates $105,000 in regional income before it leaks out of the area economy. By contrast, Knight argues, a routine production job (average salary $7,000) contributes only a fifth as much ($21,000) to the region's economy. The implication is clear:

the city's future lies not on the shop floor but in the front office. "Cleveland's future depends on whether the region will effectively compete with other cities as a base for advanced services."[60] In order to sail ahead, public and private policies must be properly aligned with the winds of economic change.

Knight's analysis of Cleveland has overtones of theories of post-industrial society that prophecy an end of ideology and a peaceful transformation of capitalism.[61] Instead of control over capital, education and skills in white collar technical functions will form the basis for social status, political power, and economic growth. Instead of avaricious capitalists bent only on profits, the separation of ownership and control will give increased power in corporate decision making to an impersonal technostructure that rules in the name of progress and efficiency. Instead of a growing industrial proletariat schooled in class conscious ideologies, a new generation of white collar employees will arise with higher skills, higher incomes, and a stake in the system; they will reject class struggle in favor of a consensus politics based on economic growth and pluralist democracy. Knight seems to be saying that Cleveland's leaders must move the city forward into this new post-industrial society.

There are many problems with Knight's analysis, however, ranging from technical problems with his calculation of the benefits of headquarter's employment to more general questions concerning the distribution of the benefits of the emerging service economy.[62] Most important, for our purposes, is Knight's failure to examine the *distribution* of the benefits of growth in advanced services. Knight looks at the beneficial effects of advanced services on the regional economy; he does not examine the distribution of the benefits and their "leakage" out of the inner city.

While many high paying professional and technical jobs are created in the service sector, there are also many very low paying clerical jobs. In 1977 in the Cleveland metropolitan area, the average yearly wage in selected services was well below that in manufacturing: in selected services, it was $9,147, in manufacturing (production workers), it was $14,350.[63] In low level service jobs, hourly pay is low and the average number of hours worked per year is less than that for manufacturing.[64] There is less capital invested per worker in the service sector than in manufacturing and productivity gains are lower. Compared with manufacturing, there is a low level of unionization; correspondingly, service workers have less control over their jobs through devices like grievance procedures, enjoy less job security, and receive fewer fringe benefits. While there are some highly skilled jobs in the service sector, it is doubtful that overall skill levels are rising. At one time a white collar was the mark of high skill and status; today a white collar job can be just as unskilled and routine as work in a factory.[65] Surprisingly, only 72 percent of jobs nationwide in manufacturing were nonsupervisory or production jobs; in business services, by comparison, 87 percent were nonsupervisory.[66]

Furthermore, there is mounting evidence that the expansion of service sector employment means greater inequality in job structures. In manufacturing, there are many jobs in the middle and upper ranges; in the service sector, more jobs fall into the high and low ranges, as Table 4 shows. Expecially in business services, a high growth sector for the city of Cleveland, there is a tendency for jobs to fall into either the high or low range, with relatively few jobs in the middle.

What about the distribution of this economic growth: Where are the new jobs located? Who gets them? Clearly, a great number of white collar jobs are locating within the city of Cleveland, mostly downtown. This helps city government cope with its fiscal crisis by generating increased property and income tax revenues.[67] But does this job growth alleviate the unemployment and poverty of inner city residents? Using the *Journey to Work Census*, the number and types of jobs located in Cleveland *that are held by city residents* can be determined. While city residents held 47 percent of the jobs located in Cleveland in 1970 (and 47 percent of the clerical jobs), they held only 31 percent of the professional and technical jobs and only 25 percent of the managerial

TABLE 4.
Percentage Distribution of Employment among Earnings Classes (Quintiles) for Manufacturing and Producer Services, U.S., 1975

Sector	Top ($12,000 & over)	2nd ($9,500– 11,999)	3rd ($7,000– 9,499)	4th ($4,500– 6,999)	Lowest (below $4,500)
Manufacturing	26.2	20.0	35.7	16.4	1.7
Producer (business services)	30.8	22.2	1.3	44.3	1.5

Source: Adapted from Thomas M. Stanback *et al.*, *Services: The New Economy* (Totowa, N.J.: Allanheld, Osmund, 1981), 71.

and administrative jobs.[68] Looking at income, the underrepresentation of city residents was even worse: city residents held only 9 percent of jobs paying over $25,000; suburban commuters held 91 percent of such jobs.[69] On the other hand, city residents held 56 percent of low level jobs paying less than $10,000 per year. Furthermore, women and minorities are excluded from many of the benefits of the growing white collar employment.[70] Clearly, the benefits of Cleveland's growing service sector employment are unevenly distributed and a great deal leaks out of the city to the suburbs.

The traditional spinoffs of a growing downtown service sector have not been as great in Cleveland as in other cities. Spurred by the increase in young professionals working in the service sector, the number of living units downtown has grown from approximately 150 in 1971 to 2,500 in 1981.[71] But there has been very little gentrification and renovation of existing housing. The only significant area of rehabilitation has been Ohio City, just across the river from downtown. But this involved a very small portion of the city's housing stock, nothing like the large areas of gentrification in Baltimore, Philadelphia, or Chicago. Also, the Ohio City phenomena seems to have spent itself.

There are many reasons for the low level of gentrification in Cleveland. As we saw earlier, Cleveland's neighborhoods developed without any zoning controls during a period of unfettered industrial expansion. Residential values are not well protected. Cleveland's housing is predominantly woodframe, which means that beyond a certain level of deterioration, the structure can only be demolished. The city lacks the historically significant brick frame structures that have been the magnet for gentrification in other cities. Finally, Cleveland has large concentrations of poor people and minorities on the East Side, where the more substantial housing stock exists. Perhaps the most important factor, however, is that Cleveland has some of the most attractive close-in suburbs in the nation. With excellent transportation facilities, commuters can get downtown from Shaker Heights by train in 15 minutes, and by car from Lakewood in 15 minutes. In short, there is little reason for the gentry to move into Cleveland, when they can enjoy all the positive externalities of suburban life and still work in the city at little extra cost.

Cleveland's retail sector has also not benefited from the expanding white collar economy. The income generated downtown does not circulate in the local economy in the form of specialty shopping and entertainment areas. There is no Faneuil Hall as in Boston, no Harborplace as in Baltimore. Cleveland's retail sector has declined faster than its population.[72] Out of twenty cities studied, Cleveland had the second largest drop in retail sales between 1963 and 1972.[73] To a remarkable extent, downtown Cleveland, which fills up with commuters during the day, empties out at night. With the exception of heavily subsidized development around Playhouse Square, Cleveland has had little luck capturing the mobile consumer dollar originating from downtown service employment.

Conclusion: The Pain of Economic Transition

Cleveland is clearly in the middle of a long and painful transition to a post-industrial economy, or at least an economy in which the goods-producing sector will play a much smaller role in generating jobs and income. The bright spot in Cleveland's economy, its expanding downtown service center, is a leaky bucket, with most of the good jobs and spin-off benefits going to the suburbs.

The agonizing question concerning the new service economy is whether it can create enough jobs, enough well-paying jobs, to fill the gap left by shrinking industrial employment. At this point, the outlook is not good, especially for displaced blue collar workers concentrated in the inner city. The question posed here is whether city governments have the power to shape their futures and redistribute the costs and benefits of the economic transition. Economic change always brings about political change. Whether or not city governments have the power, citizens will demand that they "do something" about the economic crisis.

A gutted police cruiser, victim of the 1968 Glenville riots, stands before a sign announcing the much heralded Cleveland: NOW! project of Mayor Stokes. Business participation in Cleveland: NOW! dried up after the Glenville riots. Courtesy of UPI/Bettmann Archive.

Buildings in the St. Vincent area (October 27, 1964) were later demolished by urban renewal. Courtesy of Cleveland State University, Cleveland *Press* Library.

The Metro Campus of Cuyahoga Community College (March 3, 1976) was built on land cleared by the St. Vincent urban renewal project. Courtesy of Cleveland State University, Cleveland *Press* Library.

The residential area on the East Side was demolished to make way for interstate highway I-77 (April 9, 1963). Courtesy of Cleveland State University, Cleveland *Press* Library. By Frank Aleksandrowicz.

Demolition and Construction is shown under way in Erieview, Cleveland's largest urban renewal project (February 28, 1964). Courtesy of Cleveland State University, Cleveland *Press* Library. By Glenn Zahn.

Cleveland State University, an important component of the expanding service sector, was built on land cleared of decaying housing, industry, and commerce on Cleveland's near East Side. Courtesy of Steve Cagan, photographer.

The nine-story-high central blast furnace of American Steel and Wire, a division of United States Steel Corporation, was built in 1954 in Cleveland's Flats. It was abandoned in 1978 and completely demolished in 1984. Courtesy of Steve Cagan, photographer.

Fiscal crisis has forced the city of Cleveland to close several Cuyahoga River bridges, key links between the East and West Sides. Courtesy of Steve Cagan, photographer.

Every year thousands of buildings are demolished in Cleveland, as in this picture of Benedictine High School being torn down in 1984. Courtesy of the Cleveland *Plain Dealer*. By C. H. Pete Copeland.

River Bend Condos under construction in the Flats are one of the few examples of middle-class housing reinvestment in the inner city. Courtesy of the Cleveland *Plain Dealer*.

4

Liberal Growth Politics: Starts and Stalls

> This whole program [urban renewal] has been dishonestly presented to the community. This is not low-cost housing. This is not housing for the poor.[1]
>
> *Bronis Klementowicz*
> *Cleveland City Councilman*

In an article entitled "The New Convergence of Power," written in 1964, Robert Salisbury discusses how the process of industrialization caused wealth to split off from political power around 1900, as political entrepreneurs, primarily representing working class immigrants, took political power away from the economic entrepreneurs, who had previously dominated most cities.[2] The new industrial capital, often absentee-owned and concerned only with narrow corporate interests, largely withdrew from city politics. After the Second World War, according to Salisbury, certain businesses reconverged on city politics, businesses that had major investments that were threatened by core city decay: "the major banks, utilities, railroads, department stores, large real estate firms, and metropolitan newspapers."[3] They joined forces with chief executives and technically-oriented professionals in city-related programs to form a "new convergence of power" in city politics. This new coalition focused on mobilizing public and private resources to redevelop the city and insure future growth.

Roughly speaking, this "new convergence" is what happened in

Cleveland, only somewhat later—beginning in the mid-1950s. As long as the economy grew, the caretaker ethnic regimes, which took a passive position on the economy and maintained distant, often hostile, relations with large corporations, were sure of political support. As the economic crisis deepened in the 1950s, however, the old system of conservative growth politics broke down and the victims of economic change pressured city government to "do something" about the economic crisis. Economic change precipitated political change. But business and government experienced the crisis in different ways and had different reasons for supporting political change.

For business, the crisis was one of real estate values. Although almost the entire corporate elite had moved their homes to the suburbs, they still had substantial investments within the central city, especially downtown, but also around University Circle and the Cleveland Clinic. The profitability of these investments was threatened by creeping urban blight. Since these large physical and institutional investments were immobile, moving away was not an option. Business had a serious problem. According to a congressional study, in 1960, 29 percent of the nation's mortgage debt was secured against inner city property. The study warned: "Continued central city deterioration would lead to the devaluation of these assets with serious repercussions within the national financial structure."[4]

Moreover, these substantial investments in the inner city had promising growth potential because of the transition to a service economy. If Cleveland were to have a place in the rising service economy, however, much of its physical layout would have to be reworked. The physical form of Cleveland had followed its function as a site for heavy industry and manufacturing. Sunbelt cities could build from scratch the physical plant consonant with the new function of cities in a service-oriented economy. But older industrial cities would have to rework their existing physical layouts, not to mention their policy orientations and even social relations. Clearly, private development efforts were not enough. The public sector would be needed to use its power of eminent domain to clear away the slums, to expand the area devoted to office functions, and to build highways to bring the service workers downtown. Industrial workers would need to be retrained in white collar skills. Downtown would have to be made a more attractive place to invest. Gradually, business began to see positive functions for city government. Ironically, it was the uneven and unplanned expansion under conservative growth politics that threatened investments, eventually leading sectors of business to break with conservative growth politics and support a more active role for local government.

For city government, the economic crisis was a fiscal crisis. City government relied primarily on the property tax to finance its budget. The property tax base in Cleveland was devastated by the flight of industry and the middle class to the suburbs. Figure 4 shows how property values in Cleveland stagnated; clearly much of the investment in real property was being siphoned off to the suburbs, where the tax base was booming. Under the calm political surface of the ethnic mayors, there was a crisis brewing. Cleveland's aging infrastructure (roads, bridges, sewers, water lines) needed larger investments and the concentration of dependent population left behind by suburbanization (poor, elderly, minorities) needed greater public services.[5] Cleveland's low per capita tax base eventually meant that the tax rate had to be raised; but doing so would not help stem the exodus of business and the middle class. Cleveland's conservative, and penurious, city government was pushed by forces beyond its control into a fiscal crisis, a fiscal crisis that has not been resolved to this day.

It was clear to everyone that city government did not have the resources, by itself, to mount a serious attack on the economic problems; the private sector would have to be enlisted. With its inner city investments threatened, business indeed was ready to take a more instrumental approach to city government, attempting to use it to reconstruct the conditions of growth in a period of economic transition. But to induce business to reinvest in the inner city would require substantial incentives. Local government did not have the resources to provide them. In stepped the federal government with substantial grant programs for highways and urban renewal. Pressured from above by threatened investors and from below by threatened constituents, lured by the attraction of large federal grants, Cleveland city government in the 1950s took the first major expansion of its functions since the era of Tom Johnson: *economic and community development.*

Neither city government nor business, however, was comfortable in their new roles. After decades of keeping government ignorant of even minor economic planning decisions, business found it difficult to suddenly treat the public sector as an instrument of economic redevelopment. Moreover, the new partnership between business and government was flawed by a basic contradiction: in order to smooth the economic transition and speed the flow of private investment, city government would have to carry out policies that threatened a large

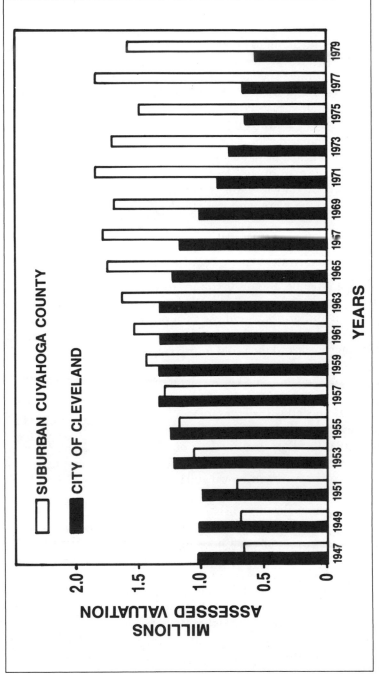

FIGURE 4. Assessed Valuation of Real Property: Cleveland and Suburban Cuyahoga County, 1947–1979, Year of Collection.* Source: *Moody's Municipal and Government Manual* (New York: Moody's Investors Services, Inc.). Adjusted for inflation using the Consumer Price Index for the Cleveland metropolitan area, as reported by the Department of Labor, Bureau of Labor Statistics, *Monthly Labor Review* (Washington, D.C.: Government Printing Office).

*In constant 1947 dollars.

part of its constituency. Those in the path of the new liberal growth machine were not about to bear the costs lying down. City government was caught between the conflicting pressures of mobile wealth and an immobile electorate. The familiar tradeoff between growth and equality would prove especially severe in Cleveland—to the point where, it seemed, economic success could only be bought at the price of political instability. A 1979 study by the Brookings Institution summed up how the new growth partnership fared: "There has been a failure to articulate the convergence of public and private interests in ways that are acceptable to the majority of Cleveland's voters, who are black, second- and third-generation white Americans with nationality identifications, poor and working class, and the elderly."[6] This is a masterpiece of understatement.

Urban Renewal: The Costs of Liberal Growth Politics

The first attempted solution to the growth crisis of inner cities was urban renewal, beginning with the 1949 Housing Act. The method was simple: local authorities would use their power of eminent domain to buy up slum properties; the parcels of land would be assembled, cleared, improved, and then sold to private developers at considerably below cost; the new owners would then build new housing, stores, or businesses on the land. The key element was the land writedown; the private developer usually paid only about 30 percent of the actual cost, providing an incentive for entrepreneurs to redevelop areas that previously had been deteriorating into slums. The federal government absorbed two-thirds of the total cost of the writedown. The program was not small; as of 1971 the federal government had committed $9.4 billion in grants for urban renewal and its successor, the Neighborhood Development Program.[7]

Throughout its history, urban renewal was marred by a fundamental ambivalence: was it aimed primarily at improving the lot of slum dwellers by providing new housing or was it designed to maximize private investment and redevelopment of inner city properties? In the beginning, urban renewal was primarily a housing program, oriented toward providing "a decent home and a suitable living environment for every American family" (words of the original 1949 Housing Act). The housing goal was written into the 1949 law in the so-called Taft provision, which required that urban renewal be confined to areas that were "predominantly residential," administratively defined as 50 percent residential before and after renewal.

As time went on, however, it became clear that developers were not primarily interested in building housing, especially housing for slum dwellers displaced by urban renewal. They *were* interested in commercial development that furthered central cities' service sector growth potential. Correspondingly, in 1954, 10 percent of urban renewal funds were exempted from the requirements of the Taft provision. It was at this point that urban renewal first really began to take off.[8] In 1959 the percentage of funds that could be used for nonresidential purposes was enlarged to 20 percent, in 1961 to 30, and in 1967 to 35 percent.[9] Nationwide statistics for urban renewal show that, in practice, the goal of providing housing was shunted aside. According to a congressional study, as of 1971 approximately 600,000 housing units had been demolished on urban renewal sites, but only about 244,000 new units had been built or were under construction.[10] Of course, most demolition occurred in the poorest areas, often black. Not without reason, urban renewal came to be known as "negro removal." As of 1962, the estimated cost of construction on 492 projects was $5.813 billion. But only $83 million (1.4 percent) was invested in public housing, one of the few places where most families displaced by urban renewal could afford to live.[11]

John Mollenkopf, in a masterful overview of postwar urban development, interprets urban renewal, along with the massive federal highway program, as the centerpiece of a powerful new growth coalition that dominated big city politics in the 1950s and 1960s.[12] Although Mollenkopf believes that urban renewal was shaped predominantly by business interests, he sees the business interests less as independent actors, cooly planning their own advantage, than as dependent variables, essentially responding to a crisis. And the solution they pursued was fraught with contradictions. Mollenkopf's central thesis is that "local government's role in stimulating central city development contradicted its role as the guarantor of social peace and political cohesion."[13] Stimulated by federal grants, new growth coalitions, led by growth-oriented mayors like Lee of New Haven and Daley of Chicago, emerged to dominate city politics. The costs of the new growth politics, however, were highly unevenly distributed: racial tensions were exacerbated as housing for poor minorities was destroyed; the pressure on existing inner city housing caused a backlash, pitting white ethnics against poor blacks; stable working class communities were disrupted by highway building and commercial projects; and the tax burden was shifted from the central business district to tenants and homeowners.[14] Eventually, the accumulated pressure erupted in the ghetto riots of the

1960s. Grassroots protests against the federal bulldozer emerged in city after city, later coalescing into the community organizing movement.[15]

Mollenkopf's focus on the contradiction between economic development and social peace and political stability is similar to what I call the dilemma of growth politics: the trade-off between growth (the need to attract investment) and equality (the need to serve low income households trapped in the inner city). While cities needed to make the transition to a new economic base, what urban renewal did, especially in its early phase, was to load the external costs of the transition onto those who could least afford to bear them while subsidizing the profits of those who would benefit the most. Further, it is doubtful that benefits or urban projects ever trickled down sufficiently to compensate those who were forced out of their homes.

Cleveland illustrates the pattern described nationally by Mollenkopf with one important difference: in Cleveland the benefits were less than in other cities and the costs were greater. The new growth politics, consequently, never dominated Cleveland the way it did other cities. The extreme disparity between the suburbs and the inner city in Cleveland made attracting development all the more difficult. Also, city government was not prepared for the complex task of urban renewal; administrative foul-ups and costly delays abounded. Perhaps most important, urban renewal in Cleveland unlike most cities was administered not by an autonomous redevelopment agency but by a department of city government, the Department of Urban Renewal and Housing. Many of the problems and delays of urban renewal were brought about by political opposition that found relatively easy expression through Cleveland's ward-based political system. Richard Green, who directed urban renewal in the Stokes administration, blamed Cleveland's urban renewal problems on an obstructionist city council: "The one thing in Cleveland that nobody really described because it is indescribable is City Council. . . . It's a problem in the city because you have thirty-three councilmen in a ward system, and their interests don't necessarily provide a city-wide view. They tend to be segmented."[16] Of course, many of these parochial opponents of progress were precisely those who would bear the costs.

Urban renewal in Cleveland started out rather benignly as an effort to clear the slums and build new housing for the residents. To be sure, projects were delayed as homeowners fought demolition and pleaded for opportunities to rehabilitate their properties.[17] Nevertheless, a sincere effort was made to build new housing in the urban renewal areas for the previous residents. Early on, however, city councilmen expressed opposition to urban renewal, suspecting that rents in the new projects would exceed the financial ability of the displaced residents. Their suspicions were not groundless.

The problem was basic: in order to make the projects profitable, rents had to be charged that were too high for the low income population in the area. On the other hand, middle class families who could afford the rents did not want to move back into the slum areas. As one reporter put it, "If one group can't afford the new housing and the other won't have it, who are we building for?"[18] Every housing development built under urban renewal in Cleveland ran into trouble. Even if housing projects could be profitable, developers could make much higher profits (given the fixed public subsidy for the land) on commercial and institutional projects.

In short, there is no need to resort to a conspiracy theory to explain the antihousing bias of urban renewal. We do not need to suppose that the corporate elite manipulated government officials in order to line its own pockets at the expense of the poor slum dwellers. Politicians had plenty of reasons of their own to go along. Mayors wanted to be able to say that they had the solution to urban blight. They wanted to boast at election time that they had expanded the tax base and brought jobs back to the city. To do so, they had to attract massive amounts of private capital. Private investment would be forthcoming, however, only for those projects that furthered the city's growth potential in the service sector. Politicians could then take credit for impressive real estate developments in the booming service sector. They could not take credit for low income housing developments that never got off the drawing boards. Well-meaning mayors, like Cleveland's Celebrezze, Locher, and Stokes, ended up bowing to the imperatives of growth politics.

Did the commercial projects ultimately benefit central cities with new jobs and tax revenues? Oddly, the question was seldom asked. Very rarely did local governments scrutinize the costs and benefits of particular projects with any care. The reason was simple: since local governments paid only a third of the subsidy (in truth, much less than that, because cities could load in various in-kind services and routine expenditures), their attitude was, the more the better. The goal was to get more federal grants. Viewed as "funny money," urban renewal distorted rational decision making in the governmental marketplace. If local governments had been forced to contribute the entire subsidy, evidence suggests that urban renewal would have been pursued with far less enthusiasm.[19]

The obvious question to ask of any urban renewal project is whether the subsidies actually attracted new private investment that would not have occurred otherwise. There is mounting evidence that many urban renewal projects would have occurred anyway, without subsidies, given the natural expansion of white collar activities in the central city.[20] The difference is that, without the benefit of eminent domain, they would have been built in different parts of the city. This suggests that urban renewal did more to fatten the profits of developers than to stimulate new investment.

Corporate planners did not rely solely on the imperatives of growth politics or the desire of politicians to take credit for new development in order to steer urban renewal in their direction. They also took active roles in planning urban renewal projects. While the neighborhoods mainly had to react to urban renewal projects, corporate planners were present at their conception. The instruments they used were the so-called nonprofit foundations, which, in Cleveland's case, supplied the Department of Urban Renewal with extensive plans and projections. The foundations formulated the alternatives from which city officials chose. The initiative came from corporate leaders.

> In 1954, Cleveland's top business leaders—the heads of Republic Steel and the top utilities and banks—decided to take action to save the city from "blight," as they called it. . . . [T]hey formed a nonprofit organization, the Cleveland Development Foundation (CDF) to promote urban renewal in Cleveland. With over $1 million in contributions from Cleveland's top 83 firms and a $5 million grant from the Hanna Fund, CDF was to provide "seed money" and planning assistance to the city government's urban renewal agency. Actually, CDF quickly supplanted the city and became the kind of private "government" for urban renewal.[21]

As Pike Sloan, former chairman of Oglebay-Norton and a CDF founder, said: "It would be a mistake to think that foundation had as its main concern housing . . . the main thing was to make land available for industrial and commercial use."[22] Blight threatened not only downtown but the valuable cultural island on the East Side. In 1960, a second foundation was formed, the University Circle Development Foundation (UCDF), with an initial grant from the Mather family. It was designed to plan urban renewal for the area around Case Western Reserve University. According to a former top staff member of the CDF, the overall strategy, or "planning concept," was to build up institutional enclaves at each end of the East Side (Erieview downtown and University Circle on the far East Side) and then join the two with a sort of white corridor, like the bar of a dumbbell.[23] Poor black residents of urban renewal areas were in no position to counter such proposals by providing city planners with glossy plans for low-cost housing.

The ambitious corporate plans for urban renewal in Cleveland were never completed, largely because their reach far exceeded the administrative and political grasp of city government. Cleveland, it seemed, still had illusions of grandeur stemming from its industrial heyday. City planners and foundation officials, captive of what pundits called an edifice complex, composed grandiose plans that looked good on paper but went far beyond the city's growth potential or management capabilities. Cleveland designated 6,060 acres (one-eighth of the land area of the city!) for urban renewal, almost twice as many acres as any other city in the country. As late as 1976, the Cleveland *Plain Dealer* reported, despite the influx of $106.9 million in federal funds, almost 30 percent of the city's urban renewal land was unsold and was yielding almost no tax benefits.[24] Urban renewal did not wipe out blight or rejuvenate the city's tax base. Even within its corporate goals, urban renewal in Cleveland was a colossal failure; and it suffered perhaps the worst delays and mismanagement of any program in the country.[25]

Urban renewal did, however, succeed in transforming the physiognomy of Cleveland's East Side. By contributing to severe overcrowding and deterioration, urban renewal worsened an already bad housing situation for Cleveland's blacks. For obvious reasons, being designated urban renewal had a severe chilling effect on private investment and maintenance in an area, even though often the land was never purchased, or if purchased and cleared, never redeveloped. City government further contributed to deterioration by withholding services. In testimony before the U.S. Civil Rights Commission in Cleveland in 1965, city officials admitted that they stopped enforcing the housing code and cut back on city services like police and fire protection in areas designated for urban renewal.[26] By allowing these areas to deteriorate, the city would be able to buy the land cheaper for clearance purposes.

In those areas that were redeveloped, thousands of families were forced to move without adequate provision for decent and affordable housing. They had to fend for themselves, moving into existing housing and contributing to its further deterioration. Black families either had to crowd into the ghetto or had to move into white areas. Racial clashes resulted as lower middle class whites girded to exclude the poor and blacks, by physical intimidation, if necessary—just as middle class whites in the suburbs had done all along by more genteel and legal means. Urban renewal set in motion a vicious game of musical chairs that disrupted stable communities and heightened racial tension.

Two projects illustrate the problems with urban renewal in Cleveland. The St. Vincent project was planned, using funds from CDF, for predominantly residential use of 118.1 acres when the contract with the federal government was originally signed in 1959. As the Little Hoover Commission dryly reported in 1966: "There was a premature exodus of families from this area. No record indicates where the premature exodus situated, but all evidence shows that Hough area was inundated by most of the premature relocations; total number approximately 1200 families." When no builders came forward to put up the new housing, the Department of Urban Renewal took action in 1963 to change the re-use of the land from partly residential to completely institutional. When it was all over, it was estimated that 1,780 families had originally resided in the project area. All left.[27] No housing was built for the persons displaced. Relocation authorities had records of only 528 displaced families and admitted that the majority of black families relocated to areas heavily segregated, more than 90 percent black.[28] Most of the land was eventually sold to Cuyahoga Community College, a hospital, and other civic institutions. Since most of these institutions are tax exempt, the St. Vincent project resulted in a net loss of assessed valuation for the city, from $2,368,383 before the project to $2,102,380 in 1972.[29] This project, which cost $9.3 million and took thirteen years to complete, was "rated a success."[30]

Erieview, located downtown near the lake, was trumpeted at its inception as "undoubtedly the most ambitious project so far undertaken under the Federal Urban Redevelopment Program."[31] It was hailed as the salvation for Cleveland's drab downtown. At the request of Mayor Celebrezze, I. M. Pei, famous New York City planner, prepared an impressive dream plan for Erieview, calling for an array of attractive office buildings, luxury apartments, malls, and fountains. Pei's plan was announced with great fanfare. The Cleveland *Press*, whose new building was located across the street from Erieview, pushed hard for the project.

Erieview I, the first phase, was considered "the city's most monetarily successful project."[32] This success, however, was bought at the cost of projects in other areas of the city, since urban renewal staff time was dominated by Erieview for years. Erieview I covered ninety-six acres. Originally to be finished by 1965, the project was not closed out until June 1973. The total project cost was $45.5 million; assessed valuation increased $35 million from 1961 to 1972. The city got considerable private investment in the area but, in order to attract developers, was forced to offer the land at ridiculously low prices. City officials overestimated the resale price of the land by $18 million. This debt to the federal government was finally canceled in November 1972.

Most rated Erieview I an overall commercial success. Some maintained, however, that by shifting the center of gravity downtown it ruined Euclid Avenue, formerly a fashionable shopping district.[33] One thing is certain: Pei's dream plan for all of Erieview was never fulfilled. Some of Erieview land still lies vacant or covered with parking lots. The rest is dominated by two boxlike skyscrapers: the Anthony J. Celebrezze Federal Office Building and the thirty-seven story Erieview Towers. Between them lies a barren, windswept fountain area, frequented by few pedestrians. Ada Louise Huxtable, the *New York Times* architecture critic, called Erieview "a kind of monument to everything that was wrong with urban renewal thinking in America in the 1960's," and described Pei's design as "long on desolate, overscaled spaces, destructive of cohesive urbanism and defiantly antihuman."[34]

Urban renewal in Cleveland must be accounted a failure. Since most of the cost was borne by the federal government, it did not precipitate a tax revolt. (But it is also clear, from Figure 4, that the federal money did little to boost the tax base.) The need to attract private investment, however, steered the priorities of urban renewal in Cleveland, as in other cities, toward downtown. It resulted in building tall office towers, command modules for the expanding public and private sector, as well as luxury apartment buildings, like Park Centre and the Chesterfield, to make downtown an exciting place for rising young professionals. But urban renewal did little for neighborhoods where blue collar workers and poor blacks lived. In fact, it positively damaged Cleveland's neighborhoods, destroying more housing than it created and further overloading the ghetto. To the list of negatives should be added the detrimental effects of interstate highways, designed mainly to benefit suburban commuters, that sliced through Cleveland's West Side, destroying valuable housing, taking land off the tax rolls, and separating neighbor from neighbor.[35] Urban renewal and highway building created a pervasive sense that politicians and planners were insensitive to the needs of neighborhoods. There was a fundamental contradiction between the imperatives of the new growth politics, designed to further Cleveland's economic transition, and the immediate needs of the average voter. Cleveland's electoral system entered a period of turbulence.

Stokes: The Promise of Liberal Growth Politics Betrayed

The relationship between urban renewal and Carl Stokes, the first black mayor of a major American city, is straightforward.[36] Massive urban renewal projects, like St. Vincent, caused a sudden influx of displaced black families into Hough, transforming it from a rundown black neighborhood into a pressurized ghetto of misery. It was only a matter of time before Hough would explode.[37] On July 18, 1966, a sign appeared on the door of a bar in Hough: "No Water for Niggers." Enraged residents gathered around the bar. When police attempted to disperse the crowd, the riots began, lasting for a full week. There was street talk in Hough that summer about rioting and arson as a form of "instant urban renewal."[38] Frightened, the business establishment turned to Stokes to guarantee peace in the ghetto. In 1965, Stokes had run for mayor with little business backing; in 1967, he suddenly had massive support from the downtown business establishment. Stokes knew what was happening: "In the backs of their minds, those white men believed that if they put me out front they would be buying off the ghetto."[39]

What is more, in January 1967, HUD Secretary Robert C. Weaver, in an almost unprecedented move, put a freeze on release of any more urban renewal funds to Cleveland, citing sixteen specific problems, primarily relating to slow progress, waste, and incompetent administration. HUD officials began to call Cleveland their Vietnam: "We'd like to get out but we don't know how," they quipped.[40] Businessmen were attracted to Stokes for his close connections to Hubert Humphrey and the Democratic administration in Washington—which bode well for Stokes's promise to get federal funds flowing back into the city.

There is more to the story than this, however. The business elite did not simply pick a new mayor. The 1967 election represented a fundamental break in the conservative social contract between white ethnics and industrialists that had ruled Cleveland politics for more than a generation. The ethnics had been left largely alone to control local government, using the formula of low taxes and minimal government. As long as both benefited from economic growth, the formula worked. Disinvestment caused a crisis for the public and private sectors. Business broke with the caretaker ethnic regime when it became clear that two basic functions necessary for growth were not being fulfilled: maintaining law and order and insuring the flow of federal money into the central city. Business, which had previously argued that city government had little political discretion to raise taxes (doing so would supposedly kill off industrial investment), suddenly supported an expanded public sector and new taxes.

More than an economic crisis, however, it was also a fundamental crisis in legitimacy. One-third of the community had been excluded, for the most part, from the benefits of conservative growth politics and urban renewal. In the 1960s, black consciousness of this deprivation was raised by the civil rights movement. A new militant civil rights organization, the United Freedom Movement (UFM), organized mass protests against segregation in the public schools and the exclusion of blacks from the all-white construction trade unions. Blacks were also excluded from positions of power within the county Democratic organization. Allowed to be council members, or even in a few cases state legislators, they were denied powerful citywide or countywide offices. Black dissatisfaction was expressed in the 1965 mayoral election, when a savvy black politician, Carl Stokes, running as an independent, came within 3,000 votes of defeating the major party candidates. In April 1966, the U.S. Civil Rights Commission met in Cleveland and put the glare of national publicity on the miserable living conditions of most blacks in the inner city. The Hough riots in July confirmed that something had to be done.

The severe crisis of economic growth and political legitimacy caused the Cleveland business community to withdraw its long-time tacit support of caretaker ethnic regimes in the last two years of the Locher administration (1965–1967). (Locher also drew business opposition because he opposed the sale of the municipal light plant). According to Roldo Bartimole, independent Cleveland journalist and modern-day muckraker, business interests were unable to handpick Locher's successor but, by withdrawing support, were able to make it impossible for Locher to govern. By fostering a crisis atmosphere, they destabilized the Locher administration and guaranteed a change. Business needed a fall guy, someone to blame for the deepening economic and political crisis in Cleveland—a crisis brought about for the most part by private investment decisions. Locher was it. (A dozen years later, Bartimole says, the Kucinich administration was destabilized in a similar manner.)[41]

One of the devices used to reshape business approaches to city problems was the Little Hoover Commission, another chapter in the efforts of good government reformers to remodel city government along the lines of the private corporation. Called "a time and motion study of every single government operation," the Little Hoover Commission was formed after proposed city income tax in 1965 was defeated by the voters (with the help of business), precipitating a budget crisis.[42] The city invited businessmen to undertake a complete study of city operations.

The Little Hoover Commission signaled basic changes in the political stance of big business. First, the business community shifted from opposing tax hikes to supporting them. Higher taxes were needed to avert fiscal crisis and to finance the additional public spending needed to aid the economic transition. This marked a shift from a conservative to a liberal growth strategy. The commission recommended that the City Council adopt an income tax, as allowed by state law, bypassing conservative ethnic voters. Second, the Little Hoover Commission signaled that corporate interests could no longer tolerate the inefficiency of the fragmented ethnic regime, with its constant need for bargaining and compromise. Blaming the fiscal crisis on the failure of urban renewal, the commission implicitly criticized the Locher administration and the slow pace of pluralist politics.[43] While city government was no more inefficient than it had ever been, business now needed a streamlined public sector to facilitate the economic transition. In place of bargaining between interest groups, the commission recommended top-down leadership to plan economic development.[44]

In March 1967, James C. Davis, an establishment lawyer of the prestigious firm of Squire, Sanders and Dempsey, gave a speech entitled "Cleveland's White Problem" in which he blamed white ethnics for the city's problems. This marked a shift in the growth coalition of top businessmen: from the peculiar conservative operating arrangement with white ethnics, they moved into active alliance with blacks and liberals and attempted to exert more direct control over city government, now given expanded authority over economic and community development.

I do not mean to give the impression that business was in control or was completely unified and conscious of what it was doing. The destabilization of Locher and the election of Stokes represented both a change in business attitudes and a coming to power of a more liberal wing of business, rooted not in industrial capital but in the growing service sector.[45] "Business," then, was not a unified actor. It did not include, of course, the small businesses in the neighborhoods, which were mainly controlled by ethnics and retained their conservative political outlook. "Business" refers to big business, the downtown business establishment that had largely withdrawn from local politics. If business did not control city government it was even more helpless when it came to the black community. Executive suites in the Terminal Tower were a long way from the black ghettos of Cleveland's East Side. Black militants and nationalists were threatening to lead a revolt. Business people had the money but not the votes. They desperately needed a streetwise politician, someone they could work with. Carl Stokes filled the bill.

Stokes was nothing if not streetwise. Growing up fatherless in the heart of Cleveland's ghetto, Stokes was fortunate to move into public housing at the age of eleven. He later worked as a liquor enforcement agent, closing down bootleg operations in black neighborhoods. A charismatic politician with more than the usual amount of personal charm, in 1963 Stokes became the first black Democrat elected to the Ohio legislature.

Stokes was also somebody business knew they could work with. In spring 1967, he had been one of the few Democrats to support Republican governor Rhodes's Ohio Bond Commission, which called for the Senate to borrow $1.7 billion for various building projects. Stokes himself labeled it "a gigantic Republican pork barrel." But, as he said in defending his position, "I had no choice but to go with a proposal that at least benefited my constituency as well as the bankers."[46] Stokes also strongly supported the sale of Muny Light in his mayoral campaign. (However, in order to mollify the unions that opposed it, he promised there would be no sales without a referendum.)[47] Stokes always spoke warmly of business, saying that city government should do everything in its power to help business grow. At the same time, he called for higher taxes to support an expanded welfare state.[48]

In 1967, business backed Stokes strongly over Locher in the Democratic primary. Reasoning that if there were a riot, Stokes would not have a chance, businessmen helped Stokes by distributing $40,000 to black militants in an unpublicized program to keep peace in the ghetto in summer 1967.[49] Stokes eliminated Locher in the Democratic primary. In the final election, business split between Stokes and Taft, a liberal Republican, and Stokes won by a slim margin.

In a sense, the election of Carl Stokes in 1967 represented a concession to the black community. Business was forced to do something it does not like to do: sanction expansion of the public sector. The normally tight reins that business kept on city government through the threat of disinvestment and control over credit were loosened somewhat. Suddenly, taxes could be raised and city government expanded without leading to a loss of "business confidence." As *Business Week* trumpeted in headlines: "Business now backs Cleveland."[50] At this historical moment, Cleveland city government was given a certain autonomy and moved off dead center to effect reforms. Cleveland was hailed as an example of how close collaboration between business and government could reinvigorate the city's economy and aid the poor at the same time. It was not long, however, as Stokes noted in his autobiography, before he was left with only the "promise of power," as business withdrew its money and local government became bogged down in trench warfare between mayor and council, blacks and whites.

Stokes was elected at the last hurrah of American liberalism, just as the Vietnam War was beginning to take its toll on Lyndon Johnson's War on Poverty. Liberal activist mayors, like Lindsay, Hatcher, and Cavanagh, were calling for massive federal aid to solve the problems of inner cities. This liberal optimism was exemplified by Stokes's statement that "there is nothing fundamentally wrong with America's cities that money won't cure."[51] Stokes proceeded to enact his cure.

Stokes attempted to take advantage of his close relations with business soon after the election. Black leadership in Cleveland was miraculously able to keep the peace after Martin Luther King's assassination in April 1968. Knowing the business community would be especially receptive at this point, Stokes called them together and founded a booster project, Cleveland: NOW! The immediate aim was to raise $11.5 million, primarily from the white business community, to leverage $165.75 million in federal, state, and foundation money for new projects ranging from job training to recreation centers. The long-range plan called for $1.5 billion over the following decade to rebuild Cleveland.

In July 1968, however, the Glenville shoot-out and riots occurred. They began with a shoot-out between police and black militants. The first evening, seven people were killed, including three policemen, and fifteen people were wounded. Stokes made a daring decision to pull out white police from the Glenville area and send in black leaders to keep the peace. There were no more deaths, but there was extensive property damage. During the five days of looting and arson that followed the shoot-out, sixty separate business establishments were damaged or destroyed. Property losses totaled over $1 million.

The honeymoon of white businessmen with the Stokes administration was over when they saw that even a black mayor could not give them the peace needed for business confidence and expansion. When $6,000 of Cleveland: NOW! money was traced to Ahmed Evans, the black nationalist later found guilty of conspiracy and first degree murder of Cleveland police, business support for Cleveland: NOW! dried up. In the end, only $5.5 million was raised.[52]

When Stokes pulled the white police out of Glenville, he earned the enmity of almost the entire police department, overwhelmingly composed of white ethnics, and lost all hope of reforming the department. It was the beginning of paralyzing conflict between the black chief executive and the white ethnics who were entrenched in City Council and led by conservative Council President James Stanton. Stokes was isolated. He had no grassroots organization to put pressure on Council or business between elections. In 1970, he pulled blacks out of the Democratic party to form the 21st Congressional Caucus. But this, like his own election effort, was based more on charismatic appeal than grassroots organization. "My second term," Stokes said, "was almost total war between the mayor and the Council, between the mayor and the newspapers, between the mayor and everyone."[53]

Even though he was successful in getting the freeze on urban renewal funds for Cleveland lifted a few months after his election, much political opposition still centered on his handling of federal programs. Resistance to urban renewal mounted as Stokes's choice as Community Development Director, Richard Green, concentrated on downtown renewal more than neighborhood assistance. An association of residents near downtown, bordering on Erieview, demanded renewal projects more suited to neighborhood needs and desires. In the first issue of their newsletter they described the situation: "Then one day, the City Inspectors showed up at the front door, demanding that our homes be brought up to City code, *immediately*. Bulldozers standing at the back door and City Inspectors at the front door!" They asked the question:

"Were we being asked by our City to fix up so that we could stay, or were we to become another urban renewal blunder?"[54] The embattled residents successfully resisted new development in their community.

Urban renewal moved to the West Side in the form of a new offshoot, the Neighborhood Development Program (NDP). Correcting some of the faults of urban renewal by supporting smaller scale, more neighborhood oriented projects, NDP still called for officially designating an eligible area as "blighted." On Cleveland's West Side, 1,300 acres were so designated. Given past experience with urban renewal, alarmists found it easy to play on people's fears. At a meeting in Ward 3, one opponent declared: "Urban renewal became a dirty word, so they had to change it, and they called it Neighborhood Development Program."[55] Another critic said a proposal for scattered-site public housing in the area meant "an undesirable element—welfare people; ADC women who are on welfare."[56] Racial prejudice was barely below the surface. White West Siders dug in to preserve what was left of their neighborhoods, but the issue gradually dissolved as federal funds never arrived.

Conflict with Stokes on federal programs was not only racially motivated, as another example of community opposition to a federally funded project illustrates. Stokes, remembering what public housing had meant for him as a youngster, was proud of his administration's record for building public housing. His pet project was an effort to build 277 single family homes for low income families in Lee-Seville, a middle class black neighborhood on the Southeast Side. The Lee-Seville project would have been the first project in the nation to provide single family homes for purchase by poor families. Local black councilmen united with white Council President Stanton to stop the project. Legislation, authorizing $4 million in community improvements necessary for the project, was pigeonholed in committee. Residents of the area contended that services for the present population were inadequate, but mostly they seemed opposed to poor people moving in. Stokes suffered defeat on Lee-Seville, but he did succeed in building more public housing than previous administrations.

Stokes's liberal efforts to help those at the bottom were constantly opposed by those a few steps up from the bottom, protecting their precarious advantages. One of the most outspoken critics was a first-term councilman, barely old enough to vote, named Dennis Kucinich. Kucinich spoke out against public housing and alleged waste and high spending in the Stokes administration. Cleveland was still in the middle of a growth crisis and, by 1971, Stokes realized that the fiscal problems of local government could be solved only by a tax increase. He proposed lowering the property tax 5.8 mills, hoping that would encourage voters to approve an income tax increase from 1 to 1.8 percent. Young Kucinich led a successful fight against "Stokes's Tax." (Ironically, Kucinich thus helped to dig the fiscal hole that he later found himself in as a mayor.) Stokes's gamble dropped property tax revenues almost a third, with no compensating increase in revenues. Stokes called this "the worst blunder I ever made."[57] In February 1971, Stokes tried again to raise the income tax and failed by a wide margin, a further demonstration of the political paralysis of his administration.

Perk: From Populist to Downtown Booster

Left with only the "promises of power," Carl Stokes decided not to run for re-election in 1971. Nevertheless, he played a major role in that election, the last partisan mayoral election.[58] In the 1971 democratic primary, the two main contenders were white: Anthony Garafoli, close associate of James Stanton, Stokes's City Council nemesis, and James Carney, millionaire downtown developer and regular Democrat. Even though Stokes wanted Arnold Pinkney, a black running as an independent, to succeed him, he called for blacks to vote for Carney in the Democratic primary in order to eliminate Garafoli. Stokes succeeded. But he found it difficult to convince these same voters that they should switch back to Pinkney in the final election. This gave Ralph Perk, the Republican nominee, the opening to pull off one of the biggest upsets in Cleveland's political history.

An impoverished ice peddler who built a political career appealing to Cleveland's ethnic voters, Ralph Perk grew up in a Bohemian neighborhood on the near East Side, just above the steel mills in the Flats. First elected to City Council from that area in 1953, Perk was a true ethnic and retained those ties even after he became mayor. (He once turned down an invitation to the White House when he was mayor because it was his wife's bowling night!) In 1962, Perk was elected County Auditor, supporting half transit fares for the elderly and accusing his opponent of giving property tax breaks to big business. In 1962 and 1965, he lost mayoral races, the latter a close one to Stokes.

In 1971, Perk ran on a platform, described as urban populist, that included opposition to tax abatements for business and a pledge to retain and rehabilitate Muny Light. Perk's platform and victory were engineered, in part, by none other than Dennis Kucinich, then serving in City Council. After the primary, Kucinich put together an organization called Democrats-for-Perk. Kucinich acted as a kind of advance man for Perk, warming up the crowds with stinging attacks on Perk's opponents. Kucinich successfully identified both of Perk's opponents, Pinkney and Carney, with Stokes and his alleged big spending, wasteful policies. Kucinich wrote Perk's speech for the traditional City Club debate before the election. In it Perk attacked Carney for advocating tax abatements: "Carney talks about tax incentives to attract industry, a tax bonanza for big business at the expense of the small taxpayers." After Perk won the election with 38.7 percent of the vote, Kucinich crowed: "The power is with the people."[59]

When Perk came into office, Stokes's failed gamble to win a tax increase presented him with an immediate fiscal crisis. At one point, Perk laid off hundreds of city employees and forced those who remained to take a 10 percent pay cut; he succeeded only in buying a little time. In an effort to balance the city budget without raising taxes, Perk pursued a number of stopgap measures, all of which made the situation worse in the long run. One method was to sell valuable city assets and to use the proceeds to cover operating expenses, as he did in 1972 when he sold Cleveland's sewer to the Regional Sewer District for $32 million.[60] Later, Perk attempted to do the same with Muny Light, but there he ran into serious political opposition that thwarted his plan.

Perk also borrowed money to meet operating expenses, although state law allowed municipalities to borrow only for capital improvements. After Perk left office, an Ernst and Ernst audit of the city's finances revealed that, as of June 30, 1978, $52 million of capital improvement funds had been misspent for operating expenses—the vast majority during Perk's six years in office. While cultivating the image of a fiscal conservative Perk increased the city's debt from $326 million in 1971 to about $434 million in 1977. More importantly, Perk increased the proportion of city debt in short-term notes instead of in bonds. Under Ohio law, cities are allowed to issue notes for capital improvements that can be renewed for up to eight successive one-year periods. During this time, the city pays only on the interest, not the principal. Theoretically, short-term notes allow cities to time their entry into the bond market to take advantage of the best interest rates. Practically, Perk used them as a painless way to raise cash to cover budget deficits. Short-term debts mushroomed from $14.6 million in 1971 to $140 million in 1976. By the time he left office, Perk had managed to convert all but about $39 million of these short-term notes into long-term bonds. Nevertheless, these notes were a time bomb in the city budget, set to go off years later when they would have to be refinanced. (The inability of the Kucinich administration to rollover some of these notes in December 1978 precipated default.)

A third way that Perk tried to avoid a tax increase was through the fortuitous influx of federal funds. Total annual federal grants to Cleveland jumped from $17.8 million in 1970 to $75.1 million in 1976.[61] By 1975, fully a third of the general fund operating budget came from the federal government.[62] Like his predecessors, however, Perk had trouble running federal programs in a way satisfactory to federal administrators as well as to local council members and neighborhood organizations. The growing neighborhood organizations, especially, became a thorn in Perk's side.

All the time, Cleveland was undergoing a veritable revolt of the neighborhoods, with grassroots community organizations springing up in most areas of the city. This new generation of community organizations focused on neighborhood economic issues and were not hesitant to use direct action tactics against corporations and governmental units that were unresponsive to neighborhood needs. Seed money was supplied largely by the Commission on Catholic Community Action, funded by Catholic Charities. Another important organization was the Ohio Public Interest Campaign (OPIC), formed in 1975 by a group of anti-war activists associated with the Indochina Peace Campaign, who turned their considerable organizing skills to state and local politics. Focusing on basic economic issues beyond the neighborhood level, such as taxes and runaway shops, OPIC, together with the neighborhood organizations, formed a growing counterweight to the pressure of corporate interest groups.

In 1975, Cleveland received its first allocation of $16 million under the Community Development Block Grant (CDBG), referred to as "block grant." Earlier programs, like urban renewal and model cities, were folded into one block grant that gave municipalities greater discretion over how to spend the money. Still, federal regulations mandated that CDBG funds should not be used to substitute for local tax monies but to pay for new programs aimed primarily at low and moderate income families. Given Cleveland's fiscal crisis, the temptation to use block grant funds for city operations was great. The first year Perk proposed using $2.25 million of Cleveland's block grant to pay salaries of 190 police officers, who otherwise would have been laid off. Neigh-

borhood groups, especially in the black community, led by Congressman Louis Stokes, Carl's brother, protested the diversion of funds for
low income neighborhoods. Eventually, HUD approved the police
program but required that it be limited to low and moderate income
neighborhoods. In essence, this subsidized normal police operations
instead of providing special services for the poor.

When Perk's budgetary gimmicks failed to solve the fiscal crisis,
many argued that the only long term solution was getting the private
sector to reinvest in the city. Since the city could not force capitalists to
invest, it would somehow have to entice them. Gradually, Perk succumbed to the logic of growth politics. He even proposed using block
grant funds for that purpose. In 1975, Perk attempted to use $1 million
of block grant money to buy the aging arena on Euclid Avenue near
downtown and lease it to private promoters for $15,000–$25,000 a
year. Community groups stormed City Hall. "Our houses are falling
down and Mayor Perk's city is deteriorating—this is where we need the
money," declared a representative of the Buckeye-Woodland Community Congress, the largest community organization.[63] Perk was
forced to back off amid charges of conflict of interest.[64] In 1976, as part
of a new program called Cleveland Works!, Perk established an Office
of Business Executives within the Mayor's office, making economic
development a high priority (indicative of his new close relations with
business). He pledged $1–2 million of block grant funds for creation of
an industrial park.[65] Since this money had already been earmarked for
neighborhood conservation, however, heated opposition developed
and Perk's proposal for block grant funds was never approved.

At the same time, Kucinich was making political hay by opposing a
scheme to build a jetport five miles out in Lake Erie for $2.5 billion—
one of the most ambitious public works proposals in American history.
James C. Davis, chairman of the Greater Cleveland Growth Association, major backer of the project, called it "the greatest single program
on the horizon to catapult Cleveland dramatically forward on business,
economic and industrial fronts.[66] An early opponent of the jetport,
Kucinich was one of two councilmen to vote against participation in a
jetport study, and in 1972 he convened hearings on the jetport that gave
critics a public forum.[67] Loss of political support, triggered by questions
concerning the need for a new airport, cost overruns, and ecological
impact, caused the jetport to die on the drawing boards, but not until
$4.3 million was spent over a five-year period for plans and studies.

Cleveland seemed unable to shake the grandiose growth mentality of her past. Kucinich built his political career opposing pie-in-the-sky development projects that seemed to benefit politically-favored architects and planners more than anyone else. And Perk's political support suffered by his association with these projects. But above all, it was his support for downtown development that hurt Perk politically.

A Downtown Development High

Cleveland was on a downtown development high in the mid-1970s. With plans originating, as with urban renewal, from foundations, private consultants, and city planners, city government was drawn into a number of schemes to revitalize the central business district. Unlike urban renewal, however, much of the funding came out of the city's own revenues, not from the federal government.

Starting in 1973, downtown revitalization became a hot topic in Cleveland. As Roldo Bartimole put it in September of that year: "So everyone, as the news media has so obligingly done, should become an echo chamber of hosannas for a revitalized Downtown. We must have progress."[68] Downtown was the new growth sector. It had to be made a more attractive place to invest. Downtown Cleveland had to shed its stodgy image and become an exciting place for the new young professionals who would lead growth in "advanced" services.

The Cleveland Foundation hired Lawrence Halprin & Associates of California, designers of San Francisco's Ghiradelli Square, to come up with an exciting plan for the central business district. The $315,000 "Concept for Cleveland" plan was announced in 1975, with ballyhoo in the media rivalling Pei's urban renewal plans fourteen years earlier. The centerpiece of the multifaceted plan was a pedestrian mall on Euclid Avenue. Neighborhood groups immediately expressed doubts about how the plan would help them. City government, the Growth Association, and the Cleveland Foundation contributed $100,000 to form the Downtown Cleveland Corporation to put the plan into action. Mayor Perk succeeded in steering $10.7 million, or 88 percent of Cleveland's federally-funded Local Public Works funds in Rounds I and II, to downtown projects.[69] A Brookings study of federal grants in Cleveland questioned "the wisdom of giving such priority attention to downtown development" when capital needs for such basic things as sewers and bridges went unmet.[70] The Downtown Cleveland Corporation received another $385,000 from Cleveland foundations to push the Halprin plan. When Kucinich became mayor, however, he opposed most of it. With the exception of refurbishing Public Square, very little of the Halprin Plan was ever realized. In 1980, the Downtown Cleveland Corporation dissolved.

Another development scheme that never materialized was Perk's 1976 proposal for a Downtown People Mover. Calling for a 2.2 mile elevated loop around downtown Cleveland, the $50 million project cost would have been 80 percent federally funded, 20 percent locally. It was strongly supported by Perk, the Growth Association, the Downtown Cleveland Corporation, and the Regional Transit Authority. There was, however, by 1977 considerable business and political opposition to the People Mover, led by Kucinich's successor as mayor, George Voinovich (at the time, Cuyahoga county commissioner), who called the project a "federal boondogle" that would harm downtown and end in cost overruns. Neighborhood organizations and the Senior Citizens Coalition criticized the priorities of spending such a large amount of money downtown instead of using it to meet the transportation needs of inner city residents.[71] Kucinich became a vocal critic of the People Mover, calling it a "contemptuous substitute" for the real transit needs of Clevelanders.[72] "We have other problems to solve first," Kucinich said, "like getting people to and from work."[73] When Kucinich became mayor he returned all $41 million to the federal government, an almost unprecedented action for a local government.

In this context of downtown boosterism, Perk moved from a frequent critic of government subsidies for business to a strong advocate of a government-business alliance to revitalize downtown. Politically, his ties changed as well. Kucinich and Perk had a falling out in Perk's first term. Kucinich refused to support Perk for re-election in 1973 and attacked Perk on the model cities scandal and Ohio Bell increases. In spring 1975, Perk broke finally and publicly with Kucinich.[74] At the same time, Perk gradually formed an alliance with George Forbes, the black city council president. Elected to the council in 1965, Forbes was a militant spokesman for black rights in the 1960s. Gradually he changed into a pragmatic wheeling and dealing politician, with close ties to the white downtown business establishment. He became the prime broker between the votes of the black community and the money of downtown business interests. In 1973, Forbes was elected city council president, eventually parlaying his control over committee assignments and city budgeting into strong, many would say dictatorial, power over City Council. Perk, with his support among white ethnics, and Forbes, with his base in the black community, were a powerful pair.

Forbes ushered Perk's development schemes through City Council, always maintaining that they were necessary to create jobs for blacks and the poor.

The most important piece of legislation in the Perk-Forbes alliance was tax abatement. "Without Forbes' active support the business community and Perk could not have gotten tax abatement legislation."[75] Tax abatement, which is treated in detail later, was much like urban renewal, only this time all the subsidy came from the local government and there was less public planning (although the plan did include the use of eminent domain). In Cleveland, all the abatements passed by City Council went for downtown projects by big corporations, like National City Bank and Sohio. The irony of taking tax revenue away from a school system and city government on the edge of financial collapse and giving it to some of the richest corporations in the country was not lost on neighborhood activists, who packed council chambers in opposition. Before the 1977 election, anti-abatement activists distributed 50,000 information sheets in key wards. Seven incumbent members of council were ousted, in what the Cleveland *Plain Dealer* called "one of the biggest political bloodbaths in years."[76] The surge of anti-abatement sentiment helped carry Kucinich, who came out strongly against tax abatement, into the mayor's office.

A Growth Association for the Neighborhoods

The agenda of Cleveland politics was dominated in the mid-1970s by issues related to downtown development. Cleveland's problems were defined as lack of economic growth and middle class flight to the suburbs. The issue often was not whether city government should offer inducements to attract corporate investment and the middle class back into the city, but simply how this should be done. Crucial in defining the political agenda in this way were numerous Cleveland foundations and think tanks, as well as the Greater Cleveland Growth Association. As we saw in Chapter 2, the private, nonprofit sector was especially powerful in Cleveland. The Growth Association, formed in 1967 out of the Cleveland Chamber of Commerce and the Growth Board, had the largest annual budget of any organization of its type in the country. "Nonprofit" organizations supplied the seed money to do the studies, draw the plans, and generate the publicity necessary to get development projects off the ground—and to attract the federal and local tax money necessary to make them go. Cleveland was desperate for solutions to its problems of unemployment and government fiscal crisis. Corporate-oriented planners and developers shaped the agenda from which the politicians chose.

"Remember that there's no Growth Association for the neighborhoods," Jay Westbrook, director of OPIC for Cleveland, once observed. Indeed, there was no broad neighborhood organization that could call on anything like the resources and technical expertise of the Growth Association. But there was a small group of thinkers and planners in addition to the above organizations, a group who effectively criticized the corporate agenda in Cleveland and who had the technical expertise to begin developing a counteragenda. They were planners associated with Norman Krumholz, appointed executive director of the Cleveland City Planning Commission in 1969 by Mayor Stokes. Krumholz is considered one of the founders, nationally, of the equity or advocacy school of planning.[77] Just as this book can be seen as a study of what happens to politics in a no-growth setting, the story of the Krumholz planners is a case study of what can happen to the planning profession in a no-growth setting. In most cities opposition to growth politics remained divided and parochial. The Krumholz planners helped gather this opposition into an embryonic alternative in Cleveland that importantly influenced Kucinich's formulation of urban populism.

One of the primary functions of the City Planning Commission was to devise "a general plan for the development and improvement of the city" (*City Charter*, 76-2). In winter 1970, Krumholz and his talented staff of young planners began this project, which had not been done since 1949. In orthodox planning circles, this usually meant a glossy collection of maps and designs outlining the future growth of the city, a kind of blueprint for an ideal future. Since Cleveland was 97 percent developed, and disinvestment rather than investment was the rule, the Krumholz planners began to consider the orthodox approach to be irrelevant if not downright destructive. What they created instead was a remarkable document, the *Cleveland Policy Planning Report*, which articulated an overall goal and approach for city planning appropriate to a contracting metropolis like Cleveland and applied it to the areas of income, housing, transportation, and community development.

As opposed to the technical orientation of the planning profession, Cleveland's equity planners considered all city planning to be value oriented. They attempted to state, as unambiguously as possible, the goals they would pursue in their planning. Their overall goal was simple: "In a context of limited resources, institutions should give priority attention to the task of promoting more choices for those individuals who have few, if any, choices.[78] Since income, in this society, is the prime generator of choices, the goal of the Cleveland planners placed them squarely on the side of the poor, increasingly trapped in the inner city. "Thus, in providing consistent support for the interests of those with few choices, the Commission is simply providing appropriate service to a large and growing proportion of the City's population."[79] Cleveland's equity planners were committed to the *people* who lived in the city, as opposed to the commitment, evident in other city planners, to the city as a collection of physical structures or as an efficient place for production.

In one bold sweep, the Krumholz planners redefined the urban problem. no longer the lack of investment or the flight of the middle class, it was now defined as the lack of choices available to those who presently lived in the city. The solution no longer centered on enticing investment or the middle class into the city (essentially increasing their choices) but improving the choices of those who had remained behind. In justifying their commitment to equality, the Cleveland planners invoked the entire tradition of Western political theory and American democracy, from Plato to Jesus, from Thomas Jefferson to Lyndon Johnson. They did not see equality as a leveling process; rather, they favored competition and choice in the marketplace. This is exemplified by their use of the modern version of contract theory developed by John Rawls, who argues that in a just society inequalities should be tolerated—but only to the extent that they improve the material lot of the least advantaged.[80] The test for any policy becomes: does it benefit the least advantaged, those with the fewest choices? Subsidies for downtown development could be justified, then, if the benefits of the new investments trickled down to those at the bottom. When the Krumholz planners analyzed specific development proposals, however, they usually found that the benefits, especially to the neighborhoods, were far less than advertised. In the context of a shrinking economy, the equity planners implied, redistribution is a necessity, redevelopment, often an illusion.

The Cleveland planners did not stop with analysis; they went beyond the orthodox role of technical adviser to formulate an advocacy role for planners. Instead of waiting for those in power to ask for a recommendation, they aggressively sought out problems and formulated issues. They made their case to the public and lobbied behind the scenes with relevant interest groups. They fed information to friends. Rejecting any hard and fast distinction between policy planning and policy implementation, the equity planners viewed themselves as actors in a continuous process from policy formulation through passage to implementation.

Above all, Cleveland's equity planners saw themselves as advocates for neighborhood interests. Taking on projects at the request of community organizations, Krumholz and the Cleveland planners did for the neighborhoods what the foundations and Growth Association did for the corporations. Krumholz and planner Janice Cogger put the matter this way in an article:

> Why do we view these [neighborhood] groups as allies? The answer is simple. They provide a countervailing political force to the incessant demands by downtown interests for capital improvements. . . . They frequently argue that neighborhood considerations are more important than regional considerations. They often insist that more grandiose programs must be set aside in favor of basic needs. And we frequently agree on all points.[81]

While Kucinich had no formal relation to the Krumholz planners, he was one of the few politicians who read their reports and, before he was mayor, he formed an effective alliance with them on transportation issues. Pointing out the heavy costs of new highways for built-up inner city neighborhoods, the Cleveland planners helped stop a proposed freeway across the East Side.[82] Instead they advocated increased mobility for the one-third of Cleveland households who were "transit dependent," that is, who lacked access to a car and were dependent on mass transportation.[83] Through carefully researched reports that argued for fare reductions and increased service for inner city residents, the equity planners became heavily involved in the sale of the Cleveland Transit System to a regional authority.[84] Interestingly, their opposition to capital intensive expenditure on fixed rail transit brought them into conflict with liberals and environmentalists. They argued, instead, for a better-articulated bus system within the city. Kucinich took up these ideas and led the five-month negotiations for the sale, winning guarantees for a 25 cent fare and expanded neighborhood service.

Conclusion: The Dilemma of Growth Politics

The economic crunch that hit Cleveland in the 1950s undermined the system of conservative growth politics that had long dominated city politics. The public and private sectors joined together in a kind of shotgun marriage to deal with the economic crisis. The union proved unstable, however. Even with massive injections of federal money through urban renewal, city government still was the junior partner, relying on the private sector and trying to anticipate and reinforce positive investment trends. In Cleveland, this meant attention to the expanding service sector, not housing for the poor. Essentially, urban renewal forced the external costs of economic growth—for example, removal of slums to build new office towers—on those who could least afford them: inner city slum dwellers and small businesses. And the benefit of the expanding service sector went mostly to downtown corporations and suburbanites. Whether urban renewal actually attracted into the city new investment that would not otherwise have occurred is questionable; what it did do was enable politicians to take credit for the only growth game in town.

The Carl Stokes administration was an attempt to humanize the new growth politics, to steer more of the benefits to the black community that had been seriously damaged by urban renewal. It was a classical form of liberal growth politics. Stokes hoped, by close collaboration with business, to stimulate economic growth and, by voluntary contributions and increased taxes, to siphon off part of this growth to fund an expanded local welfare state. Business support for Stokes signaled a switch from a conservative to a liberal growth orientation. Whereas business had previously been united against any local tax increase on the ground that it would kill off investment, now, under the pressure of an economic transition, business argued that local government had the discretion to raise taxes—that, in fact, an expanded public sector was needed to insure economic growth. Stokes, however, was unable to pass a tax increase. He was opposed especially by white ethnics who had little identification with liberal growth politics, whether in its urban renewal or welfare varients. Moreover, when business discovered that Stokes could not guarantee peace in the ghetto, they withdrew much of their support. Cleveland's fiscal crisis deepened.

Ralph Perk demonstrated even more clearly the dilemma of growth politics in a declining industrial city. Ironically, Perk began as a populist critic of liberal growth politics, promising not to increase taxes and to redirect government benefits away from downtown businesses to the neighborhoods. Other than a resolve not to increase taxes on his lower middle class electoral base, however, Perk lacked a populist economic program. When his dubious efforts to stave off a tax increase (by the sale of assets, increased borrowing, and reliance on federal funds) failed, Perk gradually succumbed to the logic of growth politics. Like others, he claimed that it was pure pragmatism. Clearly, the only long term solution to the city's financial crisis was to get the private sector to invest in the city again. Under Perk, the effort would take a more conservative turn. With the decline in federal funding, business incentive would have to come, as with tax abatement, at the expense of local taxpayers; and the Perk administration was not inclined to restrict private developers with public plans.

Nonetheless, Perk met the same problems that had faced urban renewal. In order to leverage private investment, efforts would have to be focused on the downtown service sector. But the jobs there tended to go to suburbanites more than to inner city residents, and the physical development of downtown did nothing for the deteriorating conditions in the neighborhoods. Neighborhood organizations, more broadly based public interest groups, and equity planners rose up in opposition to what they saw as the drift of the Perk administration away from neighborhood and consumer interests. Dennis Kucinich successfully appealed to this opposition in his mayoral campaign.

In short, Cleveland's economic crisis brought with it a seemingly insoluble political crisis. At the heart of the crisis was a simple conflict: corporations wanted to use government to promote downtown as a center for advanced services, but neighborhoods resisted bearing the costs. Cleveland became a city in limbo. It did not want to step forward into its liberal corporate future, but it could not step back into its conservative industrial past.

5

Urban Populism and the Electoral *Coup d'Etat* of 1977

Nothing is so powerful as an idea whose time has come.
And I think America is ready for the idea of economic
democracy built on urban populism.[1]

Dennis Kucinich

The time: October 26, 1977. The place: St. Benedict's Catholic Church Hall on Cleveland's East Side. It was candidates night at the Buckeye-Woodland Community Congress, the largest coalition of neighborhood groups. About 150 people were there to hear mayoral candidates Dennis Kucinich and Edward Feighan answer pointed questions about community concerns. No room for political doubletalk here; a boxscore of YESs and NOs was kept for each candidate with large cardboard signs on the front wall. One of the questions was very specific: if elected would the candidate hire sixty more dogcatchers? Kucinich, with a dramatic wave of his hand, answered, "You want it, you got it," drawing one of the loudest cheers of the night.[2] Small as this incident appears, it is revealing of the Kucinich candidacy: on the one hand, it demonstrated Kucinich's support for neighborhood demands; on the other hand, it presaged the difficulty he would have in meeting the heightened expectations of him as mayor.

Kucinich was not, he claimed, like most politicians, simply responding to political pressure; he was following a coherent program for urban reform that gave national significance to his administration.

119

"Urban populism," he called it. A central question of this study is whether urban populism represents a viable alternative to growth politics, conservative or liberal. But first, you may well ask, what is urban populism?

Urban populism can be best understood as Saul Alinsky-style community organizing carried into the electoral arena. "Alinsky," observed Heather Booth, well known organizer, "is to community organizing as Freud is to psychoanalysis."[3] In other words, all community organizers owe a debt to Saul Alinsky, even if they consciously disagree with his approach. He founded the craft of organizing and suffused it with his own particular style and tactics. Kucinich learned his political craft in the rough and tumble of the inner city at exactly the time that the activist neighborhood groups organized in Cleveland. He absorbed their approach to community organizing and applied it to his electoral goals.[4]

Alinsky began organizing in the late 1930s in the Back of the Yards area of Chicago. He was remarkably successful and was one of the creators of the powerful Woodlawn Organization in Chicago's Southside in the 1950s. Alinsky's commitment was to those at the bottom of society; his goal was redistributing wealth and power to the poor and the powerless. He did not believe in telling people how to use this wealth and power; it was enough to give them the resources to control their own lives. Organizers, Alinsky believed, should start where people are, with their immediate needs, not with some ideological conception of where they should be. Eschewing any ideological blueprint for society, Alinsky was firmly within the tradition of radical American populism.

> In the end he [the organizer of a free society] has one all-consuming conviction, one belief, one article of faith—a belief in the people, a complete commitment to the belief that if people have the power, the opportunity to act, in the long run they will, most of the time, reach the right decisions. The alternatives to this would be rule by the elite.[5]

The similarities to Kucinich are obvious. The speeches of Kucinich were studded with populist rhetoric: power to the people against rule by a selfish elite. Kucinich also believed in starting where people are, redistributing wealth and power, not changing people's value systems.

Alinsky's distinctive contribution, however, lay not in his concept of ends but in his system of means, his creative tactics for organizing the powerless. In *Reveille for Radicals,* written in 1946, Alinsky laid out a method for organizing the powerless in any community. To Alinsky, the Machiavelli of the have-nots, the end justified the means: "the man of action views the issue of means and ends in pragmatic and strategic terms. . . . He asks of ends only whether they are achievable and worth the cost; of means, only whether they will work."[6]

Organizers must be extremely creative about tactics if they are to overcome their more powerful opponents, Alinsky argued. With a tactical approach that has been described as a form of "mass ju-jitsu," Alinsky showed how the overwhelming power and privilege of your opponent could be used against him. The key is conflict. "A PEOPLE'S ORGANIZATION is a conflict group," says Alinsky.[7] Conflict organizes the people.

In broad outline, it works like this. Organizers start by finding out what people are concerned about —say, a missing stoplight at a dangerous intersection. A group is then formed around such a "winnable" issue and the person responsible for the problem is confronted with the demands. At this point, the organizers must *personalize* the problem; a faceless bureaucracy cannot be confronted effectively. The group's action should dramatize the issue and put the opponent on the spot: either satisfy the demand or oppose it. If the opponent delivers, the group claims victory and moves on to the next issue. If the demand is not satisfied, the group continues to confront until the demand is satisfied or the opponent counterattacks. Being attacked by an obviously more powerful opponent, such as a public official or corporation president, actually redounds to the benefit of the group, which uses it to solidify and expand its base. In the words of an Alinsky disciple, "Existing power bases make a habit of reacting against the people and the people's issues. At that point the organizer has the beginning of a new *people's power base.*"[8]

Kucinich's electoral tactics were remarkably similar to Alinsky's organizing ones.[9] Kucinich was known for not being choosy about his tactics. Some would say he fought dirty; he would probably say that the ends justified the means. Kucinich thrived on conflict. His vaunted "confrontational style" involved pointed attacks on powerful individuals as tools of the elite, feathering their own nest at the expense of the people. When these individuals counterattacked, as they were prone to do, Kucinich turned these attacks to his own advantage, citing them as proof that he was uncorruptible and expanding his electoral appeal to the powerless. Like the Alinskyite community organizations, Kucinich avoided any hint of co-optation. He built his career on exposing the problems, not on devising solutions and involving himself in their implementation.

There was, however, one important difference: most community organizations avoid electoral politics like the plague; Kucinich was a thoroughly electoral animal, running for political office nine times within twelve years. Councilman Kucinich could play the role of the outsider, the critic. When he was elected mayor, however, everything changed; Kucinich himself pointed out, "I'm confronted with a situation that is quite different than ever faced Alinsky. Alinsky was never really on the inside."[10] In short, Kucinich ran the government, a role he never got used to.

Seeing Kucinich as an expression of the community organizing movement raises the significance of the Cleveland experience. Urban populism becomes not something unique to Cleveland but an expression of a basic approach to politics that is firmly rooted in inner city neighborhoods throughout the United States. At a time when neighborhood organizations have taken over many of the functions of the ward-based political machines—at a time when many are calling for neighborhood organizations to get more involved in electoral politics— the Cleveland experience takes on added significance.[11] With great care, lessons can be drawn from the Cleveland example about the promise and pitfalls of applying the tactics of community organizing to electoral politics.[12]

Economic Theory of Urban Populism

Strategically, Kucinich would agree with the political scientist E. E. Schattschneider: "He who determines what politics is about runs the country, because the definition of the alternatives is the choice of conflicts, and the choice of conflicts allocates power."[13] Urban populism tried, first, to displace the divisive social issues that arose in the 1960s around race, religion, lifestyle, and sex, with fundamental economic issues. The claim is that issues like busing and abortion divide natural political allies. Kucinich: "Trifling with social issues evades our responsibility to face economic issues. It diminishes the potential of economic issues to rally popular support. The social issues are often divisive and play off, against each other, the very people who ought to be the beneficiaries of economic reforms."[14]

Besides displacing social issues with economic issues, urban populism attempted to reformulate the economic issue for inner cities. For growth politics, the decisive issue for city government was always economic expansion: how to attract investment and higher income residents into the city in order to expand the economic pie. According to Kucinich, the politics of growth no longer works, either economically or politically. In a no-growth setting, the cost of enticing corporations to reinvest in the city is higher than the benefits that finally trickle down to inner city residents. In the past, growth politics may have been politically feasible as the overall economic expansion created enough benefits, in the form of added tax revenues, patronage, and government contracts, to cement a winning coalition. But the transition from a growth to a no-growth economy forces politicians, Kucinich said, to choose between serving the corporations and serving inner city residents. On the agenda of local politics, urban populism attempts to displace the *growth* issue with the *distributive* issue.

While radical in support of redistributing wealth, urban populism was conservative in social values. By focusing on income redistribution, Kucinich was able to finesse thorny cultural issues and appeal to voters with highly conservative values. Urban populism addressed their material deprivation, not their conservative values. "They [economic reforms]," Kucinich said, "are substantive and enable the individual to achieve more control over his own destiny, to resolve his own fate as he wishes."[15] The underlying philosophy was individualistic, not social.

The economic program of urban populism can be seen as an aspect of "economic democracy."[16] Carefully distinguished from state socialism, economic democracy aims primarily at equalizing power within the marketplace. It is directed not against capitalism but against monopolies and special government privileges that have short-circuited the checks and balances of the competitive market.[17] Kucinich's economic pronouncements did not mention workers' control over production or changing job structures; the focus was on the sphere of distribution, not the sphere of production.

In truth, however, Kucinich's program for economic democracy was consummately vague. "We must bring democracy to the banks as we have to our political life," Kucinich once said.[18] What he meant was unclear. Certainly, he was not calling for the nationalization of banks. Nor did Kucinich ever come out strongly for the whole range of nongovernmental alternatives, such as credit unions or cooperatives, pushed by other proponents of economic democracy. Urban populism under Kucinich, in short, was characterized more by what it opposed than what it supported.

Political Theory of Urban Populism

Since urban populism was as much a response to a political crisis as to an economic crisis, it is as important to explore the political context as the economic context out of which it arose.

Walter Dean Burnham has changed the way political scientists view American voting behavior. Back in 1965, Burnham drew attention to changes in the size and shape of the American electorate that he called "unique in the contemporary universe of democratic politics": "In the United States these transformations over the past century have involved devolution, a dissociation from politics as such among a growing segment of the eligible electorate and apparent deterioration of the bonds of party linkage between electorate and government."[19] If the American electorate in the twentieth century has been characterized by declining participation, decaying political parties, and rising alienation, then Cleveland certainly seems to fit the pattern; in fact, it is in the vanguard.

Political participation in Cleveland is low and declining. Figure 5 shows the estimated turnout in Cleveland for presidential and mayoral elections from 1932 to 1979. Only two candidacies had a significant positive effect on turnout in Cleveland. Franklin Roosevelt expanded the electorate to over 70 percent of eligibles by 1940, but since then presidential turnout has declined to levels even lower than in the rest of the country.[20] Carl Stokes, who ran in 1965, 1967, and 1969, helped blacks, for the first time, to play a decisive role in citywide elections, and they mobilized as never before. In 1967, turnout in nine predominantly black wards exceeded turnout in fifteen white wards.[21] As in the South after the Voting Rights Act of 1965, mobilization of black voters produced a counter mobilization by white voters.[22] Since Stokes, however, participation in city elections has declined to below 50 percent.

Political parties, like turnout, have also declined in Cleveland. Since the late nineteenth century, Cleveland has always had fairly strong ward-based political organizations. But Cleveland early developed a reputation for political volatility and fragmentation; rarely did these separate ethnic and racial organizations coalesce into a centralized party machine. With the exceptions of the McKisson period (1896–

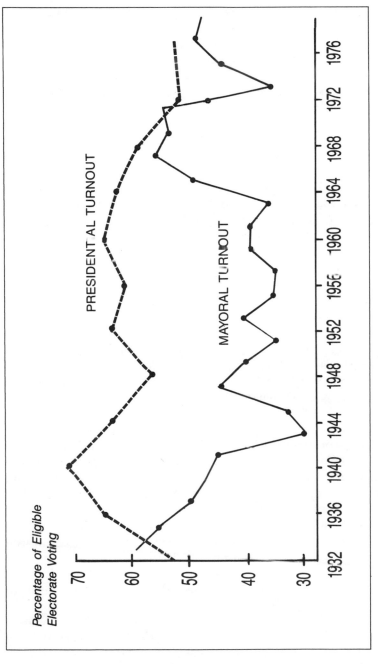

FIGURE 5. Presidential and Mayoral Turnout in Cleveland, 1932–1979. Source: Cuyahoga County Board of Elections; eligible voting population was extrapolated from decennial census population counts. (The extra mayoral election in 1962 was not recorded.)

1900) and the Maschke machine (1916–1933), Cleveland has had a "factional" as opposed to a "controlling" or centralized political machine, in the characterization of sociologist M. Craig Brown.[23] Even during Maschke's reign, however, power was somewhat dispersed and the party was split between reform and machine elements.

In 1932, FDR carried the city, establishing the Democrats as the majority party, a position they hold to this day. Since Roosevelt, no Democratic presidential candidate has lost in Cleveland. Democratic party dominance in national elections, however, did not translate into local party power.[24] Cleveland's large ethnic population gradually became less dependent on the local party for favors and established a pattern of independent voting. As the local parties atrophied, many of their functions, including recruiting candidates for office and communicating information to the voters, were taken over by mass media. All along, the newspapers had attacked the corruption and bossism of the party machines. Ostensibly nonpartisan, the mass media acquired the power to make and break candidates. The dominant force was the Cleveland *Press*.

> [Louis B.] Seltzer as editor of the Cleveland *Press* gained the informal title of "Mr. Cleveland," and in political circles the universal opinion was that he personally selected who would be mayor and then utilized the full resources of the newspaper to promote the candidate among the ethnic voters and successfully elect him.[25]

The election of Harold Burton in 1935 heralded the beginning of the era of media mayors. Burton was the choice of the newspapers. A Republican in an overwhelmingly Democratic city, he portrayed himself as an independent and in his campaigns maintained an "independent" as well as a "Republican" headquarters.

In his classic comparative study of political parties, Maurice Duverger classified American parties as "caucus parties": essentially collections of notables that come together at election time for the purpose of winning office.[26] Duverger contrasted the nonideological and decentralized American parties with the more disciplined working class parties of Europe. Today, the Cuyahoga County Democratic party, however, lacks even the unity of a group of notables held together by the common goal of winning office and sharing the spoils. In 1953, outsider Anthony Celebrezze defeated Democratic boss Ray T. Miller in the mayor's race, shutting party regulars out of City Hall patronage. Ever since, the

Democrats have tended to split between the faction around the mayor and the rest of the party revolving around county office holders and, to a lesser extent, members of City Council. Unable to control City Hall patronage and contracts, the party was never able to create a ward-based Democratic machine, as in Chicago. Knowing that neither the county Democratic party nor the mayor can affect their election chances, most council members feel free to ignore the party. They raise their own campaign funds and run their wards as separate fiefdoms. Likewise, candidates for mayor tend to run as much against the party as with it. As Robert Hughes, Republican County chairman, once lamented: "We may see the day [when] the only function of a political party is for a candidate to run against them.[27]

The Democratic party was further eviscerated by the split between ethnics and blacks. In the 1960s, Carl Stokes led a successful rebellion against the party regulars who had never admitted blacks into city- or countywide positions of power. In 1970 Carl, along with his brother, Congressman Louis Stokes, formed the Twenty-first District Caucus, which they subsequently pulled out of the Democratic party, becoming, in effect, an independent political party endorsing Republicans as well as Democrats. While the Twenty-first District Caucus was brought back into the Democratic fold in 1974, it still exists as a semi-autonomous entity, often working against the regular Democratic leadership.

The regular Democratic party in Cleveland can be thought of as the over 2,000 precinct committee members countywide (about 650 from the central city) who elect the county chairman. Incapable of regularly turning out the votes for candidates, many precinct committee members are old and out of touch; at any given time there are hundreds of vacancies. But the main problem is lack of unity. With no ideological glue to hold it together, the Democratic party is a constantly shifting web of conflicts and coalitions. Not a coherent organization, the party is more simply an arena where local notables, cheered by their followers on the sidelines, joust for supremacy.

The problem in Cleveland, however, is more than a decline in participation or even a decay of the party system. The political crisis in Cleveland is marked by the alienation of many citizens from the political process itself. Political alienation can be understood as having two basic dimensions: (1) *a perceived value conflict* between the individual and the political system (such as the belief that in a democracy the political system should operate for the benefit of the people, or the

majority, but instead it benefits a small, corrupt minority), and (2) an
accompanying *feeling of being powerless* to affect this condition.[28]
Increased alienation in the American electorate was well documented in
the early 1970s.[29] Even without a scientific survey, it is easy to spot the
symptoms of alienation in Cleveland, especially among Kucinich's
main supporters, inner city white ethnics.[30] With their once secure
position in the unionized blue collar sector constantly eroding, they see
themselves being passed over by technological trends, and there is little
they can do about it. Only a step up from the bottom, inner city ethnic
neighborhoods fear descending into a slum (symbolized by lower class
blacks). Ethnics are part of the silent majority: often too rich (or too
proud) to qualify for welfare benefits, they also are too poor to escape to
the suburbs. While their neighborhoods decay, they see all the political
attention focused on efforts to revitalize downtown. Busing, though, is
the quintessential issue of powerlessness for white ethnics. They know
their own schools are inferior to suburban schools. Yet their children
are bused across town to probably worse schools in black neighborhoods. And all this is proclaimed by a federal judge they did not even
elect. They feel their interests, the majority interests, are not being
served by the political process and there is nothing they can do about it.
Their feelings of alienation are summed up in an anti-busing bumper
sticker that reads simply: NO!

This was the political environment Kucinich grew up in: a shrunken
electorate with deep feelings of alienation and the political parties in
disarray. With high participation and strong parties, elections in the
nineteenth century resembled military campaigns, the main effort going
into drilling the party regulars to the polls.[31] Little effort was put into
going after the independent voters. By contrast, in contemporary elections with weak political parties, the large "floating vote" becomes the
center of attention. To carry over the military analogy, electoral campaigns change from a war of position to a war of movement, from a
conventional war to a guerrilla war.

Kucinich was a master at these new mobile tactics. His career
pattern was not that of the party regular loyally rising through the ranks
until chosen for elective office. Kucinich rose like a meteor from council
candidate to mayor in ten short years. He did this without the aid of the
party apparatus, running as much against the Democratic party as with
it.[32] In 1971, for example, Kucinich shocked the party by organizing
Democrats-for-Perk; in 1972, he ran for Congress as a Democrat,
narrowly losing to the Republican incumbent; in 1973, he ran five

candidates for council against regular Democrats; in 1974, he ran for Congress, this time as an independent; in 1975 he endorsed Arnold Pinkney, the Democratic nominee for mayor, against Perk. And so on. In Cleveland's political war of all against all, politicians must be prepared to shift directions at a moment's notice. No one was more adept at this than Kucinich.

More noteworthy than Kucinich's ability to maneuver in a Byzantine political system was his ability to mobilize the votes of people alienated from politics—paradoxically, by appealing to their alienation. (Interestingly, Kucinich's street campaigning concentrated on registered voters; he did not appeal to nonvoters and try to register them. In the long run, this may have been his downfall.) To the alienated voter, Kucinich's populist appeals both explained why they felt a value conflict with an ostensibly democratic political system and gave them a way to overcome their sense of powerlessness. The political analysis offered by urban populism was essentially a streetwise version of elite theory: a small closed elite, stemming from the upper economic class, uses its control over wealth to manipulate government for its own selfish purposes. The growth ideology fostered by the business elite, which claims that everyone benefits from the expansion generated by business incentives, is nothing but a smokescreen, Kucinich said. It benefits only special corporate interests, not majority interests; politicians are bought off by the economic resources of the elite. Invariably, Kucinich attacked his opponents as "tools of the elite." A leaflet in the 1979 mayoral campaign, for example, was entitled, "Who Owns Voinovich?" On the front was a cartoon depicting three "fat cats," with one quoted as saying, "Listen Voinovich, we will buy you City Hall as long as we can run it" (see p. 218). Inside were listed hundreds of wealthy contributors to Voinovich's campaign. Like Alinsky-style community organizers, Kucinich attacked his opponent's strengths (prestige endorsements, successful fund raising, close ties with big business), all the while portraying himself as a "political outsider"—the way many voters felt.

Attacks on his opponents as corrupt and powerful explained to voters why the system failed to work for them; Kucinich's own candidacy gave them a way of overcoming their sense of powerlessness about this. Essentially, Kucinich proposed replacing the ruling elite with a counterelite, led by himself, that would run the government in the interests of the people, not the special interests. The counterelite would be as tough and hard-hitting as the corporate elite, and it would be independent of established interests and able to withstand the temptation to be bought off. Kucinich portrayed himself as the only political leader independent enough to steer the benefits of government to the people in the neighborhoods. As he put it before the 1977 mayoral election: "I am the only Democrat in Cleveland who is sufficiently independent of party bosses and corrupt special interests to be able to make City Hall meet the social and economic needs of the people.[33] Kucinich did not believe in participatory democracy but in representative democracy. He would represent the people against the elite. In this way voters could overcome their sense of powerlessness while remaining in an essentially apolitical stance, alienated from politics. Urban populism did not demand much of the people between elections. As suggested in a 1979 re-election leaflet, Kucinich would fight their battles for them:

> DENNIS KUCINICH STOOD ALONE against the pressures of the banks and big business, against the political bosses and their obedient followers in City Council.

Urban populism was essentially an elite program of economic reform, stressing that the sources of injustice lay in the economic system, not the political system. Tremendous concentrations of wealth in the private economy invaded an otherwise healthy democratic system and corrupted it. The solution was to extend political democracy to the economic system. Kucinich contrasted substantive economic reforms with the hollowness of procedural reforms in the polity. Economic reforms were substantive because they actually redistribute valued resources and the life opportunities associated with them. Structural reforms of government often were "gimmicks" Kucinich said, offering only the illusion of change, or, like proposals for regional government, were actually harmful, diluting the power of inner city residents.

In sum, urban populism had no political theory as such. Politics was an instrument, a tool. Political participation was not something to be valued for itself. In the final analysis, the political theory of urban populism was nothing more than a set of tactics.

The *Coup d'Etat* of 1977

When Kucinich was elected mayor in 1977, he was still, to a great extent, an unknown quantity, a political outsider. Nevertheless, the traditional power brokers rallied around the young mayor. After all, they had heard populist rhetoric before from the likes of Lausche, Celebrezze, and Perk. All these candidates had learned, once in office, that in order to get things done in Cleveland, they had to win the cooperation of big business, the newspapers, and the political power structure. But Kucinich turned out to be different. He refused to give business any official standing in government, such as advisory committees; he spurned the consensus politics of growth that so enamored editorial writers; and he refused to play ball with most of the political leaders in town. What made Kucinich different?

The answer is that Kucinich came to power with remarkably few political debts or obligations. He seized the top political position in Cleveland suddenly, without, as was normally the case, gathering around himself a broad coalition of the area's established interest in business, the media, and politics. Kucinich's sudden seizure of power, his electoral *coup d'état*, made an almost complete end run around the established interest groups. Others had been independent in rhetoric; Kucinich was independent in fact.

This was not an easy task. The extremely low level of partisan commitments in Cleveland, however, meant that much of the electorate was floating, up for grabs, not "immunized" against the virus of urban populism.[34] As we have seen, Kucinich had a message capable of mobilizing these voters. All he needed was a way of communicating that message to the voters without relying on the political parties or the mass media (and hence large campaign contributions).

In place of a political party, with its formal charter and internal political life, Kucinich put together a labor-intensive campaign organization fiercely loyal to himself and run, in top down fashion, by his political lieutenant, Bob Weissman.[35] Lacking even the semblance of an internal political life, this organization did not debate policy; it did not endorse candidates. It had only one function: to communicate directly with the voters door-to-door using leaflets and petitions. A logical extension of Cleveland's personalist, almost feudal, brand of electoral politics, it functioned as an alternative media, an instrument used by Kucinich to connect with the voters. The antithesis of the political parties in Cleveland, which more and more had become simply arenas for power contests, Kucinich's organization was a loyal and effective instrument of electoral struggle, the ideal vehicle for the self-made political man, the political entrepreneur *par excellence*.

Above all, it was an organization that created few political debts. First, it was a labor-intensive, not a capital-intensive, campaign technology. For obvious reasons, Kucinich was not going to receive large corporate contributions. (Nor would he have desired them, being evidence of the corrupt ties he so criticized in his opponents.) Kucinich was almost always outspent by his rivals by two to one margins or greater.[36] He would have to rely on numbers rather than money. To provide those numbers Kucinich relied on patronage. Beginning with the approximately thirty-three patronage (non–civil service) appointments he acquired by winning the City Clerk's office in 1975, Kucinich put together an energetic group of campaigners. Mostly young, attracted by Kucinich's charismatic personality and populist appeal, they prided themselves on being urban guerrillas, moving swiftly through the neighborhoods mobilizing voters behind the backs of the established institutions.

The organization was egalitarian in the extreme, with everyone from cabinet officers down to garbage collectors doing the same thing: door-to-door canvassing. As patronage operations go, this one was extremely lean, including, at the high point, only 150 dedicated campaigners out of a city work force of about 10,000. The theory, at least, was that it was possible to create a patronage operation capable of winning elections while avoiding the makework and inefficiency characteristic of old style machines that were themselves a cause of the fiscal crisis. Nor was this patronage machine geographically rooted by ward. Kucinich never tried to create a face-to-face ward organization, running his campaign, instead, completely out of a central downtown headquarters. This meant that few in the organization built any independent political base; by being moved about, they were kept dependent on Kucinich. There were no power brokers in the organization to deal with. Weissman called the traditional ward-based organization "inherently corrupt." "Eventually ward organizations start making demands. Your own creation becomes a monster that comes back to haunt you," Weissman said.[37]

Kucinich used his campaign organization effectively to win the 1977 mayoral election. Kucinich ran against Perk in 1977 on much the same platform he had helped put together for Perk in 1971. As we saw, Perk had reversed himself on crucial economic issues, like tax abatement and Muny Light. Kucinich attacked Perk as a populist who had sold out, who had lost touch with the people, pointing out that Perk had promised to drive his own car but now cruised the city in two chauffeur-driven limousines and had lavishly redecorated his City Hall office. The ground was fertilized for Kucinich by the mounting community agitation against tax abatement. Nevertheless, the Kucinich forces were shocked when Perk finished third in the primary behind Edward

Feighan, liberal Democratic state representative. Perk, however, knew why his ethnic base had abandoned him as their standard bearer: "He attributed his defeat to difficult decisions that damaged his popularity, citing tax abatement and disposition of Muny Light."[38]

It seemed that Kucinich's attacking campaign style would be neutralized by Feighan, a young, relatively unknown state representative with a squeaky-clean liberal image and no City Hall record to defend. Feighan opposed the sale of Muny Light and, while giving a qualified endorsement to tax abatement, criticized specific abatements that had been granted by the city. Characteristically, Kucinich went on the attack anyhow, focusing on the fact that Feighan was the nominee of the Democratic party: "Feighan is not his own man. He belongs to the party bosses, lock, stock and barrel. If the bosses elect the mayor, who's going to be the mayor's boss? The people? No way."[39] Kucinich attacked Feighan's close association with Forbes, who, he implied, would be the real mayor, not Feighan. He attacked Feighan's big contributors with a map showing that they lived in the suburbs, not the city. He attacked Feighan's support of tax abatement as a state legislator. Kucinich portrayed himself, on the other hand, as free of all the corrupt ties that bound Feighan. "Vote for the candidate with no strings attached," his leaflets said.

Kucinich won a very close election, with less than 51 percent of the vote. Although he got only 35 percent of the black vote, he picked up the majority of Perk's constituency, the white ethnics. With less than 24 percent of the eligible voters, however, Kucinich could hardly claim a mandate. Further, while the 1977 election was called the "Tuesday Night Massacre" because seven council incumbents were ousted, many over their support of tax abatement and the sale of Muny Light, Kucinich was unable to create anything like a coattail's effect. The new council members had gained office on their own, independent of Kucinich. Burnham argues that in a fragmented electorate political coalitions tend to be office specific, that is, each office holder has to build his or her own coalition. Kucinich was a prime example of this. He could count on only three solid votes in City Council, with perhaps seven more leaning his way. In a thirty-three member council, he could not even sustain a veto.

Conclusion: Three Case Studies of Growth Politics

According to urban populism, it is the manipulations of a corporate elite, not objective economic pressures, that cause city governments to succumb to conservative growth politics.[40] Kucinich denied that irresistable growth pressures operate on city government, regardless of who is in the mayor's office. His predecessor, Ralph Perk, argued the contrary, that economic imperatives were what forced him to reverse his position on issues such as Muny Light and tax abatement.

It is precisely the purpose of this study to determine how great these structured economic pressures are and how much room there is for alternative policies. To examine this question, I have chosen to conduct detailed case studies of three issues: tax abatement, default, and community development. These were chosen not because they are the most important issues (a good case could be made that police issues were more important) but because they allow us to examine the issues of growth politics—issues largely ignored in the literature on community power, but issues that are on the cutting edge of urban change across the country today.

Tax abatement very clearly raises the issue of objective economic pressures: are cities required to enact special incentives for downtown development or suffer loss of investment to competing cities? Fortunately, this question lends itself to quantitative analysis of the role of local taxes in corporate decision making. Another question gets raised here, however, that does not lend itself to quantitative analysis: if Kucinich is right and tax abatements are not required by economic pressures, then why do so many cities enact them?

Default raises a different issue in growth politics: "politicized" investment. If lenders can attach political demands to municipal loans, then clearly the space for creative urban policies shrinks even beyond that left by economic pressures. If Kucinich is right here, seemingly his electoral appeal would be fatally wounded, for urban populist regimes would then be subject to debilitating economic blackmail. Default also raises the issue of Muny Light and whether it makes sense for cities in this day and age to compete with private corporations in productive enterprises.

Finally, community development was chosen for study precisely because it lies outside the pressures of growth politics. The rules of the federal Community Development Block Grant do not require that cities leverage large amounts of private investment with the money (as in urban renewal); in fact, the funds are supposed to predominately benefit low and moderate income neighborhoods—exactly the areas excluded from the immediate benefits of growth politics. Freed from direct economic pressures, community development reveals with spe-

cial clarity the effect of structured *political* pressures on city governments, pressures that Kucinich never acknowledged.

Although Kucinich may have captured the head of state with his
remarkable electoral *coup d'état*, the body of the state remained tied
down by a myriad of competing interest groups. The result was confrontation and *immobilisme*. In short, economic issues can never be
studied apart from political issues.

6

The Politics of Tax Abatement

You can make Cleveland the model city of the world! You can clean up Hough and Glenville with tax abatement![1]

James Rhodes
Governor of Ohio

Once confined mainly to Southern states, in recent years tax abatement has spread to many Northern states. Along with other business incentives, tax abatement has been taken up by Snowbelt states in an effort to stem the flow of industry to the Sunbelt and overseas. As used here, tax abatement refers specifically to the reduction of local property taxes. In 1974, nine states gave local counties or municipalities the power to grant abatements to corporations on some or all of their local property taxes.[2] Since 1975, at least ten more states have enacted such enabling legislation.[3] The same trend is evident for the full array of other business incentives: industrial revenue bonds, investment tax credits, exemptions on business equipment, loan guarantees. A 1979 study concluded: "Interstate competition for investment has never been more intense than at present."[4] *Business Week* called the spread of business incentives in the North, "a counterattack in the war between the states."[5]

In classic growth politics fashion, proponents of tax abatement in Cleveland argued that cities were in a race for mobile investment and unless Cleveland enacted special business incentives, it would fall

136

hopelessly behind. Tax abatement, they said, would stimulate economic growth so that in the long run everyone would benefit. Opponents argued that tax abatement was not effective in attracting new growth and, besides, it had a regressive effect on income distribution. Bucking the national trend, opponents of tax abatement won in Cleveland, putting together a grassroots anti-abatement movement that helped defeat an incumbent mayor and effectively ended abatements for downtown in the foreseeable future. This case study of tax abatement in one city examines the claims and counterclaims concerning the effectiveness of tax abatement as a tool of economic development. Equally important, it examines the *political* context of tax abatement: how growth pressures are filtered through a political system, with its own dynamic, its own pressures.

The Rise and Fall of Tax Abatement in Cleveland

Ohio's tax abatement legislation, Senate Bill 90 (Impacted Cities Bill), was enacted in November 1973. Essentially the bill authorizes municipalities that suffer from blight and deterioration (and meet certain other requirements) to: (1) exercise the power of eminent domain anywhere within their jurisdiction to create job opportunities; (2) give property tax exemptions on improvements to property in "blighted areas" to encourage redevelopment. Property tax exemptions are permitted for up to thirty years for one to three family residential structures and up to twenty years for all other uses.

Tax payments by the owner after abatement must be at least as great as tax payments were before redevelopment. Other than that, the law leaves it to each municipality to negotiate with the developer exactly how much property taxes will be forgiven. The process is simple: the developer submits a redevelopment plan to the mayor who then submits it to the local legislative body with a recommendation. Approval requires a three-fifths majority vote.

In effect, tax abatement is the successor to urban renewal. There is the same presumption that eminent domain and sufficient incentives can be used to entice private developers back into blighted central cities. At the same time, there are two important differences from urban renewal. (1) Under urban renewal, two-thirds of the subsidy was paid by the federal government; under tax abatement, the entire subsidy is borne by local taxpayers. (2) Under urban renewal, developers had to follow a plan approved by the federal and local governments; under tax abatement, developers have much greater freedom to plan and execute the project with few public controls.

In the beginning, developers in Cleveland had little trouble getting the necessary political support. The general Cleveland tax abatement ordinance passed City Council in December 1976 by an overwhelming vote of 22-8. Two public interest organizations, the Ohio Public Interest Campaign (OPIC) and Active Clevelanders Together (ACT), testified against the bill but only succeeded in getting weak amendments added to limit the life of the ordinance to three years and to recommend that 50 percent of any jobs created be given to Cleveland residents.

Public opposition mounted, however, as council considered individual abatements in summer 1977. OPIC and ACT were joined by the UAW, United Steelworkers, the Senior Citizens Coalition, and the Commission of Catholic Community Action (training center for Cleveland's Alinsky-style community organizations); the community organizations themselves, however, stayed neutral on the issue. City Council squirmed as protesters used direct action methods, stormed its meetings, and debated council members on the floor. Nevertheless, council overwhelmingly passed (27–5) an abatement for approximately $9 million for the National City Bank Building in June 1977 and one for Sohio (29–2) for approximately $21 million for a new world headquarters in August.

As we saw, Kucinich campaigned effectively against tax abatement in November 1977, promising to oppose all abatements if elected. Along with Muny Light, tax abatement was one of the two issues that contributed significantly to his victory. A few days after the election, Kucinich told a thousand business leaders at a Growth Association luncheon, "I will not equivocate in my opposition to tax abatement. Big business must pay its fair share."[6]

The history of tax abatements during the Kucinich administration can be summed up quickly: Kucinich did everything in his power to stop them and largely succeeded. He vetoed not only all abatement legislation but every piece of enabling legislation as well. Council consistently overrode his vetoes by lopsided margins. Kucinich then used his powers as chief executive to continue to block the projects.

Shortly after he took office, for example, the council passed abatements for a number of projects on the lakefront, including a $25 million 500-room Hyatt Regency Hotel, an office-apartment tower, and an office and hangar at Burke Lakefront Airport. Kucinich immediately vetoed the legislation, saying that he wanted to expand the port rather than use the lakefront for luxury hotels, apartments, and offices. After his vetoes were overridden by a vote of 28-3, he fought the projects by freezing federal money for improvements on piers, halting construction of water and sewer lines to any lakefront development, and, in general, promising to make life miserable for the projects by foot dragging on demolition, police protection, and other services. The projects died on the drawing boards. Council continued to support tax abatement legislation but Kucinich was able to prevent any more abatements from being handed out during his term.

The Equity Issue

The essence of tax abatement is the classic trade off between equality and growth: proponents call for a more regressive tax system, more inequality, to attract new investment. Taxes, they say, must be lowered on mobile wealth to promote growth. In the end every one will be better off. The issue of equity and the issue of growth both deserve careful attention.

Most experts agree that the local property tax is regressive.[7] Studies generally apportion the property tax load in relation to housing consumption. Since housing takes up a larger percentage of income at the lower levels, the impact is regressive. (Tenants, as well as homeowners, pay property taxes, with the bulk of the property tax shifted to tenants in the form of higher rents.) In effect, the property tax is more regressive than these studies indicate, because they ignore the fact that effective rates are generally higher in the poorer inner cities than in their wealthier suburbs. In 1977, for example, Cleveland's tax *rate* ranked among the top 26 percent of taxing jurisdictions in the county while its per capita property tax *base* ranked among the bottom 17 percent.[8] Clearly, property tax rates in the Cleveland area are not based on ability to pay—if anything the opposite.

At the time that tax abatement became an issue in Cleveland, the property tax load was shifting from industry and large corporations to homeowners and small businesses. In Cuyahoga County, where Cleveland is situated, the share paid by homeowners went from 39 percent in 1970 to 47 percent in 1978.[9] The tax abatement controversy in Cleveland occurred as the property tax system was perceived as becoming rapidly more regressive and burdensome. The situation was not as volatile as in California before Proposition 13, but it was close to it. Tax abatement exacerbated the situation.

In Cleveland, the distributive issue not only pitted consumers against business but different sectors of business against each other. Tax abatement was originally touted as a program that would revive Cleveland's ailing industrial sector. Ohio governor James Rhodes waxed euphoric on this point: "At $15,000 to $25,000 an acre you can fill it [Cleveland] with industry! Get the price down to where you can compete with other areas of Ohio! We've got the ready-made skilled workers there!"[10] Tax abatement, however, did little to stimulate industry in Ohio. While the legislation was written for all forms of development, tax abatement basically has been used for downtown renewal. Like most business incentives, tax abatement plays into prevailing private investment trends in order to "leverage" large amounts of private investment. With its relatively high wage rates and land prices, Cleveland is simply not attractive to industry. But the downtown service sector is booming. That's where tax abatement has been used.

The emphasis on downtown raised further distributive issues. Opponents charged that white collar jobs that were created would go to suburban commuters rather than inner city residents. They questioned using local tax dollars to stimulate the construction of downtown office buildings and luxury hotels while areas of more direct value to inner city residents, such as housing, were ignored.

Tax abatement was defended as being targeted to the poorest cities and, within them, to "blighted" areas. But developers in Cleveland had no trouble getting the most valuable real estate in town (Ninth and Euclid) designated as "blighted." And, in August 1977, Ohio passed a liberalized tax abatement law (S.B. 251) that extended abatements to suburbs and rural areas and allowed local governments to give blanket abatements to all improvements in designated areas. This removed any advantages for "impacted" inner cities.

A further distributive issue was raised by the giving of abatements to the largest and most profitable corporations.[11] Of the sixty largest banks in the country in 1977, National City was the most profitable, based on earnings as a percentage of average assets.[12] And Sohio was receiving the largesse of its Alaskan oil, which, in the words of *Business Week*, "skyrocketed 1979 profits to $1.2 billion, a phenomenal 2,200% blast in just one deacde."[13] Essentially, existing small businesses and office buildings were forced to subsidize their competition.

The equity issue concerned not only where the subsidies went but where they came from. In Cleveland, about 60 percent of the abated taxes would have gone to the school system. In many ways, Cleveland's school system was in worse shape than city government, which itself was poised on the brink of default. In 1978, the school system fell $20.7 million short and had to give up financial responsibility to a state controlling board in order to obtain needed funds. Many people questioned the wisdom of an impoverished local public sector that provides essential services, giving up sorely needed revenues to benefit some of the richest corporations in the world.

Finally, tax abatement was criticized as a peculiarly deceptive form of business subsidy. The difference between tax abatements and other business subsidies is that tax abatements are long term. Changing property values make it difficult to calculate the total abatement, and it is probably impossible for a city to compare this subsidy with future needs fifteen to twenty years down the line. Like all tax subsidies, tax abatement has the appearance of costing little because the government pays no money up front. Yet, in effect, tax abatement gives away incalculable amounts of future city revenue. Commenting on this problem, Norm Krumholz, Director of Community Development under Kucinich, said, "My feeling is, if business is going to get a subsidy, the subsidy should be up front."[14]

The Growth Issue

All of the above arguments concerning the regressive and deceptive nature of tax abatement were pretty much beside the point to supporters. For them, tax abatement was not a tax reform proposal or an instrument of economic justice; it was a tool of economic development. The pro-abatement position rested on one and only one point: tax abatement would bring jobs and investment to Cleveland that otherwise would not come. They staked everything on the expansion of the pie, not its distribution.

In a sense, the growth issue supersedes the distributive issue, for if tax abatement really does bring about new investment, then the exchange between mobile wealth and city government here has achieved its purpose: no one is worse off than before and many people benefit from the new investment. In theory, it does not cost the city anything because tax revenues remain the same as before and the additional property values and tax revenues simply would not exist without the tax abatement. Opponents of abatement in Cleveland tried to raise equity issues but, for the most part, the public debate hinged on the growth issue. Surprisingly, anti-abatement forces won their greatest victories here, on their opponents' ground. This was a major reason that tax abatement lost in Cleveland.

It is very difficult to argue for the growth benefits of tax abatement from the national viewpoint. From the viewpoint of the whole, tax abatement is a zero-sum game: one city's gain is another city's loss.[15] It is argued that tax abatement provides a way for cities that are losing investment to get even in the competition. Unfortunately, however, both rich and poor cities practice tax abatement. And, assuming that the marketplace distributes investment to the most efficient locations for production, incentives like tax abatement may only have the effect of subsidizing production at less efficient locations.[16] Regardless of its effect on the national economy, however, supporters argue that individual cities must take up the weapon of abatement or lose out. The issue here, then, is whether it makes sense from the viewpoint of an individual city to enact tax abatements. It boils down to one question: does tax abatement bring about investment in a city that would not otherwise have occurred?

Determining whether tax abatement brings about new investment is not easy. The only sure way to settle the question would be to conduct a scientific experiment: administer tax abatement to one set of cities and compare the level of investment with another control group of cities *alike in every respect, except without tax abatement.* Of course such an approach is impossible in the real world where no two cities are exactly alike and where so many factors enter the decision to invest. Three surrogate methods, however, have been developed to investigate the relationship between taxation and the location of new investment.

One way is simply to ask business executives what factors affected their decisions to invest in a locality. There is a mountain of informal testimony by corporate executives indicating the decisive importance of local taxes. In nearly all cases of tax abatement, in fact, the corporation must state that the investment would be impossible without the subsidy. However, given the obvious corporate motives for stressing the importance of special incentives, including the desire to influence future legislation, this evidence must be discounted.

Scientific surveys have been developed, however, asking executives to name the main factors behind location decisions while attempting to eliminate any motivation for self-interested replies. These surveys have uniformly ranked local taxes low on the list of factors. One of the earliest surveys, conducted in 1950 by the Survey Research Center, found that when 188 firms were asked about the disadvantages of

Michigan, taxes were mentioned by firms representing only 9 percent of employment, whereas labor costs were mentioned by firms representing 51 percent.[17] A 1958 *Business Week* study found that of 747 references to location decisions, only 5 percent referred to taxation.[18] A 1972 survey by the U.S. Department of Commerce found that only 8 percent of the respondents viewed taxes as critical in their location decisions.[19] Many more surveys point in the same direction.[20] Interviews also reveal that companies often make their decision of where to invest first and then seek tax incentives.[21]

A second method for evaluating the impact of local taxes is to compare the relative rates of investment in areas with different local tax burdens. C. C. Bloom investigated the correlation between state and local per capita tax collection with growth in manufacturing employment and capital outlays for the periods 1939–1953 and 1947–1953.[22] No significant correlations were found, except, surprisingly, a weak correlation between higher taxes and more rapid expansion of manufacturing. The Advisory Commission on Intergovernmental Relations found, in a 1967 study, "no clearcut relationship between the level of business taxes and manufacturing employment growth rates for states within the same region."[23] The fact is, states can be found with relatively high tax rates and high growth rates, and states can be found with relatively low tax rates and relatively low growth rates. Ohio, for example, in 1974, ranked twenty-fifth out of fifty states, and eleventh out of fourteen major industrial states, in business taxes as a percentage of business profits.[24] Yet Ohio has consistently had one of the highest unemployment rates in the nation and has suffered extensive industrial exodus. In Cleveland, a confidential Fantus Report, prepared for the Growth Association and leaked to the newspapers during the tax abatement controversy, concluded that Cleveland was ahead of the competition on local taxes: "At all income levels, residents of the city of Cleveland have a lower tax burden than the average of the 30 largest cities in the United States. Depending on annual earnings, Clevelanders pay from 6.8 percent to 7.5 percent less than the national average."[25] Yet Cleveland has suffered massive disinvestment and job loss since the Second World War. It is difficult to argue, in the case of a low tax city in a low tax state, that tax abatement is the key to redevelopment.

The third method, analyzing the role of state and local taxes in business costs, helps explain why the above correlations are so weak. The results have been summed up in a recent article on the subject: "State and local taxes are consistently estimated at from half to three percent of value added and from two percent to, at most, five percent of sales."[26] In Wisconsin, local property taxes were estimated at .68 percent of value of shipments for all manufacturing industries combined.[27] (Since state and local taxes can be deducted as a business expense for federal income tax purposes, their effective cost to a corporation is reduced as much as 50 percent.) By contrast, the U.S. Department of Labor estimated in 1977 that "labor is the single most important input into the production of a firm, accounting for approximately sixty percent of all input payments on a national basis."[28] It is not surprising that labor costs have a much greater impact on location decisions than do local taxes.

In short, the overwhelming weight of the evidence supports the conclusion that local taxes play a minor role in location decisions. Firms first select a region to invest in, based on major factors like markets, labor force characteristics, and availability of raw materials. (Local taxes have played almost no role in the flow of industry to the Sunbelt; "right to work" laws and wage rates have played a major role.) When companies decide where to invest within a region, local taxes may be a factor, but most studies indicate that they are a very minor factor in location decisions. But for tax abatement to be effective, local property taxes must not simply be a factor, they must be decisive in the decision to locate. The evidence strongly suggests this only rarely is the case.[29]

The evidence cited so far has been mostly for industrial location decisions. The same general results would be expected for the location of white collar and service functions. Indeed, other things being equal, one would expect local taxes to be even less important here, since service industries are more labor-intensive, with fixed capital costs playing a less important role in production.

Only a handful of studies have examined the effect of taxes on the location of service industries. With few exceptions, the results have been negative.[30] Perhaps the most damning indictment of tax abatement came out of the Comptroller's Office of New York City. New York City had probably the largest tax abatement program in the country. Administered by the Industrial and Commercial Incentives Board (ICIB), only 2 percent of tax abatements in New York City, it was found, went to industrial projects; most went for office towers in Manhattan. Covering the period from February 1977 to August 1978, the report concluded that $60 million of the $84 million granted in subsidies may have been totally unnecessary. The booming demand for office space in Manhattan meant these buildings would have been built anyway. As

Harrison Goldin, comptroller of New York City, put it: "Tax inducements for this highly desirable area of the city are as necessary as
additional sand for the Sahara desert."[31] Since Goldin's report, New
York City's tax abatement programs have been the fastest growing
items in the city budget, with the ICIB alone committing the city to over
$500 million in past and future tax expenditures.[32] Tax abatement in
New York City has come under increasing criticism in recent years,
however, leading to limited reforms, including the exclusion of certain
areas of Manhattan from the program. In 1981, Assemblyman Frank
Barbaro got 36 percent of the vote in the Democratic mayoral primary
against Koch, basing part of his campaign on opposition to tax abatement.

Even if tax abatements were effective in attracting new investment
in office buildings, the benefits may not be as great as expected. A
Cleveland City Planning Commission survey of eight new downtown
office buildings revealed that two-thirds of the firms (and 75 to 80
percent of the employees) occupying these buildings were previously
located within the city of Cleveland.[33] This largely blunts the argument
that tax abatement creates significant new long-term jobs and greatly
boosts income tax receipts. Moreover, this shuffling of tenants within
Cleveland means that tax abatement costs the city more than the actual
dollar amount of the abatements. The weakening in demand for existing office space, caused by the new buildings with tax abatements,
brings about a reduction in property valuations for older buildings,
which further reduces tax revenues. As a supply side incentive, tax
abatement may only shift existing demand to a new location, not create
new production.

Finally, a study of San Francisco's central business district concluded that the cost to the city of added services ($270,000 per down-
town block, $25,000 for all other blocks) exceeded by almost $5
million the added revenues and tax receipts from downtown. "In short:
city taxpayers subsidized the Central Highrise District that in real estate
rhetoric was subsidizing them."[34] This pulls the rug out from under the
comforting assumption that downtown building booms will lift cities
out of fiscal crisis. And this was *without* tax abatement.

Nonrational Choices: Politics and Perceptions

If the above analysis is correct, tax abatement is not an effective tool
for economic development. In fact, most of the time, cities get nothing
back economically in exchange for the substantial incentives they give

to mobile wealth—a clear case of nonrational choice in the inter-governmental marketplace. This raises the pregnant political question: why do cities pursue tax abatement with such vigor? Specifically, in this case, why did the City Council vote overwhelmingly for tax abatements?

One explanation is simple: business interests that stood to benefit used money and political pressure to influence local legislators. George Forbes, the powerful president of City Council, played a key role in getting tax abatement through council. According to Roldo Bartimole, "Without Forbes' active support the business community and Perk could not have gotten tax abatement legislation."[35] Forbes was close to James Davis, former Growth Association president and senior partner in the elite law firm of Squire, Sanders, and Dempsey, which wrote the original state tax abatement legislation. Squire, Sanders was counsel for Sohio which asked for, and obtained, a $21 million abatement. (Sohio backed out of the project in July 1978 but subsequently built its world headquarters in Cleveland, specifically rejecting tax abatement.[36] When Forbes was indicted on charges of bribery and corruption stemming from alleged carnival kickbacks, the Growth Association, in a highly unusual move, issued a strong statement in his support and the white downtown business establishment raised a legal defense fund of between $100,000 and $150,000. Defended by Squire, Sanders, Forbes was acquitted of all charges on a directed verdict in July 1979.[37]

While it is easy to explain the behavior of some members of council by the pressures and emoluments of big business, this does not account for the lopsided majorities, such as 29-2, that greeted tax abatement. There is no evidence that many council members received large contributions from businesses obtaining abatements. The explanation seems to have less to do with the economic gains of particular politicians and more to do with the general political benefits to be derived from supporting tax abatement.

In *The Symbolic Uses of Politics*, Murray Edelman describes how in certain policy areas, such as regulation of business, the tangible benefits often go to particular business interests while the supposed beneficiaries, consumers, get only "symbolic reassurrance"—the feeling that something is being done about a problem. This is especially true for policies where the public benefits are diffuse and difficult to calculate.[38] Tax abatement is such a policy. It is difficult to identify all the public benefits that would result from new growth and investment and it is equally difficult to prove that the new growth would not have occurred without the tax abatement. As we have seen, however, tax abatement mainly benefits those businesses that get the abatements. What the public gets is symbolic reassurance that something is being done about economic problems. And what politicians get is a chance to take credit for positive investment trends in the city.

In an economic crisis, people naturally turn to government. State and local tax incentives proliferated in the South in the 1930s and later spread to the North during its period of regional stagnation. Like drowning sailors, politicians in declining economic areas grasp at anything thrown their way that could be a lifesaver. Special business incentives are often seized upon, especially when there are few alternatives.

The lack of alternatives is key to understanding the attractiveness of tax abatement.[39] The local public sector in Cleveland, to put it bluntly, utterly lacks the resources as well as the organizational and political unity to plan and execute sophisticated economic development activities. First, Cleveland city government lacks the financial resources. In fiscal year 1974–1975, city of Cleveland revenues totaled $227.6 million, including intergovernmental transfers.[40] By contrast, the forty-one Greater Cleveland–based corporations that ranked among the top one thousand in the United States in 1975 had worldwide sales of $23 billion. This represented a 47 percent increase over three years, a period in which city of Cleveland revenues were stagnating. Compared to big business, Cleveland city government is in the horse and buggy days of technology. Computers have barely been introduced in most departments. Until recently, Cleveland used a single-entry method of bookkeeping that predated Medici banking. (Low technological sophistication is the pattern throughout most local governments in the United States today.)[41] And the city bureaucracy is burdened with unqualified patronage appointments. Big business—with its sophisticated technology, access to credit (much of it generated internally), oligopolistic market power, and geographical mobility—is the dynamic factor in the Cleveland economy. The local public sector is essentially in the position of anticipating, or responding to, the actions of the private sector.

Local government in Cleveland, as elsewhere in the country, also is highly fragmented, so that it cannot engage in comprehensive planning. There are seventy-one different property tax jurisdictions in Cuyahoga County alone. While the private sector is becoming more and more concentrated, the public sector is becoming more and more divided. In 1976, there were fifty-nine special government agencies in Cuyahoga County, more than twice as many as in 1945. Together, they spent more money and employed more people than the city of Cleveland.[42]

Cleveland city government, itself, is fragmented and paralyzed by the pull and haul of narrow political interests. Third behind Chicago and New York City in size, Cleveland's thirty-three member council played a much more active role in policy making than either of those bodies. With each member of council representing a small geographic ward, the tendency was to spread the benefits as widely as possible to cement a winning coalition. Economic planning, on the other hand, requires concentrating resources according to some recognizable plan. The weakness of the political parties in Cleveland accentuated the tendency toward petty bargaining and logrolling, which is ill suited to long range economic planning.

Cleveland city government, in short, lacked the economic resources, the technological sophistication, the organizational unity, and the political will to plan or execute major economic planning initiatives. Perhaps most importantly, even though citizens turned to the public sector for solutions to economic problems, confidence in city government was so low that voters were extremely reluctant to give it new resources and authority to embark on economic planning initiatives. Politicians in Cleveland must convince their constitutents that they are doing something about the severe problem of jobs and investment. Tax abatement had one overwhelming attraction: it was something the city government could do, even in its weakened state. Tax abatement purported to transform small amounts of public funds into huge amounts of private investment that would resurrect a dying city. In fact, supporters claimed that tax abatement created, as if by magic, something from nothing, for the purported cost to the public was zero. (Since the projects would not have occurred without the abatement, the city gained the amount of the new tax revenues rather than lost the amount of the abatement.) And all of this with hardly any planning by the public sector, to say nothing of putting together the kind of complex organization that would have been necessary to implement more sophisticated public initiatives.

The first big advantage of tax abatement is that it requires no up front investment. As federal subsidies for urban renewal have been cut, cities have been thrown back on their own meager resources. Tax abatement has become a popular alternative because it requires no cash reserves. It even has the appearance, as we have seen, of being costless. Tax subsidies, like tax abatements, are more politically palatable than direct payments, because they are voted on once and paid out of future tax revenues, rather than each year out of budget expenditures.

Second, tax abatement has the great political virtue of finessing thorny distributive issues. Issues such as which sectors of production should be subsidized and what areas of the city should be developed— issues that would tend to paralyze Cleveland's fragmented and pluralistic political system—are processed outside the political system by relying almost entirely on the logic of the private market. The overwhelming trend in local abatement programs is to grant invarient awards: the same award is given to each corporation regardless of the value of the development to the community or the size of the subsidy needed to influence the investment decision.[43] From an economic viewpoint, this is irrational; from a political viewpoint, it has many advantages. All corporations are treated alike, freeing the political system from charges of favoritism. Distribution of the subsidies is determined by the logic of private investment: tax subsidies go wherever they can induce the investment of the most capital (even if this means luxury hotels and office buildings at a time when neighborhood housing is crumbling). A classic form of conservative growth politics, tax abatements concentrate on expanding the pie and not on redistributing the benefits. Little attempt is made to plan development or to target the subsidies, and there is no need for sophisticated economic analysis since the same award is usually given to every applicant. Compared to a program like urban renewal, for example, tax abatement requires very little staff and no ongoing bureaucracy—a distinct political advantage, especially in view of the horrendous delays and mismanagement of urban renewal in Cleveland.

In short, politicians supported tax abatement not because it was effective but because it was a remarkably easy path to follow, one that allowed them to claim they were mounting a serious attack on the economic problems of the city. Tax abatement is like the explorer who knows of an eclipse of the sun. Encountering a group of natives, he performs an elaborate ceremony to darken the sun, and the stunned natives worship him as a man of supernatural power ever after. Similarly, nothing is more tempting for a politician than to take a bow for causing some massive private project. With tax abatement, politicians can point to towering skyscrapers downtown and say, "Without my help these never would have come about." The populace is stunned and grateful.

Conclusion: Economic Autonomy, Political Determinism

Tax abatement was defeated in Cleveland largely because people began to dispute its exaggerated claims. Kucinich killed tax abatement and, even though he defied the will of City Council on this, there was no public outcry. After Kucinich ended tax abatement, in fact, Cleveland enjoyed a downtown building boom that lasted for about five years.[44] During the two years of the Kucinich administration, over $240 million in downtown construction was planned or in progress, three-fourths of it without tax abatement, thus vindicating opponents who argued that market factors, not local taxes, determine investment in office construction. Kucinich lost his bid for re-election in 1979 but this was not because of his anti-abatement stand. His opponent, George Voinovich, came out against tax abatement, stating: "I'm convinced downtown can flourish without tax abatement . . ." (campaign leaflet). Further evidence of the irrationality of tax abatement emerged in 1983 when one of the buildings that had received a multimillion dollar abatement, the National City Bank building, was sold. Built in 1980 at a cost of $59 million, the building was sold in 1983 at a reported profit of $30 million—and the tax abatement was transferred to the new owners![45] With that kind of inflation in downtown real estate, tax abatements clearly are unnecessary.

If the analysis here is correct, Kucinich's opposition to tax abatement was an economic success: the city of Cleveland did not lose any investment because Kucinich killed tax abatement. In fact, city government did better, because it received full property tax revenues from the downtown building boom. The reason for this freedom from economic pressure was that business did not exercise political discretion in its decision around abatement. (The situation was far different in the case of default, as we shall soon see.) Business could have withheld investment, punishing Cleveland and Kucinich for killing tax abatement. But it did not. Instead, attracted by an office shortage, downtown construction increased after Kucinich killed tax abatement, in a sense confirming his position. Kucinich was able, so to speak, to use the competition for profitable investment to carve out space for his populist opposition to tax abatement without suffering economic reprisal.

Tax abatement, in many ways, shows business as a clumsy actor in local politics. The tax abatement issue exhibits business as a narrow interest group, not as a self-conscious class planning in the long term interest of economic growth. The infrastructure of older cities in the United States (sewers, bridges, water systems) is crumbling from lack of maintenance. For future growth, business needs these public goods, as well as better schools and public transportation. Tax abatement bids away the already inadequate tax bases of cities in an internecine competition for investment. Understandably, the more farseeing business advocates, such as *Business Week* and the *Wall Street Journal*, criticize local incentives.[46] Listen to the pro-business Committee for Economic Development:

> Although we continue to advocate the use of public incentives to stimulate private investment in public objectives, we question the real value of local tax incentives. There is little evidence that they significantly affect the relocation and expansion decisions of firms, and they decrease tax revenues needed to provide public services and infrastructure essential for urban development.[47]

Kucinich's opposition to tax abatement, then, was economically successful. Was it also politically successful? Was he able to overcome the political pressures that force politicians, in the absence of an alternative, to support tax abatement so that they can take credit, even if falsely, for positive investment trends and reassure voters that something is being done about the growth crisis? While this question is more difficult to assess, it seems clear that Kucinich was not able to overcome the political logic of tax abatement. Kucinich claimed that his opposition to tax abatement was a major factor in the unsuccessful drive to recall him from office less than one year after being elected. It was not so much his opposition to tax abatement itself that cost him votes, however, but the general negative impression that was created in the minds of voters in connection with Kucinich and the economy. Kucinich was aware of the problem: "As soon as you start talking against tax abatement, they say you are anti-business," he lamented. "My administration is not anti-business."[48] Kucinich's form of political organization—office specific, appealing directly to the alienated voter over the heads of established interest groups and institutions—was well suited to his negative victory on tax abatement. At the same time, aside from vague talk about economic democracy, Kucinich did not project a coherent alternative to business subsidy schemes. It is questionable whether Kucinich ever had an economic plan in mind; he stressed that local government could do little in the face of broad market trends. After leaving office, Kucinich said: "I'm fully aware that it doesn't matter who happens to be mayor. Many businesses prospered when I was mayor; many have failed since Voinovich has been mayor."[49] The administration did carry out some experiments in economic development, but they clearly did not have high priority; the main emphasis was on basic city services.[50]

While Kucinich's position that city government could do little to influence investment was more intellectually honest than that of politicians who promised to return Cleveland to its glory days, at the same time, his stand made it difficult for him to reassure voters that something was being done about the economic crisis. In fact, once Kucinich was in office, his confrontational style created a sense not of symbolic reassurance but of perpetual political crisis that many voters came to see as detrimental to the economy. Kucinich became a victim of his own rhetoric. A hostile media focused on his headline-grabbing fights with business, blaming the city's economic setbacks on bad relations between business and the administration. Business leaders played to this theme. Materially, the business climate in Cleveland had been hurt little, if at all, by the actions of the Kucinich administration. As before, industry was in swift decline while the downtown service sector was growing. "Business confidence," however, is a critical variable for any elected chief executive. Competitive pressures often deny businessmen the discretion to change their investment behavior, but they do have the discretion, at no cost to themselves, of giving reasons for their behavior, of distributing praise or blame for investment trends. Control over the public's impression of business climate is a potent weapon in growth politics, apart from actual control over mobile wealth.

In Cleveland, businessmen used this power effectively, attributing a lack of business confidence in the administration for Cleveland's economic troubles and blaming Kucinich for specific acts of disinvestment. When Diamond Shamrock, the nation's 178th largest industrial corporation (*Fortune*, May and June 1979), with headquarters in Cleveland, announced that it was moving to Texas, papers gave front page treatment to the claim of its president and chief executive officer, William Bricker, that the reason was "the political, economic and educational climate in Cleveland and particularly the anti-business attitude on the part of the city administration."[51] An editorial in the

Cleveland *Plain Dealer* on the Diamond Shamrock move opined: "Every time Kucinich speaks against tax incentives for business, he adds to the feeling that business has no place in Cleveland."[52] Overwhelming evidence shows, however, that Diamond Shamrock's move was dictated by economic considerations mostly internal to the corporation and not by city politics.[53] This did not allay the impression created in the minds of voters, though.

In other words, Kucinich won the battle on tax abatement, but he lost the war on economic development. He refused to play the game of tax abatement, but he failed to come up with an alternative program that would have reassured voters that he was dealing with the economic crisis. What is worse, his confrontations with business created the impression that he was part of the problem, an impression enthusiastically fostered by business leaders and the media. While many voters respected Kucinich's fighting stance against big business, they ultimately came to believe that such defiance was harmful to the city.

7

The Politics of Default

We had been kicked in the teeth for six months.
On December 15 we decided to kick back.[1]

Brock Weir

Early on the morning of December 15, 1978, Dennis Kucinich, mayor of Cleveland, sat at a table in the boardroom of Bobbie Brooks, Inc., a leading garment manufacturer with offices near downtown. Also seated at the table were Brock Weir (chairman and executive officer of Cleveland Trust), Maurice Saltzman (president of Bobbie Brooks), and George Forbes (president of City Council). The subject of discussion was the pressing need of the city of Cleveland to rollover (extend in time) $14 million to short term notes due that day to area banks. According to Kucinich, Weir attempted at that time to consummate a corrupt deal of massive proportions. In Kucinich's words:

> At that meeting, Mr. Weir told me that only if I agreed to sell the Municipal Light System to CEI [Cleveland Electric Illuminating Company, the area's private utility] would he agree to roll the notes. He also offered to raise $50 million in City bonds, but only if the Light System was sold.[2]

Kucinich refused. At midnight, Cleveland became the first major city since the Depression to go into default.

Kucinich makes an extraordinary charge concerning default: that

154

bankers attempted to blackmail an entire city into selling a valuable asset for the benefit of private interests. Close financial ties and interlocking directorships between the banks and CEI, according to Kucinich, gave bankers the economic motive to force Muny Light out of business in order to give a monopoly to the private utility. They also had a political motive: to discredit a populist mayor who withdrew material benefits like tax abatements from corporations and scathingly attacked the banks for disinvesting the city.

The bankers, for their part, disavowed any interest in Muny Light and denied that their refusal to rollover the city's notes was motivated by any political animus toward Kucinich. In a letter to Cleveland Trust employees eleven days after default, reprinted as a newspaper advertisement, Brock Weir asserted, "We don't care who owns Muny Light." The banks refused to rollover the notes, said Weir, because Cleveland was a poor credit risk, pure and simple.

Was Cleveland's default political? This chapter attempts to answer that question, a question potentially having far-reaching implications for local democracy. As we noted in Chapter 1, while previous students of community power studied corporations as lobbyists and campaign contributors, they ignored corporations as investors. Investment was overlooked because of the presumed separation between economics and politics in a capitalist society; political power is not exercised in the private market. This separation between economics and politics is viewed as an important guarantee of freedom in our society. Milton Friedman describes how in a capitalist society dissident political views can find expression, if they have a wide enough audience, because publishers are concerned with profits, not politics. Blacklisted Hollywood writers, for example, found employment under pseudonyms because producers wanted to make as much money as possible by hiring the best talent.[3] The same principle should apply to local governments. A city government run by a populist radical should have the same ability to borrow money as its conservative counterpart, as long as it is equally sound financially. If private investors could discriminate against cities because of their political coloration, the space for democratic decision making would shrink significantly. Corporations would then possess an instrument of power unavailable to ordinary citizens and unaccounted for in liberal (pluralist and market) theories of American politics. To the extent that this political investment exists, both the efficiency of the economic system and the freedom of the political system are called into question.

Muny Light: Public Versus Private Power

In order to understand default, it is necessary to understand how Muny Light, a small, dilapidated public utility, became the center of a raging political controversy that precipitated default. Muny Light was born in controversy during the administration of Cleveland mayor Tom Johnson (1901–1909), who recounts his struggle to form a public utility in his autobiography.[4] In 1903, Cleveland Electric Illuminating Company (CEI) blocked a $200,000 bond issue to establish a municipal light plant by influencing three Democratic councilmen to vote against it and obtaining a court injunction to prevent the issue from going to the voters. Johnson sidestepped this opposition, in 1905, by annexing South Brooklyn, thereby acquiring its small electric light plant. After voters approved a $2 million bond issue, a new generating plant was built that began operating in 1914.

Muny Light's first three decades of existence were a period of phenomenal growth.[5] Cleveland is unique among big city electrical systems: within the area served by Muny Light, customers can choose between two competing utilities. Muny began selling electricity at 3¢ per kilowatt-hour (to go along with Johnson's call for a 3¢ transit fare), while CEI charged 10¢. By 1931, Muny still charged 3¢ while CEI had cut back to 5¢. Largely because of this price advantage, Muny grew from 2,000 customers in 1910 to 52,000 in 1935, attracting many customers away from CEI. During this period, Muny turned a healthy profit and gave a significant subsidy to the city, as well, by providing street lighting at below cost.

Beginning in Cleveland's city manager period (1923–1931), Muny gradually shifted its approach and ceased its aggressive efforts to expand into CEI territory, adopting instead a "yardstick" philosophy, where its main function was simply to provide a competitive measure for CEI's rates.[6] Muny's profits were generally not reinvested in the system but were used instead for such functions as poor relief during the Depression. From 1935 to 1958, the number of Muny's customers increased only from 52,000 to 58,000.

The third phase of Muny's history, from approximately 1958 to 1977, can be called its period of decline. Owing to a lack of sufficient investment in its own generating equipment and an inability to purchase adequate amounts of electricity from outside sources, in the 1960s Muny began to have serious outages. CEI took advantage of Muny's problems with an aggressive marketing campaign to lure away customers. In 1963, for the first time, more customers shifted to CEI than to Muny. From 1970 to 1975, Muny lost about 10 percent of its customers to CEI. In 1969, again, for the first time, Muny reported an operating loss. While Muny reported profits of $31.5 million, as well as significant subsidies to the city's General Fund, in the period 1906–1968, it lost $31.1 million from 1969 through 1977. The General Fund was forced to subsidize Muny.

During the period of Muny's decline, CEI made numerous offers to buy the ailing system. CEI's first offer came in 1965, but Mayor Locher refused even to meet to discuss it. Carl Stokes ran for mayor in 1967 promising to sell Muny, but the sale was put off during his tenure. Ralph Perk ran for mayor in 1971 vowing to save Muny but, unable to sell bonds for the ailing plant, he later reversed his position and in September 1976 announced that an agreement had been reached to sell Muny to CEI for $158.5 million.[7] In May 1977, council passed an ordinance (18–15) to sell Muny Light. Meanwhile, Muny's steep plunge into the red (over $7 million in 1976) was halted in 1977, when it stopped generating its own electricity entirely and began purchasing electricity from other sources than CEI through its new interconnection.

In the meantime, Kucinich, who had been elected citywide Clerk of Courts in 1975, became a vocal, tenacious opponent of the sale. With challenges in court and before the Federal Power Commission, Kucinich attempted to block the sale. The Save Muny Light Committee, which he chaired, gathered 29,758 signatures to put repeal of the sale before the voters in a referendum, but the Election Board ruled the petitions invalid because of improper language. Kucinich appealed that decision in the courts and challenged the Zoning Board approval of the sale. With a legal cloud hanging over the proceedings, Kucinich was barely able to prevent completion of the sale until he became mayor in November 1977. As mayor, Kucinich had the power to block the sale.

One basic question hung over the entire Muny Light controversy: was Muny Light a drain on the city or was it a public asset? In other words, could Muny support itself or would it require subsidies from the city's already hard pressed General Fund? Of course, some argued that, regardless of profit or loss, Muny served a valuable function by providing a competitive check on CEI's rates. And of course the approximately 20 percent of Cleveland's households that used Muny Light benefited, because rates were still 4–7 percent below CEI's. For most citizens, however, the question was whether Muny Light was an asset or liability to the city's taxpayers. As we shall see, answering this question was not simply a matter of toting up the economic gains and losses.

In October 1978, R. W. Beck and Associates, a nationally recognized independent firm of engineers and consultants, concluded that Muny had entered the black in 1978, after it began purchasing electricity from cheaper outside sources, and would continue to show an overall profit in the next five years. Kucinich trumpeted these figures. These operating surpluses, however, did not include payments for Muny's debt to CEI and other city departments accumulated during the period of operating losses. If a reasonable payment schedule for these debts were included, Muny would be back in the red.

The general question of Muny's economic viability actually hinged on a more specific question: what was the cause of Muny's substantial losses from 1969 to 1977? If the cause was mismanagement, the losses were unrecoverable. If the cause was illegal and predatory efforts by CEI to snuff out Muny and obtain a monopoly, the losses were turned into an asset. The nation's antitrust laws would allow the city to recover triple damages—which, indeed, it is trying to do in a $110 million lawsuit against CEI, originally filed in 1975. (The first trial ended in a hung jury; the second ruled in favor of CEI. The city appealed on the grounds that the judge failed to grant sufficient time for discovery and excluded crucial testimony. In 1984, the Sixth Circuit Court of Appeals ruled against the city. The case may well go to the Supreme Court.)

The antitrust suit is intricate and difficult to assess, but a few things seem clear. One is that Muny Light was, indeed, mismanaged by its public sector owners. For political reasons, rates were kept unnecessarily low and surpluses over the years were drained away to street lighting and other city operations instead of being used for maintenance and modernization.

At the same time, it is equally clear, CEI took actions that severely crippled Muny. Even Muny's lack of investment can be attributed in part to CEI, which kept lobbying pressure constantly on council to cripple the public system. In 1972, the city sought to issue $9.8 million in bonds for badly needed capital improvements to Muny. CEI wrote damaging amendments that were attached to the bond legislation through a friendly councilman, making the bonds impossible to sell. CEI also secretly sponsored two taxpayer lawsuits against Muny for the purpose of delaying an interconnection that Muny needed with CEI. At the same time, CEI was maintaining before the Federal Power Commission (FPC) that it was cooperating on an interconnection.[8]

Evidence of CEI's predatory behavior toward Muny is well substantiated, thanks to hearings before a federal regulatory agency. In 1971, the city filed a Petition to Intervene before the Nuclear Regulatory Commission (NRC) in CEI's application for a license to build and operate additional nuclear power plants. The city charged that CEI had violated antitrust laws and requested that conditions be attached to the license that would prohibit future anticompetitive acts.[9] The NRC's Atomic Safety and Licensing Board issued its findings on the city's complaints in 1977, concluding that CEI had, indeed, violated the Sherman Antitrust Act in its dealings with Muny Light. As Figure 6 shows, Muny is completely surrounded by CEI and therefore requires an interconnection with CEI in order to purchase electricity to deal with emergencies or to shut down its own generators in order to repair them. In a section entitled "Refusal to Interconnect Except upon Unfair Terms," the NRC documented how CEI agreed to set up an interconnection only on condition that Muny fix its rates at the same level as CEI's. Muny refused. The NRC called this attempt at price fixing a "per

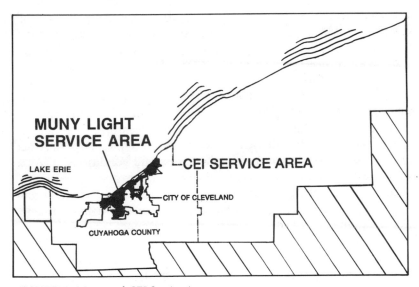

FIGURE 6. Muny and CEI Service Areas.

se violation of the antitrust laws" (that is, an act that by itself violates antitrust laws, regardless of its specific intent or effect).[10] While CEI refused to allow a permanent interconnection, in the early 1970s it did establish five load transfer points for emergency power. They were designed, however, to harm Muny Light: "When Cleveland needed power from CEI, the load transfer was operated in such a way as to cause an outage of MELP's [Muny's] system. From an operational viewpoint no outage need have occurred."[11] Afterward, CEI solicited the customers of Muny who had been affected by the outages. Muny was also prevented from taking any of its generators out of service and lack of maintenance caused further deterioration and loss of customers to CEI.

Most important, however, was CEI's ability to prevent Muny from purchasing electricity from outside sources. Surrounded by CEI, Muny needed CEI's cooperation to transmit outside power over CEI's lines ("wheeling power," it is called). In 1973, for example, Muny had the chance to purchase low cost electricity from the Power Authority of the State of New York (PASNY). CEI simply refused to wheel the power, a clear antitrust violation. In addition, CEI restricted Muny's access to power generated by the new nuclear power plants. The conditions for access demanded by CEI included that CEI control the rates at which the power would be sold, as well as that Cleveland "withdraw all formal and informal requests for antitrust review of CEI's conduct and drop its opposition to CEI's practices and policies in all administrative hearings and proceedings."[12] The NRC called these conditions an "outrageous affront" to the nation's antitrust laws.

The NRC concluded that CEI had, in fact, attempted to eliminate its public competitor through unfair and anticompetitive acts. In response, the NRC attached specific conditions to the license for the nuclear power plants, including that CEI wheel power at request and construct an interconnection "upon reasonable terms and conditions."[13] As a result, for the first time, Muny was able to purchase outside electricity. Since Muny stopped generating its own electricity in 1977 and began purchasing power through reliable interconnections, it has basically been operating in the black (apart from extraordinary legal expenses or past questionable debts).

Evidence uncovered by the NRC documents a clear example of the exercise of monopoly power in the governmental marketplace. CEI was able to construct a near monopoly over a product, which the city badly needed, by preventing Cleveland from purchasing power on the open market. Forced to purchase power from CEI, Muny had to accept conditions that damaged its operation and that eventually, without the intervention of federal regulators, would have meant elimination of the public utility as a competitor. Hardly a fair exchange between the public and private sectors, this was a clear example of power exerted over the market by a private corporation.

Mounting Fiscal Pressure and Default

Cleveland's default in 1978 was inextricably bound up with the struggle between CEI and Muny Light. Nine days after Kucinich took office in November 1977, CEI filed a certificate of judgment of lien on lands and property of the city to recover disputed debts owed CEI by Muny. The city claimed it had been overbilled. The judgment liens, however, were upheld by an appellate court and in February 1978 CEI began attaching city property—which meant the city could not use this property for any purpose. Federal District Court Judge Robert Kru pansky found the city in contempt, fined it $25,000, and ordered the Kucinich administration to pay the $18 million owed CEI by April 1 or face $5,000 per day fines and possible dismissal of the antitrust suit. Faced with a General Fund deficit of $10 million, the administration lacked the money to pay the debt. In May, the city had to draw $17.8 million from the water division's construction funds to meet payrolls. Kucinich devised a plan to pay the CEI debt by issuing bonds, but the Ohio Supreme Court declared the plan illegal in July 1978.[14] In July 1978, $7.8 million in short term city notes held by Cleveland Trust came due. Cleveland Trust refused to refinance the notes. The city was forced to purchase its own notes using funds slated for other purposes. Soon after, Standard and Poor's suspended Cleveland's bond rating and Moody's Investor Service downgraded the city's bond rating for the second time. Cleveland was gradually being shut out of the national bond market. More bad news came in August when the national accounting firm of Ernst and Ernst reported that $52 million in bond money for capital projects had been misspent for operating expenses. For the first time, the Kucinich administration became aware of the perilous financial condition of the city.

In September, $3.34 million in short term notes came due and the banks, again, refused to refinance. Kucinich was forced to dip into the city's meager cash reserves. Having narrowly survived a recall election a month earlier, Kucinich this time took the offensive against the banks with a blistering political attack containing the kind of anticapitalist rhetoric seldom heard in American politics. Challenging the banks to come to the aid of Cleveland "even if they can't make the same extraordinary profits as they do elsewhere," Kucinich concluded with a political threat:

> Unless the banks begin to respond to the needs of Cleveland residents, a tremendous uprising of anger and bitterness will be directed against them . . .
>   We must bring democracy to the banks as we have to our political life.
>   This administration will be in the forefront of a movement to severely hamper normal business operations of area banks if they do not begin to respond to the needs of the city government and city residents. The banks leave us no choice but to fight back to save our city.

Ignoring Kucinich's attack, the banks again, in October 1978, refused to rollover short term notes. The notes were refinanced internally with the few remaining city funds. Meanwhile, a time bomb was ticking in the budget: $14 million of short term notes, held by six local banks, would come due on December 15, 1978. And the city still owed $5.7 million to CEI. A Federal District Court ruled that, unless the debt was paid by the end of the year, Cleveland's multimillion dollar antitrust suit against the private utility would be thrown out.

In December, everything came to a head. United States marshals began tagging city property for CEI's debts. By December 13, about fifty of Muny's repair trucks were impounded. Coming when it did, this action gave CEI, as a Cleveland *Press* editorial put it, "the image of the flinty banker who forecloses the mortgage of a widowed mother."[16] Kucinich was able to squeeze money from operating expenses to pay CEI and keep the antitrust suit alive, but this left no money available to purchase the $14 million in short term notes due on December 15.

The administration met with bankers to try to come up with an acceptable plan. Kucinich proposed an income tax increase, which he promised could be sold to the voters. On December 14, five of the six banks indicated their willingness to rollover the notes if the city would seek a tax increase, but only if all six banks agreed. Brock Weir of Cleveland Trust refused to state his bank's position, sinking Kucinich's proposal. On the morning of December 15, council approved a plan

(20-13) to put the tax hike on the ballot on the condition that the administration sign a contract to sell Muny. Kucinich refused and offered his own compromise in an effort to shift the blame for precipitating default onto council: Muny Light would be put under the control of an autonomous board for eighteen months to see if it could become solvent; if not, it would be sold. As the clock in council chambers ticked past midnight, council president Forbes declared the time was 11:57 P.M. and called for a procedural vote on the mayor's plan. Before packed chambers, council rejected Kucinich's proposal, 17-16. At that point, Cleveland was officially in default.

If default was the dramatic climax, the period that followed was the denouement. One week after default, council worked out a compromise, placing before voters in February both the 50 percent increase in the income tax and the sale of Muny Light. Kucinich predicted that default would bring a "run of creditors on the city . . . we can expect to have our income tax attached and there would be no money to meet payrolls."[17] The crisis never occurred, however, after default, the banks backed off, promising to take no action to collect the debt until after the election.[18]

In the campaign, Kucinich led an effective grassroots effort that, according to polls, completely turned around public opinion on Muny Light.[19] The electorate voted to retain Muny Light and to increase the income tax, both by almost 2-1 margins.[20] Kucinich began paying off the $14 million in defaulted notes with the income tax receipts late in the next summer, but the city of Cleveland remained technically in default throughout his administration.

Was Default Political?

The most thorough study of Cleveland's default, a staff study for a subcommittee of the Committee on Banking, Finance, and Urban Affairs of the United States House of Representatives, concerned itself mainly with one question: was the decision by the banks not to rollover the notes for Cleveland based on factors other than an objective assessment of creditworthiness? The congressional study came, tentatively, to an affirmative conclusion:

> The interlocking relationship of Cleveland Trust Company and
> some of the other banks with much of the corporate community,
> and the deep animosities and political cross-currents in which some

bank officers became involved suggest the strong possibility that factors, other than pure hardnosed credit judgments, entered the picture. At a minimum, it is impossible to conclude that key bankers donned green eyeshades, locked themselves in their board rooms, and made dispassionate decisions based solely on computer runs.[21]

What factors, "other than pure hardnosed credit judgments," could have entered into the bankers' decision not to rollover the notes? The congressional study suggested two illicit goals in the bankers' minds when they precipitated default: one was to force the sale of Cleveland's public utility to CEI; the other was to cripple the Kucinich administration. By demanding that Muny Light be sold as a condition for rollover, they placed Kucinich on the horns of a dilemma—with either horn (selling Muny or entering default) exacting severe political damage. In the words of the congressional study:

> It is possible to suggest a scenario in which Cleveland Trust believed that the banks and the Mayor were involved in some variation of a game of "chicken" with the thought that the Mayor would swerve at the last second, accepting the sale of MUNY and thus averting a politically crushing default. Such a conclusion is clearly speculative, but if this was the game, obviously the Mayor did not swerve.[22]

There is enough evidence to move this interpretation well beyond the realm of speculation.

Definitive proof of the bankers' intentions would require access to their thoughts. Considerable circumstantial evidence exists, however, both in statements of individuals involved as well as in analysis of the material interests of the bankers, to indicate that they had an interest in city government beyond its ability to repay a loan.

Regarding the sale of Muny Light, there is, first of all, no doubt that CEI had long desired to eliminate its competitor. In fact, this was the first thing admitted by the CEI lawyers in the antitrust suit (although they denied that CEI had used any illegal methods). Second, the banks (especially Cleveland Trust) and CEI had common interests because of close financial, organizational, and social ties. The trust department of Cleveland Trust held 800,000 shares of CEI. Altogether, five of the six banks (one provided no information) held almost 1,800,000 shares, or about 5 percent of CEI's outstanding stock.

Extensive interlocks also existed between the banks and the private utility. Eight of the eleven directors of CEI during 1978 were directors at four of the six banks; four directors of Cleveland Trust were also directors of CEI (one joined in January 1979). Cleveland Trust managed CEI's pension plan, served as bond trustee and counsel, and was registrar for CEI's stock. According to CEI, four of the Cleveland banks had $72 million in lines of credit available for the utility.

Indirect links drew the net of common interests tighter. The six Cleveland banks had seventy-nine director interlocks with twenty other corporations that also shared one or more directors or officers with CEI. Top officials of CEI also had extensive social ties to bank executives through associations such as the elite Union Club and the Growth Association, Cleveland's Chamber of Commerce. Four members of CEI's board of directors and twenty-five members of the Cleveland bank boards were either officers or key committee members of the Growth Association, which campaigned vigorously for the sale of Muny. (The foregoing represents only a small part of the evidence linking the interests of the banks with CEI. The congressional study summarizes these interlocking interests in a chapter 150 pages long.) In short, considerable evidence exists of a massive conflict of interest between the banks' loan-making functions and their trust management responsibilities (and other ties) to the private utility.

Since the court rulings beginning in 1961 (*Cady v. Roberts*), it has been contrary to public policy for trust departments and commercial loan departments within a single bank to trade material inside information. As a result, banks have constructed what has come to be known as a Chinese Wall between bank trust departments, which are supposed to act solely in the interests of the institutions or persons whose money they manage, and the commercial loan department of the bank, whose purpose is to make loans solely on the basis of creditworthiness so as to protect the interests of bank shareholders.[23]

In this case, at least, there is evidence that the wall was breached— that is, the banks' refusal to rollover the city's notes was influenced by the benefits that would accrue to trust department holdings of CEI stock, as well as the economic and political interests of bank officers. In the case of Cleveland Trust, suspicions are further roused by the removal of decisions regarding city debt from the commercial bank level to an executive committee at the holding company level. This occurred in October 1979, shortly after Kucinich's verbal attacks on the banks. Thus the decision not to rollover the notes was made not on one side of the wall but by high level executive officers sitting atop the Chinese Wall.

A second possible ulterior motive of the banks in default, in addition to forcing the sale of Muny Light, was a desire to damage Kucinich politically and stop his being re-elected. This desire came not so much from the harm done to the banks by the policies of the Kucinich administration (notwithstanding Kucinich's killing of tax abatement, the Republic ore dock subsidy, and the downtown People Mover) but from Kucinich's strident rhetorical attacks on the banks that raised the ire of bank executives, who cultivated low key images of community concern through involvement in civic committees and philanthropies.

Considerable evidence exists of the bankers' political hostility toward Kucinich. At least seventy officers and directors of the six banks involved contributed to the campaign to recall Kucinich, including Brock Weir and seventeen of thirty-two directors of Cleveland Trust. (Very few, if any, lived in the City of Cleveland.) A month before default, Claude Blair, chairman of National City Bank, which Kucinich had attacked for obtaining a tax abatement, was quoted on local television news as saying, according to confidential sources, that he would not refinance the notes held by his bank because of the "Kucinich administration's antagonism toward the business community" and that he was "willing to accept the consequence to Cleveland as the price to pay to see Mayor Kucinich defeated in next year's election."[24]

Brock Weir, however, was the most visible leader in the banks' struggles against Kucinich. After default, Weir made a number of statements that indicated his intentions toward the Kucinich administration, including the one that begins this chapter. In addition, a January 1979 Boston *Globe* article, based on an exclusive interview with Weir, contained the following statement: "Although public finances are a mess and virtually all the upper middle class has deserted the city for the suburbs, the business climate remains healthy. Weir said, "The only problem is the little canker downtown."[25]

Not only is there evidence that the bankers conditioned rollover of the notes on the sale of Muny Light, thus forcing Kucinich into a choice between unpopular alternatives, there is also evidence that this *quid pro quo* was in fact communicated to the city. According to Kucinich, it was at the crucial December 15 meeting, also attended by Saltzman and Forbes, that Weir made the corrupt offer. This meeting, however, is bathed in controversy; only a tape recording could settle the issue, and no tape exists. Two participants in the meeting, however, originally supported Kucinich's version of the story. A few days after default, Saltzman was quoted as saying, "Brock [Weir] was nice. He said, 'Look, Dennis, get this [Muny Light] out of the way. Sell the building, we'll rollover the notes and I personally will help with the $50 million in bonds.' "[26] (Later, in response to an inquiry from the congressional subcommittee staff, Saltzman denied that Weir had linked rollover with Muny.)

It is unnecessary to prove, however, that the bankers communicated the *quid pro quo* to Kucinich in person, for it was communicated clearly through the media; at the time, all the principal actors assumed that the sale of Muny Light was the sticking point in default. We can look here at only a small portion of the evidence indicating almost universal acceptance, in December 1978, of this condition for rollover.[27] Certainly everyone in Cleveland who read the newspapers or watched television knew that it was Kucinich's refusal to sell Muny Light that was the cause of the banks' refusal to rollover the notes. This condition was stated repeatedly. The Cleveland *Plain Dealer*, for example, linked the sale of Muny Light to rollover of the loans in front page headlines on the day before default (Illustration 1).

With all this coverage of the story in the media, Brock Weir significantly took no action to deny the widespread stories linking the sale of Muny to rollover until eleven days after default.[28] On December 26, in a letter to Cleveland Trust employees, later reprinted as a newspaper advertisement, Weir denied that Cleveland Trust had any interest in who owned Muny Light.[29] What is inexplicable is why Weir did not make his position clear, at considerably less trouble and expense, at the time that it mattered. It would have been easy to call up the newspapers and television stations to clear up this monumental misunderstanding. The bankers' inaction implicitly confirmed reports that the sale of Muny Light was a condition for rollover. Together with Cleveland Trust's refusal to go along with Kucinich's plan for avoiding default, and the approval in executive committee of the rival plan of council president Forbes (which required the sale of Muny), the only reasonable conclusion was that the banks, and especially Cleveland Trust, wanted to send the message to the city: either sell Muny Light or we will not rollover your notes.

Another way to determine if any political motivations were involved is to examine whether the Kucinich administration was treated differently from other, similar administrations or borrowers. First, it is important to note, rollovers are routine in the financial community.

THE PLAIN DEALER

OHIO'S LARGEST NEWSPAPER

CLEVELAND, FRIDAY, DECEMBER 15, 1978

15¢

Cleveland Trust: Pay up

Bank would relent if Muny Light were sold, Forbes believes

By Joseph L. Wagner and Frederick E. Freeman

Cleveland's hopes for avoiding default were dealt a serious blow last night as Cleveland Trust Co., the city's largest bank, insisted on prompt payment today of $5 million in loans.

The five banks holding the remaining $9 million in notes due at the close of business today will be closely watching City Council — which is meeting this morning — but are apparently leaning toward going along with the city's refinancing plan.

If council and the mayor cannot

agree on a package, the other banks would be likely to refuse to refinance the notes.

Council President George L. Forbes, D-20, who met with bank executives yesterday, said he believes Cleveland Trust "could change its mind if Muny Light were sold." Mayor Dennis J. Kucinich has said repeatedly he will never sell Muny Light.

Saying "I want to save the city from default," Forbes called an emergency council meeting for 9 a.m. today at which time council leaders would push for passage of:

• Enabling legislation for the

50¢, income tax hike and a $90 million bond issue with specific language that these issues could become effective only after Kucinich sells Muny Light.

• A resolution asking the Ohio Legislature and Gov. James A. Rhodes to establish a multimember board of fiscal control to supervise city financial administration. Kucinich has opposed a board, but has agreed to establishment by the state of a single fiscal agent.

Last night, Forbes ruled out any referendum on Muny Light.

In a letter to Finance Director Joseph G. Tegreene, William J.

Clutterbuck, Cleveland Trust vice president for public investment, said the city's bailout plan was deficient. He appeared to leave the door open for new proposals that might affect the loans.

"While we commend the administration's recognition of the need for additional revenue, we still feel that the plan is too reliant on speculative contingencies which are beyond control of the administration.

"If, prior to maturity, you have any other proposal that will deal with alternatives that have more

materiality, we will be happy to review them."

Forbes said this was a reference to Muny Light.

"I spoke to the chairman of Cleveland Trust and he indicated he could go with the sale of the Muny Light Plant," Forbes said.

The chairman is M. Brock Weir.

Clutterbuck's message on the notes was officially terse:

"This will advise you of our intention to present our notes for payment at the office of the city treasurer of Cleveland on December

Continued on Page 10-A

• Ohio legislators discuss a bill that would permit Cleveland to hike the municipal income tax.

Page 9-A

• City consultant reports that the Municipal Light Plant will make a profit of nearly $1 million in 1978.

Page 10-A

• Andrew M. Juniewicz, the mayor's news secretary, says local news reporters have sometimes been irresponsible or inaccurate.

Page 11-A

Newsmen waited in vain through the day for reports on the city's financial situation.

The Plain Dealer/James A. Hatch

It's Snubsville as suburbs shun save-city session

By W.C. Miller

Dozens of reporters and businessmen flocked to University Heights yesterday, expecting to see an equal number of suburban mayors discussing Cleveland's money problems.

The television cameras whirred at Temple Emanu El. The businessmen listened. But most of the mayors weren't there.

The meeting was scheduled for University Heights City Hall, but was moved to accommodate an expected large turnout.

But only nine of Cuyahoga County's 61 suburban mayors and city managers showed up to hear an ambitious save-Cleveland plan presented by University Heights

mirror and solve its own problems.

Even Avery admitted the legality of his plan is questionable.

He asked the suburban Council of Governments to review and develop his proposal and to offer Cleveland's political leaders advice. He also asked Cleveland's business and industrial community to help the suburban council review city finances.

"The time is here for the suburbs and industry to stop sitting as complacent observers while the mother city dies," Avery said. "The time is here to stop playing the deadly game of city vs. suburb."

Avery asked Cleveland's banks to extend, for 120 days, the $14

ILLUSTRATION 1. Front Page Headlines on Muny Light Sale and Default. **Source:** Reprinted by permission of the Cleveland *Plain Dealer*.

Rollover of a short term note, as in Cleveland's case, is not a decision to lend money but a decision to extend in time a line of credit already granted.[30] Rollovers are often granted to private corporations with declining fortunes. In fact, they are a prime tool used to restore them to financial health. The congressional study describes how Cleveland Trust, during the time of default, as part of a consortium of banks, rolled over $28 million of expired notes to Clevetrust Realty Investors, even though that financially ailing company's assets had tumbled from $133 to $84 million from 1974 to 1978.[31]

Questions are also raised whether the city of Cleveland should have been forced into default, with severe damage to its future access to credit, over such a small debt ($14 million). A recent Ernst and Whinney audit appraised Cleveland city government's net worth, including all of its land and buildings, at slightly more than $1 billion.[32] While there is no doubt that the city was in a difficult financial situation, it was not overtaxed and still had considerable assets. With the full faith and credit of the city behind the notes, the banks were in little danger of losing their investment. By contrast, the New York legislature, with the implicit approval of the bankers, declared a moratorium on the repayment of $2.4 *billion* of outstanding New York City notes in 1975. Technically, this was the same as default, but New York City avoided the stigma of default even though it was more overextended and the bankers had much greater exposure than in Cleveland's case. In 1975, New York City's cumulative deficit was approximately $8 billion; soon after Kucinich left office, Cleveland's was estimated at $111 million.[33] The difference in treatment of the two cities raises the question whether it was related to Cleveland's being governed by an angry populist while New York City was led by politicians who promoted a new growth partnership between government and business.[34]

Evidence also exists that Kucinich was treated differently from the previous mayor, Ralph Perk (1971–1977). In September 1975, the Growth Association issued a report on the city's finances that contained a number of telling criticisms of Perk administration practices—using the sale of capital assets to pay for operating expenses, relying heavily on short term note borrowing, keeping chaotic books that prevented full public disclosure of revenues and expenditures.[35] Perk practiced all these fiscal sins, including misspending at least $38 million of bond funds, and yet the banks routinely and without probing questions rolled over the notes of his administration. When Kucinich took office, the books of the city were unauditable.[36] Throughout the Perk years, the books had been in chaotic condition, yet the banks never asked the city for an audit and a cash projection analysis, as they demanded of Kucinich. (In August 1978, Kucinich submitted to an extensive Ernst and Ernst audit that uncovered the missing bond funds.) While the informational demands of the banks were not unreasonable, given the city's questionable bookkeeping methods, they were clearly far greater than those made of the previous administration.

Kucinich was a radical on many issues, but on fiscal matters he was a rock-ribbed conservative. It is difficult to argue that Cleveland's finances deteriorated during his administration. Kucinich added almost no new debt to the city during his two years in office. Cleveland was the only major city in the nation to operate on a cash basis. Out of operating funds, Kucinich was able to pay off a sizeable Muny Light debt that had accumulated during previous administrations. Cabinet meetings were highlighted by competition to see who could save the most money or cut the most employees without reducing services. The city payroll dropped from 11,640 when Kucinich assumed office to about 9,500 when he left, by a process of attrition. Kucinich also began to correct abuses in federal grant programs practiced by the Perk administration.[37] Finally, the Kucinich administration did not succumb to the dubious practice of selling assets to meet operating expenses. Kucinich could have sold the water system to a regional authority and enjoyed a windfall of over $100 million.[38]

Kucinich claimed to have brought operating revenues and expenses into line during his administration. This is difficult to judge. But his administration incurred very little new debt, trimmed the payroll by about 14 percent, paid off a $14 million CEI debt (thereby preserving a multimillion dollar lawsuit), did not sell any major assets, and began an extensive audit of the city's books—reasons to believe that his administration was, at least, no less creditworthy than its predecessor.

While objective evidence indicates that the Kucinich administration was discriminated against compared with its predecessor, there is also the testimony of Brock Weir, reprinted in the volume summarizing the congressional hearings on Cleveland's default (July 10, 1979). Here Weir admits that Kucinich was treated differently from Perk and, in explaining why, as much as confesses political bias:

> We weren't asking the type of questions of them [Perk administra-
> tion] that we are asking of this [Kucinich] administration. There are
> a couple of reasons why. First, New York happened. That taught us

all a lesson about asking questions. The second reason is the *attitude of the Kucinich Administration.* The Perk Administration was not as antagonistic toward the business community and the banking community as to precipitate (a showdown).[39] (emphasis added)

To wit: the banks treated Kucinich differently from Perk for political reasons.[40]

In sum, there is strong evidence that the bankers had motives for demanding that Cleveland sell Muny Light or go into default; there is incontrovertible evidence that this demand was in fact communicated to the city; and finally, there is substantial evidence that Cleveland city government, under Kucinich, was treated differently from other borrowers, other cities, and other administrations. In short, Cleveland's default was political.

The Political Impact of Default

If the banks deliberately presented Kucinich with an untenable choice—sell Muny Light or go into default—Kucinich firmly chose to face default and to live with the consequences. What then were those consequences? In other words, what was the extent of the political power exerted by the banks?

As we have seen, the bankers very probably had two political goals when they refused to rollover the notes: to eliminate Muny Light as a competitor to CEI and to embarrass Kucinich politically, preventing his re-election. On the issue of Muny Light, the bankers lost. Voters overwhelmingly opposed the sale in the February 1979 election and Muny Light remains in the public sector today.

The bankers, however, achieved their second goal. Kucinich was defeated for re-election in November 1979 by Republican George Voinovich (56 to 44 percent). It is difficult to say how many votes default cost Kucinich, but there is no doubt that he was hurt politically. The damage came both from the general onus of default and from the tax increase he was forced to support in order to cope with default.

Kucinich had made his political career out of opposing city income tax increases. As mayor, Carl Stokes had tried twice and Perk had tried once to raise the income tax. All three efforts failed at the polls; each time young Kucinich had led the oposition. In 1975, Kucinich supplemented his antitax stance with a call for tax reform, calling for a special panel to probe "inequities" in the municipal income tax and make specific proposals for change.[41] Kucinich pointed out, correctly, that while the local income tax appears to be proportional (neither progressive nor regressive) because it is a flat rate on all incomes, in effect it is regressive.[42] In the 1977 mayoral campaign, Kucinich promised to increase city services without any tax increases. He was adamant in his opposition to an income tax increase: "I have consistently opposed throughout my whole career attempts to increase the income tax, and I make a commitment to the people that under no circumstances will I ever increase the income tax."[43]

In December 1978, however, Kucinich had little choice. According to one report, it was not until the weekend before default that he learned the true seriousness of the city's finances, including that at the current rate of expenditures, the city's treasury would run dry in February.[44] Within a few days, Kucinich had to come up with a plan that could be sold both to the banks and the voters. For years, Cleveland voters, in the face of declining city services, had refused to raise taxes on themselves. Now the banks demanded increased revenues to back up any future loans. Kucinich was caught between a rock and a hard place. He could not resolve the contradiction against the banks, for without either a loan or a tax increase, the city would soon run out of money and be unable to meet payrolls—sure political suicide. Unable to force bank capital to invest in the city, Kucinich had to persuade the taxpayers to do so. Stagnating property values in Cleveland made raising property taxes out of the question. Kucinich was forced to pick up the only instrument that lay close at hand: raising the city income tax. It must have hurt to realize that it was aimed right at the pocketbooks of his constituents. And, ironically, under Ohio law, neither banks nor utilities pay any local income taxes at all.

Kucinich campaigned successfully for the income tax increase on the grounds that the majority of it is paid by suburbanites working in the city. It is true that the income tax takes a disproportionate share of its revenues from suburban commuters, who consume city services and do not pay any city property taxes. However, to the extent that Kucinich implied that inner city residents who work in the suburbs (about 25 percent of city workers) faced no tax increase or that the tax is more progressive because it falls mainly on wealthier suburbanites, the appeal was disingenuous.[45] Because of a complex system of tax credits between Cleveland and its suburbs, nearly all suburbs lose income tax revenue when Cleveland raises its income tax. As a result they retaliate by increasing their rates or lowering allowable tax credits. That is what happened: a vicious cycle of tax increases that left no sector of the population, city resident or suburbanite, unscathed.[46]

The February 1979 referendum was the first time Cleveland voters ever approved an income tax increase. Analysis of the vote shows that Kucinich's political appeal was largely responsible.[47] Traditionally, tax levies in Cleveland succeed in the black wards but are voted down in the West Side white wards. Kucinich carried the West Side, his working class ethnic base, strongly behind the tax increase. This was a feat of dubious distinction for a populist politician, however. It is not fair to say that Kucinich simply acted as a cat's-paw for the bankers who desired a tax increase to secure their debts; Kucinich made the bankers wait in line behind city workers and did not begin paying back on the defaulted notes until late the following summer. But it is accurate to say that Kucinich was forced to take an action, increasing a regressive tax, that hurt the economic interests of his constituents. Forced to go back on a decade of antitax rhetoric, Kucinich was asked on the day before default if he had been forced to eat humble pie. He replied, "I'm on a steady diet of it."[48]

It was not just the tax increase but the general onus of default that hurt Kucinich with the voters. His electoral appeal, "urban populism," was based on the claim that he could deliver benefits to the neighborhoods that other administrations, which siphoned off resources for various boondoggles of growth politics, could not. If the argument here is correct—that Cleveland was discriminated against in the realm of credit precisely because it elected a populist mayor and chose to retain the municipal light plant—then, in the short run at least, urban populism meant economic sacrifice, not economic gain. In many ways, Kucinich had the worst of both worlds: he was forced to increase a regressive tax and, at the same time, was unable to borrow money— a debilitating condition for a city that, according to a 1979 study by the Urban Institute, faced "a backlog of some $700 million in basic improvements to its infrastructure system."[49] To be sure, Kucinich was able to save Muny Light, but the benefits of that—preserving the antitrust suit and maintaining a competitive yardstick against the private utility—were less immediate than the tax increase and denial of credit.

The particular nature of the banks' power in the cause of default should be clearly specified. They exerted power over the size and shape of the local public sector, not over particular allocations. Forced to seek an income tax increase, Kucinich, nevertheless, controlled the allocation of tax receipts and made the banks wait in line behind the city payroll. By voting with their dollars, the banks could not dictate specific policies, but they could convince many voters that keeping Kucinich as mayor would hurt the city economically. As one voter in a lower income ethnic ward said on the weekend before the election, "There's the business people and the common people. The two got to work together. I'm a straight Democrat, but you can't tell people with money to go to hell."[50]

In short, the banks did not take over city government; rather, they laid seige to it—a seige, it was implied, that would not be lifted as long as Kucinich was mayor. As we saw, Kucinich's lack of a positive economic program to reassure voters and the media's focus on his frequent confrontations with business and other interests contributed to the seige atmosphere as well. But default played a key role. The banks were able to manipulate the electoral process by using an instrument of power that goes well beyond the legitimate use of lobbying or campaign contributions: the political allocation of credit.

Conclusion: The Causes and Consequences of Investor Discretion

This chapter on default and the preceding chapter on tax abatement offer contrasting case studies of growth politics. Both violate pluralist and market theories of urban politics, but for different reasons. In the case of tax abatement, city government had the political discretion to kill it without suffering economic reprisal. In fact, after ending tax abatement, Cleveland enjoyed a downtown building boom as investors moved in, seeking profits, not political power. Growth politics was an issue because people argued that city government did not have this discretion—that's what the whole controversy was about. The example of municipal lending, on the other hand, supported the opposite conclusion: it was the investors who exercised political discretion while city government was hemmed in by economic pressures. More importantly, the banks were able, by exercising political discretion in their demand for immediate payment of a loan, to exert significant power, playing a major role in defeating an incumbent mayor. Why the difference between the two areas?

Cleveland had discretion in the tax abatement case because the market for downtown investment was not politically organized but was a highly competitive national market. Moreover, Cleveland had a highly desirable commodity: a booming downtown service sector with a synergistic mix of business services. Default, on the other hand, is an example of one group acquiring monopoly power over a needed commodity, in violation of market theory, and then exercising political discretion in withholding that commodity. In order for this monopoly power to operate, three conditions had to exist:

1. The city had to be shut out of the national bond market and forced to depend on local banks.
2. The local banks, for their part, had to possess extraordinary unity of political purpose and action.
3. Forced to deal with a united phalanx of local banks, the bargaining relationship between the city and the banks had to be highly unequal.

Cleveland was forced out of the national bond market when the two rating agencies dropped Cleveland's bond ratings below investment grade. In part, these low ratings reflected the city's long term financial problems. Yet, as we saw earlier, Cleveland's financial situation had changed little from the time of the Perk administration. Undoubtedly, the refusal of local banks to rollover notes earlier in 1978 focused the attention of the rating agencies on Cleveland's problems. Nevertheless, for whatever reason, by December 1978 the national bond market was unavailable to the city. Having exhausted its cash reserves paying the CEI debt and buying up notes the banks earlier had refused to rollover, the only place the city had to turn to finance the existing notes in December 1978 was the local banks that held them.[51]

When Cleveland turned to the area banks that held the notes, it faced a remarkably united financial phalanx, led by Cleveland Trust. The six banks that held the notes tacitly agreed that all would go forward together or none would: the highly demanding rule of unanimity was adopted as the principle of political unity. At a meeting with the city shortly before default, five of the six banks expressed a willingness to rollover the notes if Kucinich's plan were implemented. Brock Weir, representing Cleveland Trust, refused to state a position. This meant that one bank, Cleveland Trust, and probably one man, Brock Weir, was able to veto Kucinich's plan, since without the support of the banks, it had little chance in City Council. Apparently, in violation of antitrust laws, Cleveland had the benefit of only one credit judgment, not six.[52]

The unanimity of Cleveland banks is not surprising, because close ties have long existed between them and Cleveland Trust has exerted dominance over the entire financial sector. Congressional studies in the late 1960s documented Cleveland's centralized pattern of bank stock ownership and control, calling it "the most alarming of any of the 10 cities under study."

> First of all it should be noted that, according to the latest FDIC concentration statistics as of June 30, 1966, the five largest banks in the Cleveland metropolitan area held 91.7 percent of all the commercial bank deposits in the area, one of the highest concentrations in the Nation . . . However, this is only the beginning of the true picture among Cleveland's commercial banks.
>
> When one looks below the surface, the information gathered from the subcommittee's survey of bank stock ownership and control reveals an even greater concentration. . . . [T]he Cleveland Trust Co., through its trust and nominee holdings, is a major stockholder in three of its competitors. . . .
>
> It is clear from the major Cleveland banks' extensive web of stockholder links, more pervasive than in any other city examined thus far, that competition among these banks is bound to be adversely affected.[53]

Another congressional study a year later, focusing on trust holdings, found Cleveland to be one of four cities (out of ten examined) where banking was dominated by a few institutions with "permanently entrenched managements."

> All in all, it is clear from the Subcommittee's survey that not only is Cleveland banking from the point of view of commercial bank operations, dominated by the Cleveland Trust Co., but when the additional factor of trust investments combined with interlocking directorships is considered, the Cleveland Trust Co., along with the other banks surveyed in Cleveland, is probably the single most influential element in the entire economy of the area.[54]

The 1979 House Study concluded that Cleveland Trust "remains by far the dominant financial institution in the city."[55]

In short, the near-monopoly of the big banks in Cleveland, their strong ties to one another and to most major corporations through investments and interlocking directorates, as well as the intimate social and political connections between bankers in such organizations as the

Growth Association and the Union Club, created a "community of interest" among major bankers in Cleveland. Led by Cleveland Trust, finance capital in Cleveland showed remarkable solidarity throughout the December default crisis.[56] This is crucial, because if only one bank had broken ranks, Kucinich's hand would have been greatly strengthened and the city might have been able to work out a refinancing plan.

Not only did local banks have a monopoly on meeting the city's credit needs, but they were also able to exercise political discretion in the operation of this monopoly. Part of the reason, of course, was precisely the monopoly, which took away any competitive pressure to avoid losing a valuable customer. More important, however, the notes in question represented an infinitesimal portion of the banks' assets so that they could afford to exercise political discretion. In the case of Cleveland Trust, its $5 million share of the notes represented less than 1 percent of its loans to states and political subdivisions ($689 million) and less than .01 percent of its total outstanding loans.[57] With such limited exposure in the securities of their own city, even a complete write-off would have made only a small dent in the total equity of the Cleveland banks.

Indeed, it cost the banks something to force the city into default. Once default occurred, they could not be certain when they would be paid; ultimately, the banks had to wait months for the first payment and did lose some interest. Being pretty well "loaned up," however, the banks could afford to place political conditions on any exchange with the city.

While the banks had many places to loan their money, the city had only one place to borrow. A monopoly is not very powerful if the buyer has no great need for the commodity, but in this case, city government, being poor, had a desperate need for loan funds. Having to pay the notes immediately meant curtailing basic services; not paying meant the stigma of default, damaging the city's access to credit for years to come. If the default can be thought of as a complex game of chicken (as the congressional study suggested), then the banks were driving the equivalent of a Sherman tank and the city a beat-up Volkswagen. This was not a typical market exchange; the bargaining relationship between the public and private sectors here was dramatically uneven.

8

The Politics of
Community Development

Local governments' toughest task in the new Community
Development Program is deciding *where* and *on what projects* within the city to spend the limited federal funds available. There are not enough funds even to begin upgrading
all of the deteriorating neighborhoods in each city. Hence,
no matter how local officials allocate these funds, residents
of many neighborhoods are going to be disappointed.[1]

Anthony Downs

The scene was the second annual Neighborhood Conference, held
November 4, 1978 at St. Philip Neri Church on Cleveland's East Side. It
was a chance for the burgeoning community organizations, now
numbering about a dozen, to flex their muscles. At one afternoon
workshop attended by over 350 people, Harry Jump, Director of the
Ohio Department of Insurance, was the honored guest. Because of his
lack of concern for inner city insurance redlining, Mr. Jump was, as
they say, "roasted." By the time he was through, the crowd was pretty
well worked up.

Next in line was Betty Grdina, the young new Director of Community Development in the Kucinich administration. Mayor Kucinich had
been invited to speak but was out of town. Grdina refused to answer
questions until Bob Weissman, Kucinich's chief political lieutenant,
was given a chance to address the crowd. Reluctantly, Weissman was

given two minutes. He began on a cordial note: "The Kucinich Administration believes very strongly in the neighborhood concept that underlies your organizations." But Weissman, known for his abrasive personality and confrontational style, was not one to engage in idle flattery. The speech went on to rebuke the neighborhood groups for treating public officials with disrespect by refusing to make appointments and protesting at officials' homes. The crowd was getting restless. This was their chance to criticize public officials, not vice versa. Near the end of his remarks Weissman came directly to the point:

> We are not going to be able to cooperate with organizations that promote confrontation for its own sake—at our expense. Whether the Administration will be able to work with your organizations, or whether we will have to work around you to serve the people of the neighborhoods is going to depend on whether you are able to curb the excesses of the agitators who want only the escalation of confrontation.

But few heard these words. As the two minute mark approached, many in the crowd began to clap and boo, drowning out Weissman's words. Weissman continued speaking. After his microphone was yanked away by the moderator, Weissman began shouting his speech, though few could hear his words over the mounting din. Cries of "get off the stage" rang through the auditorium. Finally, Weissman stormed out a side door shouting that since the crowd wouldn't listen, the city representatives would leave. People tried to stop them; there was a scuffle outside; a woman grabbed Grdina and was, in turn, tackled by another man. Inside, Fannie Lewis, long-time black activist and Kucinich supporter, wrestled with one of the moderators over the microphone. More than a dozen people were involved in the melee. Chairs sailed through the air.

Only one of many confrontations with neighborhood groups, this incident, more than any other, symbolized the political problems of the Kucinich administration. It was one thing to be involved in noisy confrontations with banks and utilities; that was to be expected. It was quite another thing to be embroiled in angry clashes with neighborhood groups. Such conflicts cast doubt on whether the administration really represented neighborhoods interests. How did this self-proclaimed "People's Mayor" end up in conflict with his own political base? This chapter seeks to answer that question by examining how the Kucinich administration handled the Community Development Block Grant (CDBG), the federal program of most concern to neighborhood groups.

Federal Intervention: Community Development Block Grants

As we saw in Chapter 1, before the New Deal, cities competed for mobile wealth without federal involvement. Under the pressure of the Depression, which was felt most intensely in large cities, the federal government moved forcefully into areas previously reserved for states and localities. But after the federal Court of Appeals ruled in 1935 that direct federal slum clearance was unconstitutional, the national government's involvement in urban housing and related problems has been channeled through state and local entities.[2] The result is a complex system of federal grants that runs directly counter to the movement of mobile wealth in the governmental marketplace—giving more money to those urban areas that lag behind in the growth competition. These intergovernmental grants, many directly from the federal government to local governments, have dramatically changed the nature of growth politics in large cities. Over the years, however, federal grants have oscillated from one extreme to the other, as they pursued first this, and then that, contradictory objective. The urban renewal program, for example, examined in Chapter 4, required that the federal funds be used to attract private investment to declining urban areas, with the primary goal being the physical elimination of slums and blight. Not surprisingly, this approach did not serve well the needs of the urban poor and minorities, especially their housing needs, since it concentrated on highly profitable commercial and office expansion. In the 1960s, federal grants swung in the opposite direction, as the nation rediscovered poverty. President Johnson's war on poverty initiated a whole series of federal grants that shifted away from the physical private investment approach of urban renewal to direct government services for inner city poor. These grants called for a more activist role by the federal government, often circumventing local elected officials to put the money directly into the hands of the urban poor. "Creative federalism," Johnson called it. A good example is the model cities program (Demonstration Cities and Metropolitan Development Act of 1966), which offered comprehensive services for dealing with the interrelated causes of poverty and attempted to put power over the program in the hands of the residents of inner city neighborhoods.

In the late 1960s the federal pendulum swung again, as the burgeoning federal grant programs came under increasing attack. While federal grants were clearly needed to counter the uneven development of growth politics, they were criticized for putting too much power into the hands of federal bureaucrats, drowning local initiative in a sea of paperwork. Running for the presidency in 1968, Richard Nixon proposed giving state and local governments more control over federal grants. The Community Development Block Grant (CDBG) grew out of Nixon's "new federalism" approach in 1974.

Under CDBG, local governments were entitled to a certain amount of money each year, based on a formula established by Congress, using population, overcrowded housing, and poverty (double weighted). Cities had to apply for the funds, describing how the money would be spent, but approval was automatic unless the federal government vetoed the application within seventy-five days for flagrantly violating the law. CDBG, having folded seven categorical grant programs— competitive grants for specific purposes such as urban renewal and model cities—into one entitlement block grant, embodied all the conflicting objectives of the separate programs. CDBG has never been sure whether it is a program to physically eliminate slums or a program to aid the people who live in them. Closely related has been a conflict between returning power to localities (which, because of pressures of growth politics, would favor physical improvements through incentives to private investors) and the legislative goal of aiding low income families (which could be enforced only through federal regulation).

Characteristically, Congress resolved these conflicts with a compromise: the list of eligible activities was very broad, including every activity under previous categorical programs; at the same time, applicants were required to certify to the Secretary of Housing and Urban Development (HUD) that their program had been developed "so as to give maximum feasible priority to activities which will benefit low- or moderate-income families. . . ." However, two other broad objectives were allowed in place of low income targeting: "the prevention or elimination of slums or blight" and activities "designed to meet other community development needs having a particular urgency."[3] As urban renewal showed, the elimination of slums does not necessarily benefit lower income families. The effect of these vague and conflicting requirements was to place significant power in the hands of the executive branch that would administer the law.

When President Ford signed the Housing and Community Development Act of 1974, he extolled its decentralizing effects, vowing that the bill would "return power from the banks of the Potomac to people in their own communities."[4] The Ford administration proceeded to act on this decentralist philosophy by administering CDBG in an almost hands off fashion. Citizen groups criticized the loose administration of the program, however, as evidence accumulated that much of the money was not being used to benefit low and moderate income families.[5] The Carter administration, wanting to blunt criticism of its urban policies and gain points with inner city voters, especially blacks, began administering the program more tightly. New regulations, issued March 1, 1978, enabled HUD to push more explicitly for targeting to lower income families. Evidence since then indicates that social targeting did increase over the years, owing in part to enforcement of these rules.[6]

In Cleveland, CDBG was administered by the Department of Community Development, created in 1969 as a descendant of the Department of Urban Renewal and Housing. The name change was first recommended in 1966 in a revealing statement: "It is recommended that the name 'Department of Urban Renewal and Housing' be changed to 'Department of Community Development.' The words 'urban renewal' are adversely value loaded in this community and as such have a bad connotation."[7] Not surprisingly, Kucinich was an early opponent of the block grant in Cleveland. His previous experience with public housing, urban renewal, and model cities made him highly suspicious of HUD programs. In 1975, Kucinich was the only member of council to vote against Cleveland's Year I Block Grant application, which passed 29-1. He contended that acceptance of the block grant would require the dispersal of low income families into housing throughout the city. "My people don't want any low income housing and I'm going to make sure they don't get any low income housing," Kucinich said.[8] Undoubtedly, his position also reflected opposition to racial integration, although he denied this.[9]

By the time Kucinich became mayor, his stubborn opposition to the block grant had faded. Clearly, this federal program was different from urban renewal. Neighborhoods had learned to view urban renewal designation as the kiss of death; under CDBG, neighborhoods clamored to be included. The block grant favored neighborhood conservation, small projects primarily benefiting homeowners in areas of incipient decline.[10] Shifting away from the service-oriented poverty programs of the 1960s, which Kucinich often had criticized, CDBG focused more on the physical development needs of neighborhoods.

Finally, CDBG regulations mandating targeting funds to low and moderate income persons seemed little more than a codification of the promises of urban populism.

For all these reasons, and more, the block grant serves as a valuable case study of the Kucinich administration, a kind of litmus test of its political tendencies. The block grant is one arena where the extreme pressures of the fiscal crisis and growth politics are partially suspended, where local governments can exercise political discretion. Cities do not have to prove significant private sector participation in order to get the money, as they did with urban renewal. Although encouraged to leverage private investment, cities are by no means required to do so. In the block grant, attention shifts from external relations with economic actors to internal relations with interest groups in local politics. "Under the categorical grants the competition for urban aid was to a great extent *between* communities; under block grants with formula entitlements the competition is primarily *within* the community."[11] Moreover, the Housing and Community Development Act, under the so-called "maintenance of effort" provision, specifically forbade cities under fiscal pressure from using the monies to substitute for services already being funded by local taxes.[12] The funds must be used for *new* community development activities. In short, because the usual growth and fiscal pressures are deliberately limited and federal control is minimized, the block grant provides an excellent opportunity to examine the programmatic tendencies of urban populism. And more generally, it provides an opportunity to examine whether a federal grant like CDBG, specifically designed to counter the uneven investment flows of the private market, can contribute to greater economic independence for cities.

Cleveland's Housing: A Billion Dollar Problem Goes Unsolved

Cleveland has a serious housing crisis. The problem is not a housing shortage. In fact, the number of dwelling units has declined less than the population.[13] Most Clevelanders live in substantial one or two family woodframe houses. The houses tend to be old; three fourths were built before 1940. The problem is that this basically sound housing stock is deteriorating at a rapid rate in many neighborhoods. Driving around most inner city neighborhoods presents clear evidence of the problem: peeling paint, broken windows, collapsing porches. Inside, conditions are worse. The city estimated in 1972 that over 85,000 dwelling units, about a third of the total, were in "substandard" condition.[14] A housing unit was classified as substandard only if it had basic faults, such as lack of plumbing or inadequate heat, threatening the health and safety of the occupants. Eventually, substandard houses deteriorate to the point that they are abandoned and must be demolished. In the early 1970s, the City Planning Commission estimated that three housing units were abandoned each day in Cleveland.[15] Between 1976 and 1979, the city of Cleveland demolished 7,395 dwelling units under a program funded by the block grant. Clearly, this is a tremendous waste of a valuable resource, to say nothing of the social and health problems associated with occupied substandard dwellings.

In an effort to deal with these problems, the city of Cleveland enacted a housing code in 1960, making it a crime punishable by fines or imprisonment (Chapter 367) not to maintain housing in standard condition. If the code were enforced, there would be no substandard housing. Obviously, it is not. Cleveland is not unique in this respect.[16] The failure of Cleveland's housing code shows that the police powers of local government cannot deal with a basically economic problem. Housing codes treat substandard housing as a crime, but housing code violations are negligent rather than malicious in nature.[17] Moreover, codes treat the effect rather than the cause. The most important causes of noncompliance are economic. Many owners simply lack the resources to do the needed repairs.[18] Others are reluctant to invest in a house that they know will go down in value whatever they do because of neighborhood decline. Strict legal enforcement of the code may only force the poor, who cannot afford the repairs or the higher rents, to move, thus creating a housing shortage for the poor.[19] (Interestingly, many suburbs are successful in strictly enforcing housing codes. This is largely because their goal is not to bring housing up to standard but to keep good housing at a high standard and therefore limited to higher income homeowners. Housing codes become another weapon in the suburban arsenal for excluding the poor.)

Cleveland's housing problems are mainly economic. The process that leads to housing deterioration is well known. As the middle class flees to the suburbs, lower income families move into the housing that is left behind, the so-called filtering process. (Filtering also explains the problem of abandonment.) Since these families cannot afford to pay as high rents, landlords are forced either to reduce their profits or to put less money into maintenance. When maintenance falls below a certain level, housing deteriorates into substandard condition. The same process can occur with owner occupied homes, especially in the case of elderly on fixed incomes. In short, Cleveland's housing probelm is an income problem; it cannot be separated from Cleveland's growth crisis of jobs and investment.[20]

As City Planning Director under Perk in the early 1970s, Norm Krumholz began working with his staff on ways to attack the housing problem. The old method of urban renewal—bulldozing the slums and building anew—had proved a failure. For one thing, it destroyed social networks, the sense of community, that made living in the city worthwhile. For another, it was very expensive. The City Planning Commission estimated that, of the 85,000 substandard housing units in the city, approximately 67,000 were "suitable for rehabilitation."[21] The cost of bringing the older housing units into standard condition was far less than the cost of slum clearance and new construction. Clearly, rehab made economic as well as social sense.

Even though rehab was cheaper than new construction, the cost of rehabilitating the city's housing stock was still astronomical. If the 67,000 substandard units suitable for rehab were brought up to code at a cost of $15,000 per unit (a conservative estimate), the total cost would exceed $1 billion! Clearly, the residents of Cleveland did not have that kind of money. Yet the only significant public funds available for housing rehab in the city of Cleveland were block grant.[22] In 1978–1979, Cleveland received $34.66 million in its community development block grant. Of this, a little over $6 million went for housing rehabilitation. In other words, the public sector had less than one percent of the resources needed to solve the problem. If progress were going to be made on Cleveland's housing problem, additional resources would have to be found. But where?

Table 5 suggests the answer. In 1978 alone, private banks and savings and loans invested over $1 billion in housing in Cuyahoga County. Of this total, only 16 percent was invested in the city of Cleveland, even though the city contained approximately 42 percent of the total residential units in the county.[23] Redlining—the practice of refusing to lend in certain neighborhoods, regardless of the merits of individual applicants—is difficult to prove, but research indicates that it did exist in Cleveland.[24] Undoubtedly, however, most of the uneven lending was due to the greater risk and lesser profits of investments within the city compared with those in the suburbs. In any event, it was clear that the resources to deal with Cleveland's housing problem lay in the private sector. Redirecting only a small percentage of suburban housing investment would make a big difference to the city.

As a representative of the city, Krumholz became involved during the Perk administration in a series of meetings with twenty-two private lenders to increase their inner city lending. The length of the discussions, approximately thirty over a two year period, testified to the difficulty of persuading the banks to commit themselves to any affirmative lending strategy. At one point, reportedly, Brock Weir pulled Cleveland Trust out of the discussions, saying, in effect, that no one was going to tell Cleveland Trust how to loan its money.[25] Later, Cleveland Trust came back in. The group finally agreed on a program called Cleveland Action to Support Housing (CASH). CASH was designed to use CDBG monies to leverage private sector involvement in housing rehabilitation. The idea was to use the public monies to lower the interest rates on rehab loans funded mostly by the private lenders. In this way, people could fix their homes who could not previously afford to and the public dollars would be stretched by combining with private dollars. Even though the private lenders did not agree to take on riskier loans, it was hoped that their participation in CASH would increase their inner city lending. To reassure the lenders, CASH was set up as a nonprofit corporation, independent of City Hall, and controlled by a board of directors and loan review committee dominated by private lenders.

About the time negotiations for CASH were drawing to a close,

TABLE 5.

Investment in Housing by All Banks and Savings & Loan Associations in Cuyahoga County, 1978*

Location	Home Mortgages	Home Improvement Loans	Total
Cleveland	138	28	166
Suburban Cuyahoga County	819	49	868
Total	957	77	1,034

Source: Northeast Ohio Areawide Coordinating Agency, *Residential Investment and Sales: Indicators of Change, Cuyahoga County, Ohio, 1977–1979* (Cleveland: NOACA, 1981).
*in millions

Kucinich was elected mayor in November 1977 and appointed Krumholz director of the Department of Community Development. Krumholz immediately began to make a case for including CASH in the block grant. CASH was billed not just as a vehicle for leveraging private investment but as one component of a concentrated and comprehensive approach to neighborhood revitalization. Studies of the block grant had shown that cities had a strong tendency to spread the money out for maximum political effect, the so-called "Law of Political Dispersion."[26] As a result, CDBG spending was often spread so thinly throughout cities that it was unable to stem neighborhood decline and was overwhelmed by the general disinvestment of the area. Krumholz proposed scrapping the politically popular 3 Percent Loan Program, which covered twenty-eight of the city's thirty-three wards, and replacing it with CASH, concentrated in five target areas, benefiting only about a third of the wards.[27] The strategy called for selecting subtarget areas within the target areas for door-to-door housing inspections to concentrate CASH resources further. Blocks that agreed to door-to-door inspections would be rewarded with free sidewalks from the block grant. In general, it was hoped, by choosing target areas where the deterioration was not too far advanced—areas of so-called "incipient decline"—and by concentrating other block grant improvements in those districts, the negative investment psychology that gripped certain neighborhoods could be turned around.[28]

Krumholz succeeded in getting CASH ($2 million) and the concept of targeting included in the CDBG application passed by City Council in February 1978. This meant that a significant portion of the block grant would be spent according to a targeted plan, a welcome respite from the usual practice of scattering the funds to satisfy political interests. The administration's success in block grant planning, however, was due less to political adroitness than to the circumstance that Cleveland's block grant more than doubled in size that year (from $16 million to over $34 million).[29] This meant that the administration could implement new programs without threatening established clienteles attached to the old programs. The old spread-out 3 Percent Loan Program, for example, was continued at the same time that new spending was targeted to a handful of neighborhoods.[30]

The CASH program started out with great promise: it was a rare example of targeted planning of expenditure; it sought to leverage private funds (an absolutely necessary step if any significant progress was to be made on the problem); and it aimed to benefit low and moderate income homeowners. How well did CASH accomplish its goals?[31]

In its ability to leverage private resources, CASH was not simply a failure, it was a dismal failure. The concept was essentially the same as urban renewal or tax abatement: use public subsidies to stimulate private investment in the inner city that would not have occurred otherwise. In this case, however, there was one big difference: CASH subsidies—lower monthly payments on rehab loans—went entirely to low income homeowners, not to wealthy commercial developers. The Kucinich administration could hardly object to this. Originally, it was hoped, every dollar of block grant money would leverage three to four dollars of private rehabilitation funds. According to the 1978 CASH Annual Report, however, the actual leveraging rate was less than 23 cents of private funds for every public dollar.[32] This compared poorly to other cities. HUD's second annual report on the CDBG program stated, "More than half of the cities surveyed are using leverage techniques to stimulate private investment and extend the impact of the CDBG dollar. Overall, communities have been able to stimulate $2.40 of private funds for each dollar of CDBG funding."[33] By comparison, Cleveland's leverage ratio was extraordinarily low.

In fact, the leverage ratio is a highly deceptive measurement. For one thing, it does not indicate whether the reported private investment was new investment caused by the program or whether the private money would have been lent anyway without the program. What this means, of course, is that CASH's leveraging might have been worse than the reported 23 cents: some of the private loans might have occurred without CASH.

A second problem with the leverage ratio is that it only reports *direct* leveraging. The hope was that, by concentrating block grant expenditures (not just rehab loans) in targeted neighborhoods, homeowners would be encouraged to fix up their homes, whether by taking out a conventioanl loan, using savings, or doing the work themselves, and that as a result, there would be a general rise in property values in the neighborhood. Is there any evidence that these indirect effects occurred in the CASH target areas? Indirect leveraging is, of course, difficult to measure. In the case of Cleveland, however, data has been collected that can shed light on the question. Using information supplied under the Home Mortgage Disclosure Act on private lending and data on home sales supplied by the County Auditor, a measurement called the loan/sale ratio was developed and applied to

Cleveland. Measuring the total number of property sales that were covered by conventional mortgage loans, the loan/sale ratio is a valid indicator of private lenders' involvement in a community. Looking at the change in this loan/sale ratio from 1977 to 1979 for the CASH target neighborhoods indicates that there was no consistent change upward. In fact, the loan/sale ratio actually declined in more target neighborhoods than it increased in, suggesting a continued withdrawal of the private lenders.[34] Data on appreciation of single family homes between 1977–1978 and 1980–1981 presents a more complex picture. In some target neighborhoods (Ohio City, Glenville), home prices went up faster than in the suburbs; in others (Tremont, Broadway), sales prices actually declined.[35] In short, there is no consistent pattern. A definitive answer would require more detailed analysis of the data. At this point, however, the data indicate that CASH did not result in a general investment turnaround in the targeted neighborhoods.

Undoubtedly, it was difficult to get the private lenders to invest in inner city housing because the applicants were poor and their homes had low market values, making the loans riskier. The average sale price of homes in the block grant target areas for 1981 (slightly expanded from the Kucinich administration) was only $15,855 (using sales between 1977 and 1979).[36] The average sales price in the suburbs was about four times that amount. Furthermore, an analysis of CASH loan applicants for the Department of Community Development in 1981 showed that about half of them could not afford to make monthly payments at all. The failure of CASH can be partly attributed, then, to what might be called the dilemma of leveraging: while it is relatively easy to leverage large amounts of private capital for investment in highly profitable areas, such as downtown service sector expansion or suburban housing, it is much more difficult to leverage private investment in less profitable inner city housing. CASH could have improved its leverage ratio simply by serving a higher income clientele.[37] As it stood, the CASH program did target the benefits for those who most needed it—at the expense of leveraging additional private resources.

Still, it is fair to say that CASH could have done better in leveraging private investment. The private lender's contribution represented about two loans per institution per year, totaling approximately $12,000.[38] To say that for the participating private lenders such an amount was a mere pittance is not hyperbole. The Kucinich administration, indeed, possessed both carrots and sticks it could have used to increase the private contribution. As carrots, the city could have established a loan guarantee fund to persuade the private lenders to cover applicants with poor credit records. It could also have drawn down the CASH funds from the federal government at the beginning of the program year and deposited the lump sum with the private lenders as a further incentive to contribute. The big stick the city could have employed was the Community Reinvestment Act (CRA). Passed in 1977, CRA charged each private lender with "meeting the credit needs of its entire community, including low- and moderate-income neighborhoods."[39] Community groups or local governments may file a challenge with the appropriate federal regulatory agency to stop a private lender from taking certain actions, such as opening a new branch, if the lender is not meeting the community's credit needs. The Kucinich administration was successful in using CRA to negotiate an agreement with one savings and loan to increase its inner city lending.[40] But, in general, the administration was more successful at confrontation than at negotiation with the banks; it was not successful with the twenty-two lenders in CASH, at least, in delivering economic benefits for lower income neighborhoods.

In addition to leveraging problems, CASH suffered from administrative disruption and political manipulation during the Kucinich years. Midway through Kucinich's two year term, Betty Grdina, a Kucinich political operative, replaced Norm Kurmholz as Director of Community Development (a change discussed in more detail shortly). When Grdina took office she immediately considered dismantling the CASH program because of the low level of private funding, especially in view of the control exercised by private lenders over the program. When the director of CASH, Stanley Freeman, heard about this, he resigned. (Grdina charged that he had resigned because she was exerting tighter fiscal controls to counter corruption in CASH.) Unilaterally, Grdina hired the next director, Terrance Roberts, bypassing the search committee set up with the banks. By this time, Grdina may have hoped that the lenders, objects of her public criticisms, would pull out of CASH and she could then blame them for its collapse. Ironically, the lenders, who had been very reluctant to join CASH in the beginning, were now unwilling to leave it: they needed CASH as evidence of their commitment to the inner city in case of CRA challenges. CASH became a political football between the administration and the banks, each trying to blame the other for its failure. The new director, Roberts, resigned shortly before the November election, charging that Grdina and Weissman had ordered him to deny loans to anyone who supported the recall of Kucinich. Predictably, Grdina accused Roberts of corruption.

Roberts's charge that the loan program was used for political effect was undoubtedly true. The Kucinich administration was fighting for political survival and Grdina used the block grant, whenever possible, to win votes and punish enemies. (She may have reasoned that, after all, the Kucinich administration had been discriminated against by the bankers, who refused to rollover city loans on political grounds.) Nevertheless, the attempt to manipulate government programs for partisan advantage disrupted operations, as qualified technocrats left the Kucinich administration in disgust.

By the end of the Kucinich administration, the CASH program was in shambles. Door-to-door housing inspections were not being carried out at all. Inspectors were back responding to complaints, the old legal approach that had proved ineffective. The only CASH inspections were done by request, which meant they were scattered throughout the target areas instead of being concentrated on certain blocks in the subtarget areas. Site improvements (curbs and sidewalks) were not coordinated with CASH loans. The staff at CASH was far too small to process the applications, let alone coordinate the door-to-door inspections. The time required to process a loan application had increased drastically and a serious backlog had developed. These problems were noted in HUD monitoring reports on Cleveland's block grant.[41]

Perhaps the most serious indictment was that the administration was unable to spend the small amount of money under its control, even though there was a crying need for the investment. Slow spending plagued Cleveland's entire block grant program throughout the Perk and Kucinich administrations. HUD frequently threatened to reduce Cleveland's entitlement if it could not spend the money in a timely fashion. Through the first five years of the block grant, Cleveland received $120,913,786; as of December 31, 1979, only $72,713,060 had been spent. This left almost $50 million in the federal treasury losing value at a rapid rate because of inflation.[42] The situation was even worse for the housing rehab programs. Through the first five years of the block grant, $23,873,754 was budgeted for rehabilitation; as of December 31, 1979, only $11,541,203 had been spent—less than 50 percent. One other program, the 312 Loan Program, had $987,000 allocated to Cleveland, separate from the block grant. But program progress was so slow under the Kucinich administration that HUD cut $250,000 from the program in April 1979.

In conclusion, Cleveland had a huge housing problem crying out for relief. With the solution carrying a price tag exceeding $1 billion, it is not fair to expect the Kucinich administration to have solved the problem with a few million dollars in federal funds. Nevertheless, the resources existed to make progress in the area. No progress was made. At least in the area of housing, the Kucinich administration did not deliver on the promise of urban populism: to bring additional economic benefits to lower income residents of the city.

Neighborhood Imbroglio: A Conflict of Turf

The failure of the Kucinich administration to deliver better housing to the neighborhoods does not explain the bitter fight that erupted between it and many of the neighborhood groups. In fact, the Kucinich administration generally favored neighborhoods in its spending patterns; there was never a hint of spending the block grant for big downtown or commercial projects. It was not economics that caused the fight with the neighborhood groups but politics.

Kucinich started on the right foot with the neighborhood groups, appointing Krumholz as Director of Community Development. Generally, Krumholz was highly regarded by neighborhood activists as one of those rare city planners sensitive to neighborhood needs. As a planner, Krumholz did not hesitate to use politics to further his policy goals, but he was not committed to Kucinich's political ambitions nor was he close to Kucinich's inner circle. Perhaps Krumholz's major contribution during his short tenure at Community Development was the targeting of block grant expenditures. It was his professional judgment that targeting would increase the effectiveness of the block grant.[43] Unlike most planners, however, Krumholz did not stop at simply advocating targeting; he devised a strategy to use existing political forces to further his targeting goal. The new target areas were selected by Krumholz and his staff on the basis of a number of objective planning criteria, such as majority low and moderate income, high proportion of owner occupied housing, and low levels of foreclosures, abandonments, and welfare dependency. But there was one final criterion that was political: the existence of active community organizations. The community groups would serve as a kind of buffer between Community Development and City Council, Krumholz reasoned. By putting pressure on city government for service delivery, the Alinsky-style community groups would, in effect, enforce the targeting strategy. Moreover, in Krumholz's view, it was easier to work with neighborhoods that were already organized.

Community groups could, for example, exert peer pressure to persuade recalcitrant owners to fix up their homes.

In the first year, the plan worked to a great extent. Block grant expenditures began to be concentrated in target areas and much of it was funneled through existing community organizations, or at least spent with their advice. But a political problem was brewing. Krumholz was essentially engaging in a kind of political theatre with the neighborhood groups. Willing to take heat from the community organizations if it helped enforce his priorities, Krumholz, at times, even encouraged attacks on the administration for this purpose. What this meant, however, is that the Alinsky-style community organizations took credit for the increased spending in their neighborhoods, not the Kucinich administration.

In August 1978, less than a year after taking office, the Kucinich administration had its back against the wall. Under attack by the banks, faced with a difficult recall election, Kucinich did not appreciate his administration being attacked by neighborhood groups that, after all, were getting more block grant funds than ever. Kucinich decided to call in his IOUs. The St. Clair–Superior Coalition was asked to join the campaign against the recall.[44] It refused. This result should not have been a surprise. Neighborhood organizations rarely got involved in partisan electoral politics for two reasons: (1) Doing so threatened the tax exempt status through which they got their foundation funding; (2) they feared that politicians they had opposed would, once in office, cut them off completely. Community organizations tended to treat all politicians alike: as part of the system that they must pressure for benefits. Furthermore, in the case of St. Clair–Superior, the organization was split by supporters and opponents of Kucinich.

The failure of the community organizations to come to the aid of Kucinich, under sharp attack from banks and large corporations, was a bitter pill for many in the administration to swallow. Looking ahead to the re-election campaign after the recall, Kucinich, following the advice of Weissman, decided to replace Krumholz, a city planner, with Betty Grdina, a political loyalist.[45] Krumholz had refused to subsume his priorities for the block grant to the electoral needs of the administration. Why should we continue, the administration reasoned, to fund organizations that refused to come to our political defense? They decided to follow the age old political maxim: reward your friends, punish your enemies. Shortly after the Grdina appointment, Kucinich met secretly with City Council leadership to negotiate a new working relationship; one of the demands: "a free hand in the use of Community Development money."[46]

After Grdina's appointment, the conflict with the neighborhood groups, which had been simmering beneath the surface, burst into public view. For many years a new fire station had been promised for the Broadway area. The Kucinich administration continued the string of promises. After Finance Director Joe Tegreene noticed in October 1978 that the bond funds for the fire station were missing, the administration decided to use block grant funds. By this time, the community groups had lost their patience and Citizens to Bring Back Broadway led an angry protest outside the apartment of the new Director of Community Development. Grdina was enraged at the pressure tactics and invasion of privacy. The next clash was the tumultuous citywide Neighborhood Conference, described at the beginning of this chapter. Afterward, Weissman declared City Hall "off limits" to three groups: Citizens to Bring Back Broadway, Buckeye-Woodland, and St. Clair–Superior. The conflict escalated. In May 1979, the St. Clair–Superior Coalition dumped garbage at the office of the Director of Public Service. In June, Kucinich refused to walk across the street to meet with five hundred senior citizens demanding a special police unit, blaming the protest on "professional agitators."

After the melee at the citywide conference, the Kucinich administration counterattacked, trying to destroy the offending organizations by establishing counter organizations loyal to Kucinich. After nine of nineteen executive board members of the St. Clair–Superior Coalition resigned, an alternative group was set up in the area, called Neighbors United, to siphon off strength from the established group. While cooperating with Neighbors United, Kucinich refused to sign off on a grant application submitted by St. Clair–Superior to start its own housing rehab corporation. Grdina said the city already was spending millions on housing rehabilitation "so there is no need for any group to start its own housing business."[47]

The neighborhood groups tried to protect themselves. Buckeye-Woodland testified in Washington before the National Commission on Neighborhoods, asking that federal aid be channeled directly to neighborhood groups rather than through City Hall. The whole controversy had an impact at the national level when Mary Rose Oakar, Democratic congresswoman from Cleveland's West Side and Kucinich opponent, successfully introduced an amendment to the new Neighborhood

Self-Help Development Program mandating that 10 percent of the $15 million program be set aside for direct grants to neighborhood groups not approved by City Hall.

The confrontations with the neighborhood groups hurt Kucinich politically. The three groups that Weissman banned from City Hall— Buckeye-Woodland, St. Clair–Superior and Citizens to Bring Back Broadway—primarily served four wards: 14, 15, 16, and 23. Between the recall in August 1978 and the re-election effort in November 1979, Kucinich lost 12.5 percent of his expected strength citywide; in the four wards most affected by the fights with community organizations, Kucinich lost 18.8 percent of his expected strength.[48] And these were inner city wards where Kucinich, generally, tended to hold his strength. But much more important than any quantifiable loss of votes was the incalculable damage to Kucinich's image as a defender of neigborhoods.

In an article in the Cleveland *Plain Dealer*, Betty Grdina tackled the difficult task of explaining the anomalous situation of a "people's mayor" fighting with people's organizations. She began by arguing that "the Kucinich record on neighborhood issues is unequalled," listing a series of new benefits Kucinich had delivered to the neighborhoods. She blamed the conflict on professional organizers who whipped up neighborhood residents in phony confrontations against their natural ally, Kucinich. Significantly, she argued that these confrontations were manipulated by the corporate elite: "The corporate establishment, acting through the charity foundations, is trying to undermine Kucinich's neighborhood support by subsidizing the salaries of organizers who train neighborhood people in street confrontation tactics."[49] Members of neighborhood organizations were dupes of what she called "organized manipulation by the corporate establishment." The conflict was a political attack on the administration, she said, and was not based on legitimate economic issues.

While Grdina was correct to argue that the conflict was more political than economic, there was no need to resort to a convoluted conspiracy theory to explain events.[50] The conflict can be better understood simply as a conflict over turf between two similar, but differently situated, community organizations, each seeking to take credit for delivering economic benefits to the neighborhoods.

As we saw in Chapter 6, Kucinich's political approach resembled closely the organizing strategy of the Alinsky-style neighborhood groups. Both emphasized economic demands, not cultural values or issues of political structure. Both relied on confrontations with established powers to mobilize their political base. Both tended to personalize their enemies and to articulate a populist instrumental theory of politics that pitted "the people" against a "corporate elite." When Kucinich was elected mayor, he suddenly became, for the community groups, an *ex officio* member of the corporate elite. But Kucinich, of course, did not see himself this way. He saw himself as the head of a new citywide community organization, which would represent the neighborhoods in larger struggles against the banks and corporations. Kucinich set forth his approach to the existing community groups to a *Plain Dealer* reporter shortly after he was elected mayor: "Activist community groups are unnecessary with a mayor who understands their needs."[51] Above all, Kucinich needed to be perceived as the initiator, as the one who delivered the goods, in order to solidify his electoral base. The problem was that Kucinich had raised expectations with his promises during the campaign far beyond what he was able to deliver. And the economism of urban populism, with its elite instrumentalist theory of politics, did not lend itself to educating people about the structural limits of city government or the need to moderate demands in the short run in order to achieve greater gains in the long run.

The community groups, for their part, were in no position to moderate their demands. Even if Kucinich had been one of their own (and there was great debate about this among community activists), it is doubtful whether the community groups could have shifted their strategy. They had their own organizational imperatives: they thrived on confrontations with established powers; they also needed to deliver the goods. Such victories were their *raison d'être*. The community groups could not afford to let Kucinich take credit for delivering all the benefits to the neighborhoods. Moreover, their tendency to personalize issues meant that whoever was in power was held responsible for the problems. Kucinich, therefore, was fair game. In fact, the Kucinich administration in many ways was an inviting target because it did not back away from confrontation with co-opting behavior (a tactic that could be frustrating to community organizers) but actually sought out confrontations.

In short, with the Kucinich administration and the community groups each playing their natural roles, a clash was inevitable. It was a conflict over turf. And in the restricted realm of Cleveland's growth crisis, there was little turf to share.

Conclusion: Who Governs Community Development?

This case study of community development in Cleveland seems to confirm the pluralist thesis that separate arenas exist in city politics, pretty much insulated from one another, where different sets of plural elites wield power. Community development was run differently from taxes or municipal bonds, arenas where large corporations exercised decisive power with their ever present threat, real or imagined, to withdraw investment. There is no evidence that Brock Weir, or any other corporate leader for that matter, played an important role in block grant spending priorities. Grdina's thesis, that the corporate elite exercised power indirectly by manipulating the neighborhood groups, does not stand up to critical scrutiny. In fact, decision making in community development was shared by many different groups in almost classic pluralist fashion. Generalist elected officials (the administration and City Council) wielded the most power over block grant spending, followed by activist interest groups (such as community organizations and social service agencies) and specialist planners and experts (Krumholz and Community Development staff).

As mayor, Kucinich exercised considerable power over the block grant, showing a bias against economic development subsidies of any sort and a basic orientation toward public works à la the New Deal.[52] In his administration's first block grant application, Kucinich proposed cutting out all funding for local development corporations (LDCs)— which aided small businesses on commercial strips—and proposed using the money instead to fulfill a campaign promise to build sewers in areas where flooding of basements was common. The attack on the LDCs, which had close ties to many City Council members was the first round in a series of conflicts between Kucinich and council over the block grant.

The council also exerted significant power over block grant decision making. In case studies by the Brookings Institution of sixty-two large cities for the first year of the block grant, almost two-thirds were rated as having "minimal" involvement by the local legislature; the involvement of Cleveland's council was ranked "extensive."[53] Local legislatures have two formal, nontransferable responsibilities with regard to the block grant: (1) approving participation in the program in the first place; (2) approving each year's CDBG application. Cleveland's council went one big step further, requiring a council ordinance for each and every expenditure of funds contained in the approved application.[54] (This is like requiring congressional approval every time the Secretary of Defense buys airplane parts.) Council's ability to halt spending at any time proved a valuable weapon for gaining concessions from the administration.

Council had no overall plan for Cleveland's block grant, but it did represent well the many interest groups mobilized by the available federal funds. This included the LDCs and many small social service agencies funded by CDBG. Although the social service contracts represented only about 20 percent of Cleveland's block grant, they were important for the City Council.[55] Each year, applications for social service contracts far exceeded available block grant funds. No attempt was made to evaluate the applications on the basis of need or past performance. Instead, Council President George Forbes used his control over funding to reward loyal members of his council majority, who were allowed to pick which social service contacts would be funded in their wards. Social agencies or churches with close ties to their local ward organization were rewarded.

During the Kucinich years, a basic conflict developed between the public works orientation of Kucinich and the social service orientation of Forbes and the council majority. Basically, it was a conflict between inner city ethnics and blacks.[56] Kucinich rewarded his ethnic constitutency of small homeowners with new sidewalks and sewers; Forbes primarily rewarded his poorer, black constitutency with social service contracts.[57] As Figure 7 shows, Kucinich succeeded in increasing the percentage of block grant funds devoted to public works as opposed to social services. Nevertheless, Kucinich was forced to compromise continually with council over block grant issues. The typical pattern each year was for Cleveland's CDBG application to be held up until the last moment, when the administration and council would "cut a deal," each giving up something to get something in return. It was a classic case of pluralist bargaining. Moreover, council retained significant control, in pluralist fashion, over the management of the block grant.[58] Whether it was telling housing inspectors where to inspect or stretching the regulations as they applied to a specific social service agency, council continuously influenced the way the block grant was implemented.

On the one hand, Cleveland's block grant was relatively democratic, giving many different groups access to decision making; on the other hand, the same process severely handicapped the city in pursuing one important goal. As we saw, the CDBG program had two contradic-

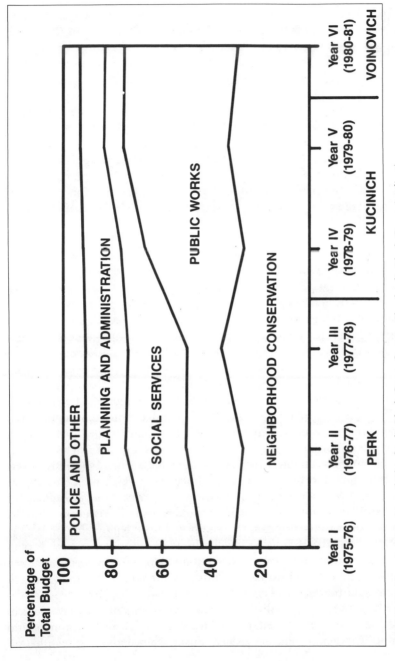

FIGURE 7. Changing Priorities of Cleveland's Block Grant. Source: Cleveland's Block Grant Applications.

tory objectives: to *redistribute* resources to poorer cities and households, and to aid in a process of community *development* that could stem disinvestment and decline. The pluralist process of block grant decision making served redistribution (policy was responsive to votes, not to money), but it did not serve redevelopment.[59]

Redevelopment would have required spending the money according to a long term plan, one that concentrated resources and involved many different elements of the community in a comprehensive effort to leverage investment, create jobs, and lessen economic dependency. The one effort at planning, CASH and the targeting concept, became the victim of political pressures. CASH was crippled by the conflict between the banks and the administration and, over the years, the target areas were expanded to give decision makers greater latitude in making political payoffs.

Cleveland's block grant responded to immediate political pressures instead of to comprehensive planning. The main decision makers were the administration, City Council, outside interest groups, and professional planners. With the possible exception of planners, who had the least power, no actor cared much about the block grant program as a whole; each cared intensely about that part of the program that directly affected its constituency. The focus was not on long term redevelopment but short term political payoff. With mayor and council elected for short two year terms, projects had to show immediate results.[60] Instead of expanding the pie, which would take too long, participants were preoccupied with dividing up the existing pie in the most politically efficacious manner. As a result, CDBG monies were scattered about the city according to the pull and haul of narrow political interests.[61]

Neither the public works program of Kucinich nor the social services orientation of Forbes and council were designed to lessen the economic dependency of city residents; they were designed to garner votes, to make the beneficiaries beholden to politicians. Essentially, both took a welfare approach: traditional pork barrel liberalism. The block grant revealed that Kucinich, urban populist or not, had no plan for community redevelopment; what he did have was a political plan for winning votes. However, Kucinich's effort to use the block grant to solidify his political base, machine style, backfired. The tendency of the block grant to activate demands well beyond its ability to satisfy them (political overload) is well documented.[62] Kucinich's "You want it, you got it" campaign promises exacerbated the problem. In effect, Cleveland's block grant became a zero sum game between the administration, the council, and the neighborhood groups: the gain of one became the loss of the others. Kucinich attempted to unite lower income voters in a war against corporate power. Instead, Commander Kucinich became bogged down in crippling rearguard actions, as his own troops fought each other over scarce public resources.

At one level, then, block grant decision making in Cleveland seemed to conform to the pluralist thesis: many different (plural) interest groups played a role in how the money was spent. Seen in the context of the crisis of growth politics, however, these immediate facts take on a different appearance. For one thing, it is precisely the pluralist fragmentation of policymaking, the weakness of the political parties, that makes it so difficult to put together a coherent program to attack Cleveland's economic dependency. Moreover, the smallness of the block grant in relation to the problems it was designed to solve, made the whole effort almost absurd—as the $6 million housing program to solve a $1 billion housing problem demonstrated. In this context, the title "community development" takes on an exceedingly hollow ring. Instead of a haven from growth pressures, Cleveland's block grant could more accurately be termed a ghetto.

Cleveland on the brink.

A series of cartoons in the Cleveland *Plain Dealer* satirized Kucinich by portraying City Hall as an outhouse. Courtesy of Ray Osrin and the *Plain Dealer*, August 4, 1978.

On the beach

Constant battles between Kucinich and Council President George Forbes were viewed as paralyzing city government in dealing with Cleveland's problems. Courtesy of Bill Roberts and the Cleveland *Press*, July 20, 1978.

Kucinich's confrontation politics was lampooned in the media. Courtesy of Bill Roberts and the Cleveland *Press*, October 3, 1978.

The press blamed Kucinich and not the banks for default. Courtesy of the Cleveland *Press*, December 18, 1978. By "Victory."

Muny Light was viewed by many as a huge drain on the city's finances. Courtesy of Ray Osrin and the *Plain Dealer*, January 19, 1979.

Nader Man and Blunder Boy

Ralph Nader was ridiculed in the press when he came to Cleveland to defend Kucinich. Courtesy of the Cleveland *Press*, January 29, 1979. By "Victory."

The $200 million Sohio headquarters building under construction in 1983—without tax abatement. Courtesy of the *Plain Dealer*, September 21, 1983. By Marvin M. Greene.

Following the February 27, 1979 Muny Light election, Mayor Dennis J. Kucinich lays a wreath at the statue of Tom L. Johnson, Cleveland's progressive mayor from 1901 to 1910. Councilman Gary J. Kucinich looks on. Courtesy of the *Plain Dealer*. By Ray Matjasic.

9

From Urban Populism
to Race Politics

I like fat cats. I want as many in Cleveland as I can get.
Cleveland needs their tax dollars and the jobs they bring.[1]

George Voinovich

George Voinovich has proven conclusively . . . —he is the
candidate of the fat cats . . . and he would love to become
the mayor of the fat cats so he can repay their generosity.[2]

Dennis Kucinich

In fall 1979, Kucinich faced an uphill battle to be re-elected mayor.
His opponent was George Voinovich, who had stepped down as Lieutenant Governor of Ohio to take on Kucinich. His only drawback was
that he was a Republican in an overwhelmingly Democratic city. (Damage here would be limited by a nonpartisan ballot.) A big asset was his
strong ethnic ties in Cleveland. And, above all, he had money—over a
half million dollars, raised mostly from generous corporate contributors. Kucinich would spend only $175,000. As the campaign pro-
gressed, evidence accumulated that Kucinich was running scared, as
disturbing incidents came to light about his campaign.

In October 1979, campaign leaflets, all with the same style and
content, were distributed from Kucinich headquarters for a number of

pro-Kucinich council candidates.[3] All attacked the incumbent for "voting three times for forced school busing when George Forbes desperately needed his (or her) votes." Actually, the votes back in May 1979 were not for "forced busing" but for distributing a film on desegregation. Kucinich vetoed the legislation and council never voted to override the veto, apparently fearing just this kind of retaliation. Many in the community, supporters as well as opponents of Kucinich, viewed these leaflets as an irresponsible manipulation of racial fears in the white community at a dangerous time—just as the first phase of court-ordered school busing was being implemented.

In the last days of the campaign, trailing badly in the polls, Kucinich played race politics again. On the white West Side, he distributed a leaflet featuring two prominent black politicians who supported his opponent (see Illustration 2). The ostensible message was that big business had bought off these black Democrats to support Voinovich: the leaflet even proclaimed, "Vote Against Racist Politics." But the subliminal message was clear: Voinovich was the "black" candidate, Kucinich the "white" candidate. At the same time, on the East Side, a leaflet was distributed featuring prominent blacks endorsing Kucinich, including again, George Forbes—who in fact supported Voinovich— criticizing Voinovich as "an anti-black Republican." Such two-faced campaigning rankled many.

Playing race politics is a time-honored game in Cleveland politics. Carl Stokes won the mayoralty in 1967 by subtly segmenting his campaign appeal: "On the east side the slogan was 'Vote for Carl Stokes because he is a Negro.' On the west side the slogan was 'Don't vote for the Negro; vote for the man.' "[4] Kucinich was well schooled in race politics. When opponents would smear him as antiblack, he would nimbly turn around and distribute the *same* leaflet on the West Side, deriding it as racist smear tactics while benefiting from the white backlash. Kucinich did this with a primary day leaflet distributed by his opponent in the 1977 mayoralty campaign and with a leaflet distributed by the Recall Committee in the black community. Top aides attributed his narrow victory in the recall to the latter leaflet.

Regardless of its success, Kucinich's manipulation of racial symbols directly contradicted his theory of urban populism. According to urban populism, genuine reform is possible only if "divisive social issues" are downplayed and basic economic issues, which unite people, are put in their stead. After the Muny Light election, Kucinich crowed: "What we've done is of great significance. We've united ethnics and black

BLACK DEMOCRATIC OFFICIALS ENDORSE REPUBLICAN FOR MAYOR

Arnold Pinkney

George Forbes

WHY ?

Who are the Black Elected Democratic Officials?

This is the same City Council clique that followed George Forbes blindly in opposing every-thing Mayor Kucinich tried to do. Add a few political opportunists like Arnold Pinkney (former School Board President) and W. O. Walker (publisher of the Call & Post) and they call it the Black Elected Democratic Officials.

WHY HAVE THE BLACK DEMOCRATS TURNED REPUBLICAN?

This is the $64 question! What do you think is going on here?

VOINOVICH DENIES EVEN MEETING WITH GEORGE FORBES. NO ONE KNOWS WHAT VOINOVICH PROMISED TO GET THIS ENDORSEMENT.

CITY COUNCIL CONTROL CAN BE CHANGED

Throughout the City voters are ready to dump the Councilmen who went down the line with Forbes and Russo against the Mayor. The Cleveland Press reported that "Cleveland Council is due for a house-cleaning in November."

City Council chooses one of its members as Council President. If enough Forbes Councilmen are defeated — Forbes can be replaced as President. That's why Forbes is now financing the campaigns of his supporters in Council, on the west side as well as the east side.

WHO'S PAYING THE BILLS? The same business interests who support Voinovich.

Vote Against Big Business Control of City Government.
Vote Against Racist Politics.

THE REAL DEMOCRATS SUPPORT KUCINICH

The top Democrats from Cleveland in Ohio politics are Secretary of State, Anthony Celebrezze, and the recent Democratic candidate for Governor, Dick Celeste. Both Celebrezze and Celeste endorsed Dennis Kucinich for re-election.

Celeste, who is now Director of the Peace Corps urged the re-election of Mayor Kucinich because "HE STOOD UP FOR ALL CLEVELANDERS."

FOR MAYOR . . . Re-Elect:

| X | DENNIS J. KUCINICH |

DEMOCRAT

Blanche Nofel, Secretary, 10605 Bernard

ILLUSTRATION 2. Leaflet Distributed by Kucinich Campaign in White Neighbor-hoods

people on economic issues. No one in Cleveland or in the country has been able to do that and that's really the coalition of the future." The promise of racial harmony in February, however, gave way to the reality of racial manipulation in November. Why?

Destabilization

After seeing the movie, "The Battle of Chile," Kucinich remarked that "some of the dynamics in the fall of Chile have their parallels in the current situation in Cleveland. Cleveland Trust and CEI have made a concerted effort to use their economic power to destabilize the municipal government."[5] The basic idea of destabilization as illustrated in Chile is that the ruling elite and its international allies, while unable to oust Allende themselves, were able to withdraw enough support from the government, through actions such as an international economic boycott and support for a disruptive truckers' strike, to make it impossible for Allende to govern. The ensuing social conflict and chaos prompted a third party, the military, to step in to stabilize the situation.[6] The analogy to Cleveland is not farfetched. Kucinich emphasized the economic pressures placed on his administration. Equally important, however, were the paralyzing political conflicts that engulfed his administration, conflicts heightened greatly by his own confrontational style. The political paralysis that seized Kucinich demonstrated the limits of populist, Alinsky-style politics, with its infatuation for political independence, disdain for political parties, and reliance on personal confrontations.

Default, as we saw, was a serious blow to the administration. Unable to borrow money, the Kucinich administration was forced to rely on a depleted tax base to make ends meet. Default was essentially an economic boycott of the city for political reasons. In the general area of investment, however, there was no organized boycott. While investment proceeded pretty much as before (only with a fortuitous boom in downtown construction), business was able to exercise political discretion over a key variable: "business confidence"—the perceptions of the average voter of the causes of investment and disinvestment. By manipulating the business confidence factor, business leaders created the impression that Kucinich was an obstacle to all forms of investment. It was as if Cleveland was under economic seige, a seige that would not be lifted as long as Kucinich was mayor.

The seige atmosphere was heightened by the political conflict sought by the Kucinich administration. Kucinich based his electoral appeal on confrontation with established powers. Once in office, he did not change. As mayor, Kucinich found himself the object of intense pressure by clamoring interest groups—with their demands far exceeding the resources of city government. What is more, Kucinich's independent political organization severely hampered his ability to discipline these interests. His antiparty, office specific coalition gave him little support in City Council or the other levels of government. His political organization made an end run around existing interest groups and appealed directly to the alienated voter. Not surprisingly, Kucinich had little clout in the established interest groups—certainly not in the banks and corporations, but also not in the political parties, neighborhood groups, municipal unions, or social agencies that played crucial roles in Cleveland politics. Coming into office with few political debts, Kucinich also had few political credits that he could cash in to moderate demands. Having seized the top office in an electoral coup, Kucinich lacked the broad power to govern effectively. Like Gulliver in *Gulliver's Travels*, the Kucinich administration became immobilized by thousands of tiny ropes representing the aroused interests of Cleveland politics.

We have already seen how Kucinich became enmeshed in clashes with City Council and the neighborhood groups over the block grant. Relations with the police were equally hostile. The incoming Kucinich administration faced the ticklish task of negotiating the first contract with a new police union anxious to prove itself, the Cleveland Police Patrolmen's Association (CPPA). In December 1977, dissatisfied with progress in the negotiations, the CPPA organized a sudden outbreak of the "blue flu." About 90 percent of police officers stayed home. (William McNea, CPPA President, was close to Forbes and the action may have been designed to embarrass the administration.) "Mayor calls them 'crybabies'," read newspaper headlines that afternoon. Two days later, after the City Council leaders promised a better wage and benefit package, the wildcat strike ended. While much-feared looting and rioting never occurred, the whole incident shook confidence, at the outset, in Kucinich's ability to govern.

Just before the blue flu epidemic, Kucinich had appointed Richard Hongisto, San Francisco's liberal, pro-gay sheriff, as Cleveland's new Chief of Police. Hongisto turned out to be a surprisingly popular police chief, developing strong support in Cleveland's conservative, largely ethnic, police force. By singlehandedly capturing criminals and rescuing motorists from snowbanks, Hongisto also became a media darling. This probably was the main reason that Kucinich decided to fire him, a decision apparently made on the spur of the moment in a bizarre live press conference. Hongisto had charged the administration with six cases of "unethical conduct." None of the charges was serious enough to warrant a legal investigation, but Kucinich's reputation as a nonpolitical politician, a populist reformer, was seriously damaged. (The Hongisto firing touched off the recall campaign.)

This was not the end of Kucinich's problems with the police. In response to high crime in public housing projects, Kucinich set up special police patrols in summer 1978. Police refused to obey the order to patrol the projects singly and on foot, calling the assignment "too dangerous." When the administration suspended thirteen officers who disobeyed the order, the CPPA voted unanimously to go on strike, the first official police strike in the city's history. That night, Kucinich drove around trying to persuade officers to return to work; he was greeted by loud boos, derisive laughter, and obscene gestures. Once again, the city was threatened with disorder. The strike ended nineteen hours later when a judge reinstated the thirteen men, pending arbitration, and the administration agreed to two-officer patrols. Coming just before the recall election, however, the police strike created further doubt in the minds of many voters about Kucinich's ability to govern.

Conflict during the Kucinich administration came from political weakness, not political strength. Time and again Kucinich was compared to a dictator; Councilman William Sullivan even compared him to Adolf Hitler. The example of the police, however, illustrates how far this was from the truth. Far from being an all-powerful dictator, Kucinich lacked the power to carry out even basic governmental functions, such as borrowing money or ordering the police on patrols. Confrontation requires a standoff. If Kucinich had possessed effective political power, there would have been no standoff. The source of Kucinich's appeal, his vaunted political independence, was at the same time the cause of his political weakness.

As damaging as these conflicts were, the mass media blew them all out of proportion, creating the impression that city government was on the brink of anarchy and collapse. Kucinich was no newcomer to this process. He had skillfully used the media to build his own political following. Adroitly attacking the Stokes and Perk administrations,

Kucinich helped to drain power from both while gaining exposure as a courageous critic. Now the tables were turned. Kucinich should have known what would happen. In fact, he was something of an expert on the subject, having written his Master's thesis on the role played by newspaper reporters in escalating the crippling conflict between Carl Stokes and Council president James Stanton.[7] Kucinich showed how some reporters, far from neutrally reporting the news, actually fostered political conflict through exaggerations and speculations. Kucinich made the instructive point that inner city dailies thrive on political conflict while suburban weeklies tend to stress community consensus. Cleveland newspapers, however, have always expected mayors to act like "Growth Statesmen," standing above the fray, promoting civic projects "to make Cleveland great again." Kucinich refused to play the role of Growth Statesman and instead engaged in conflict with nearly every interest in city politics. The result was predictable.

By the end of Kucinich's term, the electorate, which had been kept in a constant state of political excitation for two years, was exhausted. The seige atmosphere created the impression that city government was paralyzed, that nothing would move—loans, investment, or even City Council legislation—until Kucinich was removed as mayor. By November 1979, the destabilization process had reached the point that many voters agreed with an anonymous bumper sticker that began appearing around town: "Anybody But Kucinich."

A Second Recall

The Kucinich administration was also debilitated by the frequency with which it was forced to go to the voters for support, four times in two years: election, recall, Muny Light/income tax referendum, and re-election. Of the four, the recall election was the most difficult. The two year mayoral term was short enough but, with the recall, Kucinich's first term essentially lasted only nine months. All policy initiatives were put in abeyance by the recall: no one wanted to bargain with what might be a lame duck administration. Supported by the Democratic party, the Republican party, the AFL-CIO, the Teamsters, twenty-four of thirty-three council members, most other elected officials, and both newspapers, the recall was especially difficult for Kucinich to campaign against. Recall gave the angry alienated voter the chance to throw out an incumbent politician without having to embrace a positive alternative. By its very nature, recall made Kucinich the issue and turned the political distrust, which Kucinich effectively mobilized for his candidacy in the past, against himself. Nevertheless, Kucinich went on the offensive, trying to make the issue whether voters wanted George Forbes to be mayor and smearing the recall organization as a tool of party bosses and the corporate elite. While Kucinich survived the recall, the campaign drained the administration of energy. And the razor-thin margin (236 votes) hardly represented a mandate for populist policy initiatives.

Weissman called the 1979 mayoral election "a second recall."[8] There is a great deal of truth to this. The destabilization process had proceeded to the point that, for many voters, the only issue was Dennis Kucinich. Kucinich's opponent, Republican George Voinovich, played skillfully into this atmosphere by projecting a low key, nonpartisan image. As much as Kucinich tried to go on the offensive, he was continually forced back on defense.

Early in the campaign Kucinich attacked, jumping on a Voinovich quote ("I like fat cats") that had appeared in the *New York Times*. Voinovich meant, of course, that the wealthy had to be attracted back into the city for the jobs and investment they controlled. Kucinich took it as evidence of corruption, a chance to hone his longstanding attack on growth politics: that it benefited only a small elite at the expense of the vast majority of city residents. Under the title "Who Owns Voinovich?", Kucinich produced a detailed four page leaflet, distributed citywide, that listed over 400 different contributors to Voinovich campaigns from the banks, utilities, real estate industry, law firms, and industrial corporations (see Illustration 3). The theme was that Voinovich would be beholden to these interests, not to the voters.

On the growth politics issue, however, many voters had begun to suspect that maybe Voinovich was right. Few inner city voters liked Fat Cats, but many believed the city needed them. No one knew for sure, but there was evidence that because of Kucinich the Fat Cats were staying away. There was plenty of evidence that default was directed against Kucinich; frequent statements in the media about a lack of "business confidence" caused people to believe that the entire economy was hurting because of Kucinich. While many voters continued to respect what they saw as Kucinich's courageous stands against the big banks and corporations, ultimately they came to believe that it was precisely those stands that were hurting the city.

ILLUSTRATION 3. Kucinich Campaign Leaflet Attacking Voinovich

Voinovich made it easier for traditionally Democratic ethnic voters to support his candidacy by retreating on the populist economic issues that led to the ouster of fellow Republican Ralph Perk. Symbolically, Voinovich began his campaign standing outside Muny Light, pledging to defend it.[9] Stressing delivery of better services to the neighborhoods throughout his campaign, Voinovich rejected tax abatement, stating that downtown would flourish without it.

The issue that Voinovich did raise against Kucinich was ending the chaos and confrontation at City Hall, which, he claimed, was holding back civic progress. Voinovich accused Kucinich of using the powers of government for his own partisan advantage. Tapping into a long tradition of good government reform, Voinovich proposed to replace partisan politics with evenhanded administration. "I look at the city of Cleveland as a public administration challenge," said Voinovich.[10] Promising to replace politics with administration helped Voinovich downplay his Republican affiliation in a heavily Democratic town. "There really is no Republican way to clean the streets or a Democratic way to run a government," Voinovich asserted. "When you get down to it, there is just a right way and a wrong way . . . and I'd like to run it the right way."[11] Voinovich ran not under the banner of the Republican party but under the banner of Order and Efficiency. Promising "to make Cleveland great again," Voinovich focused on unifying themes with the campaign slogan, "Together we can do it."

Voinovich's low key campaign, downplaying distributive issues while emphasizing progress and efficiency, made it difficult for Kucinich to go on the attack. Like a boxer who never comes out of his crouch, Voinovich was not an easy target to hit. Kucinich came out swinging, anyway, hoping to draw his opponent into the open with attacks on his integrity as a tool of big business. Midway through the campaign, however, a tragic accident occurred that forced Kucinich to abandon this strategy: Voinovich's young daughter, Molly, was killed by a hit-and-run driver. Personal attacks on Voinovich now would only create sympathy votes. It seemed as if everything was conspiring to make Kucinich the issue; the administration would have to defend its record.

Given the economic theory of urban populism, this would seem a natural thing to do. Kucinich put the matter succinctly at the end of his major speech on urban populism: "Can a city government, based on the support of the poor and working people, increase services, improve the standard of living and the quality of life . . . without the support of big business and even with active opposition?"[12] Kucinich answered, yes. Looking back, it is possible to see if he was right.

Could Kucinich Have Won?

Elections foster the illusion of change. All the hype and hoopla belies the limited nature of the contest. After all, with very few exceptions, people vote on who will occupy the structure, not on the structures themselves. Kucinich, with his elite-instrumentalist understanding of the local state, played into this illusion. Picturing previous mayors as instruments of big business in league with party bosses, Kucinich implied that if people elected their own mayor—that is, himself—local government could be turned around and the benefits would start flowing toward ordinary working people. Perhaps the overriding theme of Kucinich's career was: one man *can* make a difference.

This study has focused on the structures of political economy that limit the ability of local governments to redistribute income. Suburbanization is one of the most important. Suburban governments were able to erect barriers in Cleveland to keep the poor in the city while the middle class continued to pour out, depleting the city's economy and tax base. There was nothing Kucinich could do about this. And federal policies continued to favor the suburban exodus as well the movement of capital to the Sunbelt and overseas. There was nothing Kucinich could do about this. Finally, there was nothing Kucinich could do about the basic transformation to a service oriented economy that was rendering much of Cleveland's industrial base obsolete.

But what about those factors that the mayor of Cleveland could control? Kucinich promised that by ending corruption in city government and stopping the rip offs of growth politics that diverted resources from the neighborhoods to downtown, he could improve the quality of life for inner city residents. On the one hand, Kucinich's refusal to play growth politics cost the city dearly, as the banks, anxious to get rid of Kucinich, pushed the city into default. Moreover, Kucinich was forced to seek a 50 percent increase in the income tax to pay back the banks. On the plus side, he managed to save Muny Light (and the antitrust suit) and to end tax abatement. It is hard to put a dollar value on these but the benefits were substantial; now, for example, the school system and city government will benefit from millions of dollars of property taxes from the unabated downtown construction boom during the Kucinich years.

The fact was, however, there were not many local government expenditures directed to downtown that could be diverted to the neighborhoods.

The big victories of the Kucinich administration, Muny Light and tax abatement, were negative ones, stopping something—achievements well suited to the executive centered, office specific coalition that Kucinich led into power. Forming a positive program was a different matter. The administration claimed to have made substantial savings by eliminating padded contracts, corrupt employees, and mismanagement. The city payroll was cut 14 percent without a cut in services, they claimed. While government was leaner, there was no perceptible improvement in services. It seemed that illegal corruption and outright incompetence were only a small part of the problem. And the zeal of the administration for confrontation politics, as we saw in the case of community development and housing, sometimes resulted in administrative disruption and inefficiency. Kucinich did not have an innovative program for economic democracy, a program for expanding the resources of government or for meeting the economic crisis of the city. Even if he had possessed such a program, it is doubtful whether it could have been implemented. When Kucinich was elected mayor, he did not take his place at the head of a rational bureaucracy that could easily be turned this way or that to serve the people. Cleveland's executive branch was, in pluralist fashion, riven by political interests—in council, in the unions, in social agencies—interests that effectively tied down the policies of various sections of the bureaucracy. Kucinich could not change this; as a result, city government, contrary to press reports, rolled along pretty much as before.

On the whole, it is very difficult to say whether the city's poor and working people were better off or worse off during the two years that Kucinich was in office, compared to previous years. Certainly, however, it is safe to say that there was no substantial improvement in their basic services, standard of living, or quality of life. Events of the campaign, nonetheless, forced Kucinich to defend his record, which he did with a four page leaflet entitled, "The 'Hidden Record' of Mayor Kucinich." Conditioned by months of crisis headlines, however, voters were not about to have their perceptions reversed by a partisan political pamphlet. Kucinich had not absorbed his voters into a party or any kind of face-to-face network that could counter the destabilizing effects of the media. Appealing to their anger and alienation, Kucinich had not educated his supporters into any positive political commitments; they were ready to believe the worst about government. The positive approach would not work.

Conclusion: Shifting Electoral Support

With the economic theory of urban populism having proved wrong, at least in the short run, and lacking a grassroots organization to fall back on, Kucinich and Weissman turned to the only lever available in the last stages of the campaign to pull out the election: race. They saw that Kucinich's middle class white ethnic support was swiftly being eroded by Voinovich, who appealed to their middle class aspirations and desire for stability. Kucinich and Weissman decided to attempt a drastic shift in their electoral coalition, a daring move that only as nimble a politician as Kucinich would attempt. In order to win, they would appeal strongly to the black electorate while trying to hang on to as much of their white support as possible. Kucinich would need to go from 35 percent of the black vote in 1977 (31 percent at the recall) to about 60 percent. Meanwhile, his white support could slip from 60 percent, in 1977, to less than a majority. Kucinich would be transformed from a candidate basically representing white ethnics to a candidate unifying lower income blacks and whites.

Ironically, the goal—a coalition of black and whites around a populist candidate—was pursued by playing on racial fears and divisions. The leaflets passed out on the West Side, which played on racial fears by smearing Voinovich as the "black candidate," were an attempt at a holding action among white voters. Meanwhile, Kucinich put most of his energies into the black community. Only in a city like Cleveland, where the Cuyahoga River marked a dividing line between two almost separate societies, could such a strategy ever hope to succeed. Of course, communication across the river did exist. Kucinich lost support on the white West side when they found out he was wooing the black electorate; and his black support suffered when the word got to the East Side that Kucinich was race baiting in the white community.

In the final election, Kucinich lost by a substantial margin, 56 to 44 percent. As Table 6 shows, the racial strategy was partially successful.[13] Kucinich increased his vote significantly in the black community (with the crucial help of Carl Stokes, by the way). But Kucinich's white support fell too precipitously to salvage a victory. Ironically, given Kucinich's racial manipulations, the 1979 mayoral election was one of the least racially polarized in recent Cleveland history: each candidate got about the same percentage of the white and black vote.

TABLE 6.
Changing Racial Support for Kucinich, 1977–1979*

Kucinich Supporters	12 Black Wards	19 White Wards
1977 General Election	35.2	60.0
1978 Recall Election	31.1	57.3
1979 General Election	44.5	43.3

Source: Cleveland City Planning Commission, *1970 Census Population and Housing Data by Wards and Neighborhoods* (Cleveland: City Planning Commission, June 1972); Cuyahoga County Board of Elections records.
*percentage

A second question concerning the 1979 election is whether Kucinich did gain the support of lower income voters. Under the impact of the economic issues fought out during Kucinich's term, there was a kind of sorting out of his support along class lines.[14] Basically, Kucinich held his support in the poorer inner city wards but lost big in the middle class wards (see Table 7). Since turnout in the middle class wards was 150 percent higher than in the lower income wards, defeat was unavoidable.[15]

More significant than the class composition of the vote, however, was the shifting character of Kucinich's electoral coalition. One technique used to examine electoral coalitions is auto-correlation, the correlation between support by geographical area for a candidate, and support at a previous election for that same candidate (or a different candidate). High correlations indicate coalitional stability; low correlations indicate a realignment of groups behind the candidate.[16] The very high correlation (+.926) in Table 8 between support for Kucinich in 1977 and support for Perk in 1975 indicates that Kucinich put together substantially the same coalition that Perk had formed, centering on the

TABLE 7.
Changing Class Composition of Kucinich Voters, 1977–1979*

Kucinich Supporters	10 Middle Income Wards	10 Lower Income Wards
1977 General Election	56.4	49.9
1978 Recall Election	53.5	52.9
1979 General Election	39.0	48.2

Source: Cleveland City Planning Commission, *1970 Census Population and Housing Data by Wards and Neighborhoods* (Cleveland: City Planning Commission, June 1972); Cuyahoga County Board of Elections records.
*percentage

TABLE 8.
Changing Composition of Kucinich Electoral Support, 1975–1977*

Kucinich Supporters	For Perk—1975 General Election	For Kucinich—1977 General Election	For Kucinich—1978 Recall Election
1977 General Election	.926	—	—
1978 Recall Election	.884	.962	—
1979 General Election	−.033	.197	.354

Source: Cuyahoga County Board of Elections records
*coefficient of correlation

white ethnics, who were for the most part conservative small home-owners. Kucinich's coalition remained fairly stable through the recall. But the most interesting figures in table 8 are the extremely low correlations between Kucinich's support in 1979 and earlier elections. Normally, the correlation between one election and the next, for the same politician, is very high. These extraordinarily low correlations indicate a radically shifting electoral base. Rather than a fundamental realignment of the electorate, however, what was going on was simply the changing, and highly personal, appeal of a populist politician. Such shifting sands were poor ground on which to build a radical new structure like urban populism.

10

Growth Politics and the Space for Change

Nothing turns out to be so oppressive and unjust as a feeble government.

Edmund Burke,
Reflections on the French
Revolution *(1790)*

The economic situation in America's central cities today is highly contradictory. On the one hand, many observers are trumpeting an urban renaissance based on renewed private sector interest in central business districts and bordering gentrified neighborhoods.[1] On the other hand, there is continuing evidence that the urban crisis has not gone away—in fact, that it is getting worse.[2] The suburbanization of the middle class is still much stronger than gentrification. And manufacturing jobs continue to disappear faster in many cities than they can be replaced by white collar jobs. Especially troubling is the acute mismatch between the types of jobs that are locating in central cities, often highly skilled professional jobs, and the job skills of inner city residents, especially minorities.

The political situation in central cities is also contradictory. Many mayors, like Koch of New York, are succeeding by cutting social expenditures and handing out deep subsidies for white collar corporate expansion, arguing that the benefits will eventually trickle down to benefit everybody. Even in cities with dynamic white collar economies, like New York, Boston, and Chicago, however, populist issues keep rising to the surface. In New York City, the cries of those left behind by growth can now be heard above the paeans to Manhattan's renaissance. The contrast between a gentrified Manhattan and the outer boroughs is simply astonishing. Between 1979 and 1981, commercial construction, almost all of it in Manhattan, totaled $6 billion—$850 for every man, woman, and child in the city. Yet, at the same time, in large areas of Brooklyn and the Bronx, housing was being abandoned at a rapid rate, with city government forced to take possession of thousands of tax delinquent properties every year. In these areas, disinvestment feeds unemployment, crime, and social decay. The warm glow of Manhattan's renaissance has not reached all New Yorkers. Not surprisingly, a black political rebellion is brewing against Koch and the regular Democratic organization. Meanwhile, Koch has begun to pull back on some of his conservative growth policies, severely curtailing tax abatement in Manhattan's overheated real estate market and even appointing a commission to look into the possibility of requiring developers to contribute to a housing construction and rehab fund.

The same thing has happened in Boston, another seeming winner in the growth competition. Notwithstanding phenomenal growth in the downtown service sector and its spin-offs, including celebrated Faneuil Hall and Quincy Market, Boston has one of the highest poverty rates in the nation and is in the midst of a severe fiscal crisis. In the 1983 mayoral election, the candidate backed by downtown businessmen with a slick media campaign was defeated in the primary. The two finalists ran on populist platforms that included full rent control, a halt to all condominium conversions, and neighborhood empowerment. The eventual winner, "Plain" Ray Flynn, advocated, like Kucinich, avoiding divisive social issues and uniting inner city residents around economic issues. Harold Washington's victory in Chicago, while primarily the result of a black political resurgence, was also made possible by strong support from neighborhood organizations who responded to Washington's platform calling for neighborhood economic development.[3]

The contradictory situation in American cities represents both a danger and an opportunity. The danger is that extreme uneven development will generate a tale of two cities: white versus black, skilled versus unskilled, downtown versus neighborhoods. The opportunity is that the renewed attractiveness of central cities as generators of wealth and culture will make it possible to address the needs of the dispossessed and repair the social fabric of the city. In this chapter, I argue that cities have the economic space to begin to spread the benefits of the down-town growth machine. This requires, however, political leadership that can engage in long term planning and hard bargaining with investors in the interest of inner city residents. The example of Cleveland shows, I believe, that structural barriers stand in the way of such reforms. Fortunately, these structural barriers, both economic and political, are not rooted in the nature of a mobile market society, but were created by deliberate policies. They can be changed.

Elitism in One City: The Limits of a Case Study

A neat separation between economic and political decision making, as predicted by pluralist and market theories of urban politics, is not what we have found in this case study of Cleveland, Ohio. Instead, we have encountered a curious admixture of economics and politics. Power and politics often intervened in economic decision making to distort the free market exchanges between cities and their economic environs. And economic elites sometimes intervened in political deci-sion making on the basis of their technical expertise in promoting growth. Indeed, in Cleveland itself, the boundary between economic and political decision making was a constant source of controversy. This mixture of economics and politics is what I call growth politics.

Over the years, Cleveland has offered a rich variety of growth politics:

1. In the late nineteenth century, Cleveland city government kept taxes (and services) to a bare minimum, based on the mistaken argument of business elites that higher taxes would kill the industrial boom.

2. During the same period, according to Mayor Tom John-son, the business elite used its control over land and municipal franchises to monopolize the positive externali-ties of urban growth, with part of the returns being used as boodle to corrupt the political process.

3. Similarly, in the twentieth century, Cleveland suburbs

evolved ways of capturing the positive externalities of urban growth while keeping the negative externalities bottled up in the central city.

4. In the 1950s and 1960s, the federal urban renewal program was twisted to benefit corporate and commercial interests, wreaking havoc on neighborhoods, minorities, and private housing.

5. In the 1960s and 1970s, Cleveland's private utility used its monopoly over the production of electricity in an effort to force the city's public utility out of business and gain a monopoly over the sale of electricity.

6. In the mid-1970s, Cleveland city government gave large tax abatements to downtown developers, even though, the evidence now shows, they had little or no effect on new investment.

7. During the same period, corporate elites publicly blamed the Kucinich administration for disinvestment that would have occurred no matter who was mayor.

8. In December 1978, Cleveland banks precipitated the city's default for political reasons: to facilitate the sale of the public utility and help defeat a radical populist mayor.

Each of the above involves a clear example of the intrusion of power or politics into the governmental marketplace. The list could be extended.

While contradicting pluralism and market theory, growth politics seems to confirm elite-stratification theory of community power. The examples of growth politics above show various elites using their control over investment, or the business climate, to manipulate the political process for their own benefit. Until recently, because of the presumed separation of economics and politics, the investment context was overlooked by students of community power. Partly as a result, Robert Dahl was able to conclude that New Haven "is an example of a democratic system, warts and all."[4] The existence of growth politics does not just add another wart to the kindly visage of pluralist democracy. Growth politics gives those who control mobile wealth an instrument of power unaccounted for in pluralist or market theories of urban politics. Fundamentally, growth politics involves the corruption of the democratic process by wealth.

But how far can the results in one city, Cleveland, be extended to other cities? Since Cleveland is one of the most distressed inner cities in the country, the implications may be limited. According to three well known urban scholars, however, Cleveland is not unique. "Cleveland is unusual only in degree; in many ways, it is typical of large, older urban areas throughout the Northeast and Midwest."[5] The results in Cleveland may be representative of the approximately fifteen cities that fit in this class. Even here, though, caution should be exercised since every city has a different political structure and a different political culture. Perhaps the only sure implication of this case study is that future community power studies, if they are to claim completeness, must critically examine the investment context.

There is one way, however, that the implications of this case study can be systematically analyzed. Traditionally, elite theory, with its instrumental theory of the state, has focused on the political organization and intentions of elites—often ignoring the structural conditions that enabled the elite to exercise power in the first place. Growth politics, I argue, is preeminently an institutional phenomenon, rooted in the structures of political economy; questions of personal relations or individual intention are largely peripheral. Structures in the economic and political system generate growth politics, largely without regard to who occupies those structures. Moreover, by identifying the structures or conditions that underlie growth politics, we can see to what extent other cities share these conditions and, therefore, to what extent the conclusions about growth politics in Cleveland apply to other cities.

The Meaning of Default

Perhaps the most striking finding of this study is that Cleveland's default was political. Sufficient evidence was presented in Chapter 7 to prove, beyond a reasonable doubt, that Cleveland bankers had political intentions (to force the sale of Muny Light and damage Kucinich politically) and that a *quid pro quo* to that effect (sell Muny or default) was communicated to the city.

Cleveland's default could be seen as a simple act of corruption, in which bankers attempted to use their control over municipal credit to bribe an elected official to sell a public asset for their private benefit. Short of pursuing the legal implications, the question of individual blame framed the basic approach taken by a United States congressional hearing and earlier congressional staff study of Cleveland's default.[6] Kucinich also took this approach to the affair, as evidenced by his frequent attacks on the bankers, and especially Brock Weir, as power hungry and corrupt individuals.

What makes Cleveland's default so intriguing, however, is that it took place completely outside the normal context of political corruption. Far from being carried out by shady characters behind closed doors, default was acted out in full public view by leaders of the most respected institutions in the city; it involved an attempt to bribe an entire city, not just one individual; and in this case, institutions on both sides stood to benefit more than individuals. Furthermore, the motivations of the bankers were completely understandable. After all, before default, Kucinich had kicked the bankers around rhetorically for failing to invest in the city; predictably, the bankers wanted to kick back. If an instrument of power lies close at hand to achieve a desired end, it is only human to use it. The bankers did. The central question becomes, then, what conditions enabled a handful of bankers to exercise this extraordinary political power? How did the loaded gun get on the table?

In Chapter 7 were listed three conditions necessary before private lenders can exert monopoly power over a city government: first, the city in question has to be shut out of the national bond market and forced to depend on local banks; second, the local banks have to possess extraordinary unity of political purpose and action; and, third, the bargaining relationship between the city and the banks has to be highly unequal. At this point, a fourth requirement could be added: there must be city leadership that is willing to resist the demands of the banks. My analysis of the default indicates that if Mayor Kucinich had refrained from attacking the banks and had been willing to sell the public utility, default would never have occurred. But Kucinich's entire career was based on confrontation politics. The die was cast.

As we look at the four conditions necessary for a local financial elite to exercise power through the political allocation of credit, it becomes clear that only rarely in American politics does a city possess all four. Direct political allocation of municipal credit is a rare phenomenon in American politics. But if this example of power over the governmental marketplace cannot be immediately generalized to other cities, nevertheless, I believe, it has important implications.

Of the four conditions necessary for the exercise of monopoly power in the municipal credit market, all of them, apart from the exceptional unity of the local banking establishment, resulted directly from Cleveland's severe economic and fiscal crisis. (This includes the fourth condition—the election of an angry populist mayor willing, even eager, to resist the demands of the banks). The causes of Cleveland's growth crisis are many and complex, but this much can be said: the crisis was not caused by spendthrift mayors or malevolent capitalists. Cleveland's fiscal crisis, like that facing many American cities, is rooted in the structure of modern political economy, including factors such as the labor intensity of local government services, the formation of autonomous suburbs, the transition of the economy from manufacturing to services, and, especially, the uneven development of American capitalism.[7]

This study of Cleveland's default indicates that structurally induced urban fiscal stress has profound (if largely unexamined) *political* as well as economic and service implications. Investors, for the most part, do not exercise political discretion in their decisions to disinvest cities like Cleveland; they are simply seeking the higher profits available elsewhere. In the long run, however, their structurally based decisions have a profound political impact, creating the preconditions, both subjective and objective, for the instrumental domination of local politics by a financial elite. Peterson's market politics—the competition between cities for mobile wealth—generates nonmarket politics, or political control by investors. Indeed, the market competition between cities is not free and equal; cumulative inequalities in the governmental marketplace generate a veritable class stratification of places.[8] The result is a kind of dialectic between structure and agency: a pluralist political system of competing interests is transformed, by a series of unintended but structurally induced market decisions, into a political system where a financial elite can instrumentally dominate.

Ironically, among Western liberal democracies, it is in the United States, where local governments have probably the greatest formal powers, that the structures of political economy most seriously threaten local political autonomy. The United States, for instance, unlike most Western European countries, lacks any coherent policy to counteract the uneven geographical development of modern capitalism.[9] In fact, as we saw in Chapter 1, many policies of the federal government actually worsen uneven development. Furthermore, unique among advanced capitalist countries, the United States leaves local governments almost totally dependent on wealthy private lenders for their credit needs.[10] In Western Europe, most central governments lend money directly to local governments; in many countries, municipalities band together to establish lending cooperatives; and almost every major West German city government controls its own municipal savings bank from which it can borrow.[11]

Without reform, capitalism may be incompatible, if not with democracy generally, at least with local democracy in distressed cities. In the United States there are indications that over the long run urban fiscal stress will intensify.[12] If this happens, Cleveland's default will cease to be unique and the proud American tradition of local democracy could give way, in our most distressed cities, to the embarrassment of municipal banana republics.

Downtown Development: Symbol and Substance

Default is a clear example of political discretion exercised by investors. Fortunately, the conditions necessary for the exercise of this kind of monopoly power do not exist in most markets. Consider downtown development. The study of tax abatement in Chapter 6 demonstrated that investors in this market do not have the ability to pull a "capital strike," as do municipal lenders. After Kucinich killed tax abatement, in fact, downtown enjoyed a building boom. The market for downtown development was not a political cartel; it was highly competitive, with many investors poised to take advantage of profitable opportunities in office development. Where in default investors could exercise political discretion, in taxation the city could exercise political discretion, rejecting tax abatement without fear of economic reprisal.

Tax abatement, when enacted, represents the interests of small elites. While providing windfall profits to downtown developers, tax abatement provides few, if any, benefits to the city as a whole. If tax abatement is such an ineffective tool for economic development, why do so many cities pursue it? Obviously, it is not for economic reasons but for political reasons. The political pressures behind conservative market approaches to urban development are worth exploring in detail.

The economic crisis of central cities, of course, results primarily from decisions made by the private sector. Nevertheless, citizens, especially those who suffer the most economically, quite naturally turn to local government as the unit of government most open to their influence and responsive to their needs. By themselves, however, there is little local governments can do; they simply lack the necessary resources. Especially since the cutbacks in federal funding, it has become clear that cities can make progress on their problems only by cooperating with the private sector. "Public/private partnerships," they are called. The goal is to use limited public sector resources to leverage additional private investment.

The leveraging strategy, however, is fraught with contradictions and trade-offs that are as immutable as the laws of physics. Using an ordinary lever, it is possible to move objects of great weight but only over short distances: speed and distance are traded for power. The same is true of leveraging private investment. The central trade-off is between leveraging and targeting. It is possible to leverage large amounts of private investment, but normally the investment will benefit the least needy. If cities target the benefits of public-private partnerships to an area in great need, say inner city housing that has experienced massive disinvestment, the leverage ratio will naturally suffer. In Chapter 6, we saw that Cleveland's CASH program, targeted to low and moderate income housing, reported a leverage ratio of only .23 to 1 (23 cents of private money for every dollar of public money). On the other hand, tax abatement, which was focused on some of the choicest real estate in downtown Cleveland, claimed impressive leveraging on the order of 10 to 1.[13]

What do you do if you are a local politician in a distressed city? What many do is concentrate resources on programs that have a high leverage ratio, so that at least they can claim to be making a significant dent in the problem. In even the poorest cities there is expansion in the downtown service sector; to achieve high leveraging, resources must be concentrated there. Ultimately, the rationale is a variation on the trickle down theory: the benefits of downtown development will radiate out to the neighborhoods, with new jobs and tax revenues eventually benefiting the whole city.

The pursuit of high leveraging, however, has a decisive drawback rarely noted by downtown boosters: the higher the leverage ratio, other things being equal, the greater the likelihood that the leveraging is spurious. In other words, the smaller the public subsidy in relation to the private investment, the greater the likelihood that the subsidy was not actually the reason for the new investment. This was precisely the conclusion I drew in regard to tax abatement in Chapter 6: local property taxes are simply not a big enough factor in overall business costs to influence investment location decisions.

Nevertheless, while the economic pressures to support tax abatement are weak, the political pressures are strong. One of the lessons of growth politics that emerges from this study is that although capitalists rarely exercise political discretion over where they invest, they do exercise discretion over something that is just as important politically: how the public *perceives* private investment decisions. Their explanations of the causes of investment and disinvestment can be highly political. Kucinich, of course, killed tax abatement, and although the city was not hurt economically by this, Kucinich was hurt politically. Each time a major corporation moved out, as corporations had been doing for decades, the move was blamed on the political business climate. Kucinich was blamed for disinvestment that would have occurred no matter who was mayor. Unsure of the truth, voters gradually began to doubt that Cleveland could afford to keep a radical populist as mayor.

On the other hand, if Kucinich had supported tax abatement during the downtown building boom of his two years in office, he undoubtedly would have been hailed by the media as a growth statesman of great vision. Investors would have claimed (as, legally, they must) that the developments would not have happened without the abatements. Tax abatement enables politicians to take credit for positive investment trends without setting up a complex bureaucracy or engaging in sophisticated economic planning. And tax abatement requires almost no up front investment—economic development under the installment plan. Ultimately, however, tax abatement is nothing more than a form of symbolic reassurance, a modern rain dance.

While the pressures on local governments are great when they use their own money to subsidize the symbolic politics of downtown development, the pressures can be overwhelming when certain types of federal grants are involved. The urban renewal program, begun in 1949, is a case in point. The idea behind urban renewal was that, if the cost of large parcels of inner city land were heavily subsidized, real estate investors would be attracted back into the city. The federal government paid two-thirds of the subsidy, and local governments, one-third. In reality, however, local governments usually paid much less because they could load in routine expenditures and in-kind contributions. Given fixed subsidies—private developers usually paid only about 30 percent of the actual cost of land assembly and clearance—it is not surprising that developers pursued highly profitable office developments and not housing for the displaced residents. Also, given the strong trend toward office development in the central city, it is not surprising to see mounting evidence that many of these projects would have been built anyway (see Chapter 4). Since the program cost local governments little, they had little motivation to scrutinize individual projects—especially to consider whether the subsidy was necessary to make the project happen. In short, urban renewal grants skewed local decision making in the direction of conservative growth politics.

The distorting effect of federal grants did not stop with urban renewal.[14] The Urban Development Action Grant (UDAG) program, enacted in 1977 by the Carter administration, is an even more glaring example of writing conservative growth politics into the very structure of federal programs. While some of the more obnoxious aspects of urban renewal, like massive displacement of inner city residents, were avoided in the UDAG program, in some ways UDAGs bias local decision making more than urban renewal. Like urban renewal, UDAG grants are linked to the city's leveraging significant private investment. In the case of a UDAG, however, not only does the federal grant cost the city little (other than staff time) but, when the highly subsidized loan is repaid by the developer, the money usually goes to the local government to spend as it sees fit within the Community Development Block Grant regulations. Obviously, local governments have little motivation to scrutinize projects to be sure that the subsidy is necessary. Indeed, given that the likelihood of getting the grant increases with a higher leverage ratio, local governments have every motivation to tag along for the ride on massive private projects that would have occurred anyway. Following the law, federal regulations called for a "reasonable balance" between neighborhood, industrial, and commercial projects.[15] The Carter administration, however, required a minimum leverage ratio of 2.5 to 1, with average leveraging of 5 to 1.[16] Understandably, neighborhood projects, unable to achieve this kind of leveraging , were slighted.

The Community Development Block Grant (CDBG) program, examined in Chapter 8, does not have the same biasing effect on local decision making as the federal grants described above. The main reason is that cities are not required to leverage private investment to obtain the grant. In fact, the regulations mandating that block grant expenditures benefit primarily low and moderate income persons tend to push expenditures in a redistributive direction, cutting against the pressures of conservative growth politics. (Loose enforcement by the Reagan administration is changing this.) Of course, cities still feel pressure to leverage private investment, but at least under CDBG they have reason to examine the projects carefully because the subsidy comes out of the city's own money; it is not "funny money" like urban renewal and UDAGs. Under block grant, cities are free to target the expenditures to those who need them most, even if that means little or no leveraging.

Certainly this is a choice that should be available in a democratic system.

We may hope that, ten years from now, local economic development efforts, especially those suffering under the distortions of federal grants, will have the same reputation among economic development experts that urban renewal has today among city planners. The problem of the city is the problem of good jobs. For all their talk about jobs, programs such as urban renewal, tax abatement, and UDAG's are not serious efforts at economic development. They are subsidies for real estate deals—showy brick and mortar developments, complete with ribbon cutting ceremonies. Even if the subsidies actually were effective in causing new real estate developments (a dubious promise, as we have seen), their economic effects would still be limited. The job provision claims tend to be grossly inflated: there is little evidence that the subsidies are sufficient to attract new jobs into a city; many of the jobs in the new buildings have simply moved from older buildings in the city; and suburbanites, not inner city residents, get the best jobs.

Cities do not have to succumb to the logic of conservative growth policies, however. The economic space exists, I argue, for redistributive programs designed to ameliorate the worst aspects of uneven development in cities. My argument cuts against the suppositions of both the left (structuralist Marxism) and the right (neo-conservativism), which maintain that there is little room for redistributive policies at the local level within the "logic of capital accumulation" or the "imperatives of the free market" (take your pick). In these views, urban populism, with its redistributive focus, is inherently irrational or even damaging to the city as a whole. However, just as in certain circumstances such as default, investors can exert power over cities by exercising political discretion over investment, cities have the opportunity in other circumstances to exercise political power over investors.

The first lesson, according to Robert Mier, Chicago's new commissioner of economic development, "is the possibility of an authentic bargaining process taking place in which the public sector recognizes that it has something to give so that it shouldn't hesitate to get."[17] Central cities have a strong market position with regard to certain forms of economic activity; they need not approach the bargaining table with hat in hand. The reason for this is that not all economic activity is hypermobile. While there are deep centrifugal forces in the economy dispersing manufacturing and routine back office service sector jobs, at the same time there are deep centripetal forces pushing certain forms of service activity into central business districts. The dense interweaving of advanced business and professional services in downtowns creates a synergy that is more than the sum of its parts. Even though land rents are much higher than in the suburbs, firms want to locate downtown to capture part of that synergy. This economic activity is a natural resource that is relatively immobile and can be tapped by cities for redistributive efforts. Neighborhoods do not need to be locked into a zero sum game with downtown; they can benefit from downtown. While the economic resources available in this manner are insufficient to solve the economic problems of central cities, they can contribute to a solution—which is more than can be said for the largely symbolic policies of conservative growth politics.

The economic argument can be simply stated: if reductions in local property taxes will not leverage new service sector investment, as we saw in examining tax abatement, *ipso facto*, similar increases in taxes will not choke off investment. Of course, city governments cannot raise taxes to confiscatory levels without economic losses; there are limits. The point, though, is that there is room for political discretion. Since many of the services locating in downtown are essentially export services, paid for by the final consumers of the product, by raising taxes on this sector, cities will tend to shift the tax burden to consumers outside the city—much like severance taxes on coal and gas.

Besides economic arguments, there are also moral arguments for the public sharing in the wealth created by downtown development (beyond the usual argument that many commuters work in the city but do not pay taxes there). The logic is similar to that used by Tom Johnson in applying Henry George's theory to cities: that the unearned increment should be taxed away from the monopolists and used to benefit the public. Similarly, the positive externalities of concentrating advanced business and professional services in one central location generates an unearned increment. This is reflected in rising downtown land values, beyond the value of the buildings. Skyscrapers, in fact, are a function of high priced land. The entire synergistic environment is made possible, in large part, by the public sector, especially through the system of roads and mass transit. Since it is partly publicly created, part of this value should go back to the public sector, where it could be used to reduce some of the tremendous inequalities in urban development.

The problem, of course, is how to tax this sector more heavily than other sectors despite constitutional strictures against unequal taxation.[18] One traditional solution is a city income tax, which, because many suburbanites work in the city, tends to fall more on suburban commuters. Using a slightly different approach, Chicago enacted a 1 percent tax on services in 1981, which Mayor Byrne called a "growth tax." Boston is trying to enact a parking tax. In another wrinkle on the same theme, the New York legislature in 1981 passed a 10 percent capital gains tax on real estate transactions in New York City above $1 million. The proceeds went to the city's transit system, with the rationale that mass transit, in part, made possible these inflated real estate values. Deliberately hindering its implementation, Mayor Koch eventually succeeded in getting the tax repealed. In 1983, however, Governor Cuomo inserted a similar tax into the state budget.

Taxation is not the only means of spreading the wealth. Since 1981, San Francisco has required that all office developments over 50,000 square feet contribute to a fund for low and moderate income housing in the city. By late 1983 the program had subsidized 2,600 dwelling units, exacting $19 million in contributions from twenty-seven developers.[19] One of the boldest approaches was taken by Hartford, Connecticut, in the 1970s under the leadership of Nicholas Carbone. In an explicit effort to capture the benefits of downtown job creation and property appreciation for inner city residents, Hartford negotiated a series of deals for downtown projects involving major insurance companies in which the city offered tax inducements but, in return, received an equity share in the development. As a result, Hartford city government benefited directly from the profits and capital gains.[20]

But cities should not just sit back and wait until developers come to them. They must use the tools of public policy to create an attractive urban environment. Reducing taxes will not do this. Providing high quality services will. Beyond providing basic services, the public sector has a special role to play in nurturing cities as dynamic generators of wealth and culture. Americans have only begun to understand what makes cities work. The key to building great cities, as Jane Jacobs ably demonstrated so many years ago, is diversity. "This ubiquitous principle is the need of cities for a most intricate and close-grained diversity of uses that give each other constant mutual support, both economically and socially."[21] Mixed uses—work, residence, shopping, and entertainment—in the same area are what make cities efficient, innovative, and exciting.

Too often in the past, governments, through rigid zoning codes or the insular project approach associated with urban renewal and large government centers, destroyed rather than nurtured the delicate fabric of cities. It is possible, however, for public policy to promote diversity instead of kill it. The problem, for example, is that work uses have been separated from other uses in many downtowns, making them deserted after the hours of 9 to 5. The centralization of employment, however, creates an opportunity for public policy. While local governments, for the most part, cannot influence the location of primary economic activity, they can enact local land use controls and targeted incentives to promote spin-offs from primary office development. Vertical zoning can be used to require that office developments have retail outlets on the first floor. Cities can also market downtown housing for office workers, so long as this does not lead to substantial displacement of existing residents. Cities are only beginning to understand the policy options available.

There are two reasons why mixed use development is so important. First, the externalities, or spin-offs, of downtown office employment can boost the city's tax base and provide jobs for central city residents. Inner city residents, for example, often do not qualify for jobs as lawyers or accountants, but they can get jobs in restaurants or retail outlets that serve the downtown market. Second, by nurturing a diversity of uses local governments create an urban environment that will have investors and residents clamoring to get in. As a result, the bargaining position of the city will be strengthened for addressing inequalities.

The Underdevelopment of Local Politics

While the economic space for redistributive reforms exists, the political space is much more restrictive. The reason for this has to do with the political requirements of urban populist reform. The argument described here says only that cities can exercise political discretion to redistribute some of the benefits of the expanding service sector. It does not say how that political discretion should be exercised. While the germs of an urban populist program exist in various experiments around the country, as yet there is no coherent program. Essentially, however, it is implied that distributive decisions that were formerly made by the automatic workings of the market must now be made by the political system in the interest of the majority of inner city residents. Whether the funds should be used for housing rehabilitation, producer cooperatives, or energy conservation, however, has not even been addressed. Suffice it to say that if the program was designed to over-

come the economic dependency of central cities it would have to be
invested in job creating enterprises according to a long term plan and
not squandered on welfare type expenditures. In short, an alternative to
conservative growth politics would require sophisticated democratic
planning.

For the most part, however, the highly fragmented and pluralistic
nature of most city governments prevents them from engaging in any
coherent economic planning. Successful planning requires the coordination of different policies and the concentration of resources over an
extended period of time. The pluralistic political process, however, has
its own imperatives requiring that resources be widely distributed
according to the automatic workings of an internal political marketplace based on the truck and barter of narrow interest groups. With
weak political parties city governments are unable to achieve autonomy
from narrow political interests which tie down public policy. At the
other extreme, to the extent that planning does exist in city governments, it tends to be isolated from the democratic process.

Americans tend to view political institutions in instrumental terms,
as means to the end of individual freedom or happiness. One of the
corollaries of this instrumental view or politics is that political development follows economic development.[22] Samuel P. Huntington has developed a concept of political development that does not make this
unwarranted assumption; he judges political institutions by their own
nonderivative standards. Huntington defines political development as
"political institutionalization"—the extent to which specifically political institutions have acquired value and stability over time. One component of political institutionalization is autonomy:

> Political institutionalization, in the sense of autonomy, means the
> development of political organizations and procedures that are not
> simply expressions of the interests of particular social groups. A
> political organization that is the instrument of a social group—
> family, clan, class—lacks autonomy. . . . Political organizations and
> procedures which lacks autonomy are, in common parlance, said to
> be corrupt.[23]

When politics becomes an arena for the untempered assertion of private
interests, then sound policymaking capable of serving the public interest is impossible.

Perhaps the foremost institution of modern political development is the political party. By bringing disparate interests into an overarching set of political commitments, parties are able to achieve autonomy from particular interests. Parties can knit together the fragmented institutions of urban government and achieve a modicum of policy consistency and follow-through. One philosopher of the city has reflected on the consequences of weak political parties for urban politics:

> In the absence of strong parties that can provide a force for integration, one might say that the functional character of the city is likely to be the source of sharp conflict and division, which could break down the restraints of civility and community and aggravate the main problems that already mark the condition of cities.[24]

This is precisely what happened in Cleveland.

Politics, in Cleveland, has undergone a process of underdevelopment, not development. The Tom Johnson era (1901–1909) was probably the high water mark of Cleveland's civic culture. The political parties were at their zenith and Johnson built his own "machine" that won him four straight terms in office, even though he was under constant attack by powerful business interests. Possessing the political strength to call the bluff of conservative growth politics, Johnson was able to raise taxes and expand the functions of government to work toward his vision of a City on the Hill. His tent meetings stirred involvement by working class voters, and trust in government grew to the point that voters approved major expansions of public responsibility, such as Muny Light—something that would be unheard of today.

The fall of Tom Johnson coincided with the rise of the good government reform movement in Cleveland—a movement that, ironically, led to the decline of Cleveland's civic culture. Fearing what an organized working class majority could do with city government, reformers sought to remove policymaking, as much as possible, from partisan politics. Reformers were motivated, in large part, by a kind of market theory of politics—the belief that in an increasingly mobile capitalist economy, governments in order to compete effectively needed to be organized in a more businesslike fashion. Civic boosters played a large role in Cleveland's short lived adoption of a city manager system. Economic growth could not wait for pluralist bargaining and democratic delay. Likewise, political parties were viewed as playing upon ethnic and class divisions that only got in the way of pursuing the shared goal of growth and efficiency.

While the reform movement was designed to insulate city government from corruption, the overall effect was to undermine the autonomy of local politics and contribute to its deeper corruption. Distinctively political methods of decision making were denigrated. It was as if local government had to make no value choices or distributive questions; governance was reduced to efficiency. The ability of political institutions to make difficult distributive choices (so necessary in economic planning), to aggregate interests, discipline demands, and generate consent for broad public initiatives was eviscerated. The effect was to weaken local government and open it up to economic influences—or, more precisely, to enthrone economic thinking within the political institutions themselves.

Interestingly, in Cleveland, political parties came under attack not only from above by middle class reformers but also from below by populist politicians. Attacks on the "party bosses" became standard fare in every race for mayor beginning in the 1930s. Populist politicians portrayed political parties as unnecessary, manipulative mediators between the people and their representatives. The populist ideal was a kind of plebiscitary democracy in which voters would commune directly with politicians. No need for party monopolies; in a system without parties political entrepreneurs could rise up spontaneously from the people to defend the dispossessed. The reform movement had its populist side as well (initiative, referendum, recall). It furthered the tendency toward a long ballot, well developed in northeast Ohio, where judges and routine officers, such as city clerks, are elected instead of appointed. (Shortly after Kucinich left office, the populist attack on parties was reflected in a referendum, put on the ballot by Kucinich supporters, to have the council president directly elected by the voters instead of chosen by the majority party caucus in council. The proposal was defeated.)

In recent years, Kucinich led the populist attack on political parties. It was not that Kucinich rejected parties *in toto*; nominally, he was a Democrat. His political career, however, showed a tendency to treat the Democratic party in an instrumental manner: Kucinich attached himself to the party when he thought it was useful to do so and, more often, attacked the party when he saw advantage in that. Kucinich played on the distrust many inner city voters felt toward politics and political parties. He taught an instrumental approach to politics: politics was not about values; it was not about participation; it was about *power*. The goal was simple: power to the people—or at least to his people. Any actions to acquire power were justifiable—as long as they were not illegal or economically corrupt. Like many politicians today, Kucinich learned the trade of politics almost completely outside any party organization. He never acquired the obligations, the party discipline, and reciprocal commitments that politicians routinely pick up in a long process of apprenticeship. For Kucinich, political parties—in fact all political processes—were simply a means to an end.

Kucinich's political opportunism raises the question of whether he was himself corrupt. Kucinich scrupulously avoided any hint of economic corruption, of personally enriching himself while in office. But was he power corrupt? His opponents would argue that he was: "You could never trust him; he would do anything to win power." There is a great deal of truth to this; Kucinich was the political opportunist *par excellence*. However, just as our focus in analyzing default was not on whether Brock Weir was a corrupt individual but on the conditions that enabled him to exercise extraordinary power, the focus here is not on the qualities of Dennis Kucinich but on the system and ideas he represented. Kucinich was not the only opportunistic politician in town. He simply carried to an extreme tendencies that were inherent in Cleveland's decaying political system—a system characterized by alienated voters, disaggregated interests, and weak parties. And Kucinich did not get his instrumental view of politics out of thin air. The Alinsky-style neighborhood groups had for years taught that politics is inherently corrupt and that the best approach is to stand outside the process and make economistic demands.

Kucinich's short term as mayor demonstrated the political limits of urban populism. Even if Kucinich had possessed a long term economic program (which he did not), he would have been unable to implement it for political reasons. Kucinich's electoral *coup d'état* catapulted him into the top city office in a short period of time, but his office specific coalition, outside the political parties, left him isolated and unable to mount any sustained policy initiatives. Relying on Alinsky-style confrontational politics to appeal to the voters, Kucinich was bogged down in stultifying political conflict throughout his term. In the one area where economic pressures were minimal, the block grant, Kucinich fell into classic pluralist politics, spreading the resources around to buy political support. Lacking the political organization to discipline the demands of his fragmented electoral base, especially the turf conscious neighborhood groups, Kucinich became trapped between their rising expectations and his limited resources.

The populist call for "economic democracy" suggests that the solution lies in extending the equal right and privileges of democracy into the economic system. But democracy in Cleveland hardly inspired confidence; few Clevelanders were willing to give the warring factions of local politics additional power over the economy. The inability of urban political systems to engage in long term economic planning is a major reason why politicians routinely succumb to the pragmatic illusions of growth politics. The beauty of growth politics is that it converts political planning issues into technical questions, finessing distributive issues by letting the market decide and concentrating the subsidies whenever they can leverage the most private investment.

Ultimately, growth politics involves a breakdown in the strict separation between economic and political decision making. In tax abatement, for example, a policy presumably chosen because it creates new economic growth is actually chosen for its political effects. Traditionally, a breakdown in the boundaries between economic and political decision making is treated in urban politics under the rubric of corruption. Similar to growth politics, municipal corruption is understood as the exercise of political discretion in supposedly economic or technical areas—such as when a political machine hires a favored contractor, instead of going out for competitive bidding. Growth politics, then, seems to be nothing but an extension of the problem of municipal corruption.

While the corruption framework does suggest the threat to democracy posed by growth politics, it does not really provide a useful way of approaching the problem. The traditional solution to the problem of municipal corruption is to cleanse the corrupted organ of political discretion and subject it to neutral bureaucratic decision making. The reform solution is justified, once again, by a strict separation between economic and political decision making. Applying this solution to growth politics, the idea would be to keep politics separate from the technical questions of growth. The goal would be to eliminate growth politics as I have defined it.

The entire effort to separate economic from political decision making is wrongheaded, however. All growth issues have distributive implications; the expansion of the pie cannot be separated from its division. If the downtown service sector is going to grow, homeowners will have to be displaced. The goal should not be to eliminate growth politics but to subject it to the will of the majority. Indeed, it is precisely the tendency of reformers to turn to narrowly economic or technical decision making as an all purpose solution to urban problems that has contributed to the decline of political parties and the inability of the political process to deal with difficult distributive issues.

In the years ahead, the political conflicts inherent in growth politics will be especially acute in older central cities as the gentry of the expanding service sector is deposited, both to work and live, in the midst of deteriorating neighborhoods with only a marginal place in the new economic order. The economic space exists for redistributive reforms to begin to address the inequalities that threaten the social peace and quality of life in our cities. This requires, however, that tough political choices be faced, that resources be distributed according to a conscious democratic plan—not according to the automatic workings of an internal political market or an external economic market. This requires, in turn, political institutions that are sufficiently autonomous from special interests to engage in long term economic planning, yet are, at the same time, capable of representing the democratic aspirations of the majority of inner city residents. The political challenge of our cities is at least as great as the economic challenge.

Afterword

Cleveland: Comeback City?

Question: What is the difference between Cleveland and the Titanic?
Answer: Cleveland has a better orchestra.

Cleveland has been the butt of jokes for years. At President Reagan's first inauguration, comedian Rich Little cracked that the Soviet invasion of Poland could be stopped by renaming it Cleveland—because nobody wants to go there. The "Mistake on the Lake," it was called—an image confirmed when the Cuyahoga caught fire in 1969. The mayoralty of Dennis Kucinich represented, for many, the nadir of Cleveland's image. "Dennis the Menace" (as the press often called him) and his "antics" (another frequent term) were blamed for default and the city's economic slide, reinforcing the image of Cleveland as an almost comical loser.

No more. The defeat of Kucinich and the election of George Voinovich marked the beginning of a dramatic turnaround in the national image of Cleveland—what *Town and Country* magazine called, "THE OVERNIGHT MUNICIPAL SUCCESS STORY THE COUNTRY IS CHEERING ABOUT!"[1] The local media has been replete with renascent boosterism since Voinovich's election. As the Cleveland *Press* editorialized in 1981: "Cleveland is on a roll . . . and has earned its stripes as a comeback city."[2] The national press largely agrees. *Time* magazine plays a popular theme about who is responsible for the dramatic turnaround:

246

"The principal architect of Cleveland's renaissance is George Voino-vich."[3]

Has Cleveland made a comeback? Has city government pulled itself out of fiscal crisis and has the city really reversed its economic decline? In order to answer these questions, we must separate fact from fancy, underlying trends from media hype.

Financially speaking, there is no doubt that Cleveland has made progress from the dark days of default. One year after Voinovich was elected mayor, the city officially ended default when area banks agreed to refinance $36.2 million in short term debt, including $10.5 million in defaulted notes ($4.5 million had been repaid earlier), through twelve year bonds at a low 8.875 percent interest rate. After failing once, Voinovich persuaded the voters, in February 1981, to approve a 33 percent increase in the income tax—an increase that he promised would enable the city not only to balance its budget but also to improve city services and rebuild the infrastructure. Gradually the city's bond ratings were hiked to investment grade and, in July 1983, for the first time since 1977, Cleveland entered the national bond market.

Cleveland also made a much acclaimed effort to increase efficiency of local government operations through the Operations Improvement Task Force, a private sector management review of city operations involving eighty loaned executives from area corporations. Costing nearly $4.25 million in cash contributions and loaned executive time, the Task Force made 650 recommendations for improving the efficiency of city government. According to the Task Force report, if all goes well, after four or five years the benefits could reach $57 million a year in city funds.[4]

For these accomplishments, as well as for approving four year terms for mayor and council and reviving Playhouse Square, Cleveland received one of ten coveted All-America City Awards for 1981–1982 given by the National Municipal League. In a general atmosphere of civic uplift and optimism, it is not surprising that Voinovich, a Republican in an overwhelmingly Democratic town, had no trouble getting re-elected in 1981 with 76.5 percent of the vote.

The issue, however, is not whether Voinovich has been politically successful, or even whether he has done a good job of running the government. The issue here is much broader: has Voinovich been able to put together a public-private partnership capable of turning around Cleveland's depressed economy, creating new investment that would not have occurred otherwise? This is the implication of the Comeback

City theme. (The corollary, of course, is that under Kucinich Cleveland experienced an investment boycott and that this boycott has been lifted by Voinovich.)

Indeed, Cleveland has experienced some of the signs of private sector reinvestment. As we saw, downtown office construction has boomed; Ohio City, a small area on the near West Side, has been partially gentrified (but the process seems at the moment to have played itself out); Playhouse Square, a downtown area of elegant old theaters, has revived as advertised (but only with deep federal subsidies); and there are even some condominiums being built in the Flats. These positive trends, however, do not compensate for the negative trends that are draining the economic life of the city.

A recent analysis of urban decline in the United States used a simulation of the Cleveland economy to study the effect of public policies designed to stem decline. Five separate policies to aid the inner city of Cleveland were studied: a $63 million per year job stimulus package; a $59.2 million per year housing rehabilitation package; a fiscal equalization package centered on tax base sharing between Cleveland and its suburbs; a transit package including $260 million in capital improvements and $36 million in added services; and a suburban growth control package that would reduce the growth in suburban households by 25 percent. The study concluded that if all five were implemented for the decade 1980 through 1990 (a politically improbable if not fantastic assumption), they would only cut Cleveland's severe job loss in half and cut its population loss by 62 percent (the city would still lose about 40,000 residents). Acknowledging the difficulty of calculating the effects precisely, the authors, nevertheless, conclude: "It is very unlikely that Cleveland's decline could actually be fully arrested through any feasible policies."[5]

For obvious reasons, Mayor Voinovich has been unable to implement any policies of this magnitude (in fact, federal aid has declined significantly since Reagan took office). It is not surprising to learn, therefore, that Cleveland's decline has continued apace. According to one study, the greater Cleveland area lost 262,000 jobs between 1978 and 1982.[6] Voinovich himself admitted that the central city alone lost 15,000 jobs in 1983.[7] News of plant closings and layoffs is an almost daily occurrence in Cleveland. The motivation is profit, not politics. The machine tool company of Acme-Cleveland, for example, known for its advertising slogan, "My heart's in Cleveland," laid off hundreds of Cleveland employees while planning to build plants in the South, where the absence of unions makes for a cheaper labor force. In a 1984 speech, the mayor pointed out that the city had almost 40,000 unemployed, 15.4 percent of the labor force—twice the national average.[8] According to the 1980 census, the percentage of families below the poverty line increased in Cleveland since 1970, while, at the same time, the city's population declined almost 24 percent. There is no reason to believe that these underlying negative trends have slowed down, let alone reversed.

The crisis atmosphere that surrounded Kucinich did, indeed, galvanize the private sector for a time behind Voinovich; the Operations Improvement Task Force and the refinancing of the defaulted debt are good examples. However, as the crisis atmosphere has faded, Voinovich has often failed to gain minimal private sector cooperation. A case in point is the $200 million Sohio headquarters building recently constructed downtown. The city provided crucial aid to the project, including the threat of eminent domain, demolition, speeded up permits, and other favors. Where San Francisco, in exchange for constructing a major new office building, got Sohio to agree to finance 500 units of new or rehabilitated housing. Cleveland got almost nothing. In a letter to the president and chairman of Sohio, Voinovich described the "unbelievable cooperation" given to Sohio on the project and implored Sohio to buy its electricity from Muny Light. "On a very personal basis, I also ask, as a favor to me, that you take this step. Your action will symbolize to so many others the resurgence of Cleveland physically, economically and emotionally." Sohio refused.[9]

Even with a pro-business mayor, CEI has not stopped its efforts to take over Muny Light. In 1982, Voinovich, who has been successful in improving Muny's ability to compete with CEI, charged that CEI was trying to cripple Muny Light by lobbying in council against needed legislation. "We still have a battle going on," said Voinovich. "They [CEI] are as dedicated as ever to laying away the Municipal Light system."[10] In 1984, however, the Voinovich administration began negotiations for CEI to take over all of Muny's private customers in exchange for various benefits, including a cash payment of $40 million and a promise from CEI not to move its over one thousand employees to the suburbs, as threatened, but to locate them instead in a major downtown development. CEI applied public pressure on the mayor to accept the deal by publicizing its advantages in a full page newspaper advertisement and a letter to every Cleveland resident. Acknowledging that he had been "leaned on by everyone in this town," Voinovich, perhaps fearing a Kucinich comeback, killed the deal saying, among other things, that CEI's decision over where to locate its headquarters should have nothing to do with Muny.[11] CEI's attempt to link staying in Cleveland with the sale of Muny Light was another blatant example, like default, of political discretion in investment. Three days after Voinovich killed the deal, CEI, in another effort to cripple Muny, filed a taxpayers' suit against the city seeking to force Muny to pay back at least $24 million supposedly owed the city's general and other funds.

Despite the best efforts of the Voinovich administration, underlying investment trends have not changed. In the area of housing, for example, private lenders are still hesitant to lend in inner city neighborhoods. Cleveland's CASH program, as we saw in Chapter 8, did as poor a job at leveraging private investment for housing rehabilitation during the Voinovich administration as during the Kucinich one. Subsequently, the Voinovich administration changed the program to serve a much more middle class clientele, thus guaranteeing a better leverage ratio. But this does not mean that the Voinovich administration succeeded in bringing about new private investment that would not have occurred otherwise. As evidence of Comeback City, many observers point to the downtown building boom. What they fail to mention is that this boom began during the Kucinich years, and there is evidence that an over-supply will call a halt to the boom during the Voinovich years. The harsh reality is that private actors are motivated primarily by private interest, not politics. And mayors simply do not have sufficient incentives at their command to change the direction of these private interests.

The question remains, then, how has the impression of Comeback City been generated when the facts point so overwhelmingly in the other direction? Big business was extremely grateful to Voinovich for delivering them from the attacks of the radical populist Kucinich. However, as we saw earlier, business, for the most part (default is an important exception), does not and cannot exercise political discretion in its basic investment decisions. What it can exercise discretion in, however, is in presenting those decisions to the public and the media. Whereas Kucinich was blamed for negative trends and got no credit for positive trends, Voinovich has received just the opposite treatment. When Diamond Shamrock moved its corporate headquarters out of Cleveland in 1979, the decision was blamed on the antibusiness climate created by Kucinich. Clearly, this was an absurd claim; the move had to do with changes in the corporation, not changes in city government (see Chapter 6.) When the same company decided in 1984 to phase out its remaining administrative offices in Cleveland, no attempt was made to blame the Voinovich administration.[12] In a similar vein, Voinovich continues to blame Kucinich for the failure of the city to obtain better bond ratings, when clearly the dominant factor is the area's distressed economy—a point made by a local business publication.[13]

For the most part, the media has simply played the business climate issue the way businessmen have portrayed it. Direct business booster efforts, however, have also redounded to the benefit of Voinovich as he nurtured the Comeback City image. The Cleveland *Plain Dealer*, for example, donated $100,000 to the "Cleveland's a Plum" promotional blitz in 1981. (Local wags distributed counter bumper stickers: "If Cleveland's a plum, no wonder the *Plain Dealer* is the pits.") Employing $3.5 million in funds contributed by big business, the New Cleveland Campaign is a more substantial effort to shape the image of Cleveland. The group claims to be apolitical. Founded in 1977, the New Cleveland Campaign, however, did not begin serious work, including a national advertising campaign, until one month after Kucinich left office. Focused on the theme, "A new frame of mind," the low key ad copy reads in part: "There's a new frame of mind on Cleveland. A frame of mind clearly displayed by the voters in their choice of a new mayor."

As Cleveland's image has improved dramatically, however, the reality of negative economic trends has begun to reassert itself. Even with the tax increase, the city government faced a $17 million deficit in 1984. Twice in 1984 Voinovich went to the voters to increase the income tax again and twice he was defeated, the second time by an almost 2 to 1 margin. During the campaign, Voinovich threatened massive layoffs if the tax increase failed to pass. Voinovich later admitted that he had exaggerated the probable extent of the layoffs in an effort to persuade the voters; the actual layoffs were much smaller than he had threatened. This prompted perhaps the first crisis of public confidence in the Voinovich administration, with the *Plain Dealer* issuing a rare critical editorial on the mayor.[14]

While the national image is that Kucinich almost bankrupted the city and Voinovich has orchestrated a remarkable turnaround, locally the situation is more complex. Voinovich is still extremely popular but Kucinich also has a devoted following. Reports of Kucinich's political death, as Mark Twain would say, were greatly exaggerated. In 1982, Kucinich ran, on a shoestring budget, for the Democratic nomination for Ohio's Secretary of State and garnered almost a quarter of a million votes. And in August 1983, Kucinich staged his own comeback, winning election to City Council from the Twelfth Ward, an ethnic working class district on the near East Side overlooking the steel mills in the Flats. Kucinich was handed his re-election issue on a platter when a secret Growth Association report was leaked to the media. Analyzing how best to defeat Kucinich, the report called for sacrificing the incumbent councilman and putting "all available resources" behind a third candidate, pointing out that it might require two or three times the normal campaign expenditure to defeat Kucinich. This effort by the establishment to manipulate the votes of working class ethnics played perfectly into Kucinich's populist appeal.

As a member of City Council, Kucinich has generally played a low key role. He took a prominent part in one issue, however, demonstrating that the populist issues of inequality and business favoritism are not dead. In 1983, the Voinovich administration sponsored a $7.5 million Urban Development Action Grant (UDAG) for a low interest loan to a private company to build a highly automated bar steel mill in the Flats. Kucinich joined forces with the United Steelworkers to oppose the grant, gathering 25,000 signatures to put the issue before the voters. Opposition centered on the contention that the new mill would take business away from existing bar mills and substitute low wage non-union labor for higher paying unionized jobs. After voters narrowly approved the project (53 to 47 percent), Voinovich lashed out at Kucinich, calling his actions "absolutely despicable" and charging that he had tarnished the city's positive image with business.[15]

Dennis Kucinich claims to have changed his confrontational political style. Only time will tell. Urban populism has shown little sign as yet, however, of having a coherent program to deal with the severe problems of a declining industrial city. At the same time, conservative growth politics seems just as far from a coherent approach. And no amount of imagemaking and media hype can cover over for long the problems and conflicts built into growth politics.

Notes

Introduction

1. William Greider, "Detroit's Streetwise Mayor Plays Key Role in City's Turnaround," Cleveland *Plain Dealer*, July 3, 1978.

2. Harvey Molotch first focused attention on the centrality of growth politics at the local level and originated some of the concepts I employ in this study, such as "growth machine" and "growth statesman." See his seminal article, "The City as a Growth Machine: Toward a Political Economy of Place," *American Journal of Sociology* 82, no. 2 (Sept. 1976): 309–32. G. William Domhoff builds upon the insights of the growth politics approach in Chapter 6 of *Who Rules America Now: A View for the 80's* (Englewood, N.J.: Prentice-Hall, 1983).

3. Ken Auletta, *The Streets Were Paved with Gold* (New York: Random House, 1975), chap. 9.

4. Advertising supplement, *Business Week*, Oct. 30, 1978, 75–121.

5. Interdepartmental memorandum from Jerry Finch to Carol Bellamy, Sept. 29, 1981, p. 3. Cited in Frank Domurad and Ruth Messinger, *Citizen Program to Eliminate the Gap* (New York: City Project, 1983), 54.

6. Ed Koch, interview, *Playboy*, April 1982, 72.

7. Boston College's Social Welfare Research Institute estimated there would have been 210,000 *more* individuals on the city's welfare rolls in 1978 without the tightening of administration. "City Reports 18% Drop in Family Relief Rolls," *New York Times*, Oct. 4, 1981.

8. Ed Koch, interview, 82.

9. For an analysis of pragmatic illusions at the national level, see Bruce Miroff, *Pragmatic Illusions: The Presidential Politics of John F. Kennedy* (New York: David McKay, 1981).

10. T. Harry Williams, *Huey Long* (New York: Alfred A. Knopf, 1969), 681.

11. *Default* literally means the failure of a borrower to make payments on a loan at the time contractually specified. Strictly speaking, New York was the first city to go into default. But the New York legislature, in Madison Avenue fashion, declared the failure of the city to meet payments, for $2.4 billion in outstanding notes on time in November 1975, a "moratorium" rather than a default.

12. Mayor Dennis J. Kucinich, press release, Sept. 18, 1978.

Chapter 1

1. Nelson Polsby, *Community Power and Political Theory*, 2d ed. (New Haven: Yale University Press, 1980), 117.

2. Milton Friedman, *Capitalism and Freedom* (Chicago: University of Chicago Press, 1962), 115.

3. *Ibid.*, 23.

4. Robert Dahl, *Who Governs?* (New Haven: Yale University Press, 1961).

5. E. E. Schattschneider, *The Semisovereign People* (New York: Holt, Rinehart and Winston, 1960).

6. Thomas J. Anton, "Power, Pluralism and Local Politics," *Administrative Science Quarterly*, March 1963, 452–53.

7. Wlodzimierz Wesolowski, "Class Domination and the Power of Interest Groups," *Polish Sociological Bulletin*, Jan.–June 1962: 53–64.

8. Peter Bachrach and Morton S. Baratz, "Two Faces of Power," *American Political Science Review* 56 (Dec. 1962): 948.

9. The contending elite-stratification school of community power, it should be pointed out, also overlooked important economic relations. Focusing with pluralists on the power approach to urban politics, elitists tended to concentrate on proximate relations of command to the exclusion of broader systems of political economy. In this vein, Marxists have criticized elite theorists for developing a narrowly "instrumental" theory of the state. At the same time, it is clear, elitist theorists such as Mills and Hunter were more sensitive to economic factors than pluralists. For an attempt to merge elite methodology with Marxist and pluralist approaches, see William Domhoff, *Who Really Rules* (Santa Monica, Calif.: Goodyear Publishing Company, 1978).

10. Robert Dahl, "Critique of the Ruling Elite Model," *American Political Science Review* 52 (1958): 463–69.

11. My criticism is aimed at the basic pluralist approach to community power; it is not aimed at specific scholars. Perspicacious analysts often have insights beyond the bounds of their basic approach. In the pluralist classic *Who Governs?*, for example, Robert Dahl observes that if an employer seriously threatens to leave a community, "political leaders are likely to make frantic attempts to make the local situation more attractive" (250). Still, this insight is clearly not central to Dahl's analysis.

12. Nelson Polsby in a companion volume to Dahl's *Who Governs?* makes this assumption explicit when he asks a basic question about power analysis: Would knowing *who benefits* be helpful in determining who has power? He answers: No. In explanation, Polsby points to a community "collectively fed, clothed, employed, and sheltered" as the result of countless individual decisions coordinated by the market. No individual intended the final result. Polsby concludes: "There is at least one sense, then, in which many payoffs of community life must be considered fortuitous and *beyond the control* of actors in the system." In other words, power does not exist in the private market. Polsby, 133 (emphasis added).

13. Michael J. Crozier, Samuel P. Huntington, and Joji Watanuki, *The Crisis of Democracy: Report on the Governability of Democracies to the Trilateral Commission* (New York: New York University Press, 1975).

14. See, for example, Richard D. Auster and Morris Silver, *The State as Firm* (Boston: Martin Nijhoff, 1979); and Richard Rose and Guy Peters, *Can Governments Go Bankrupt?* (New York: Basic Books, 1978).

15. President's Commission for a National Agenda for the Eighties, *Urban America in the Eighties* (Washington, D.C.: Government Printing Office, 1980).

16. Paul Peterson, *City Limits* (Chicago: University of Chicago Press, 1981).

17. Formally, Peterson defines a policy as being in the best interest of a city if the marginal benefits of the policy to the average taxpayer exceed the marginal costs. The average taxpayer is defined as the individual or business with the mean benefit/tax ratio (always less than 1.0). When computing the mean, each taxpayer is weighted according to the amount of taxes paid (42).

18. Interestingly, pluralists treat politics within cities in market images: political entrepreneurs (politicians) support policies in exchange for votes from citizens, viewed as relatively passive consumers of government. (For an explicit statement of the market model behind pluralism, see Dahl, *Who Governs?*, chap. 8.) This means that pluralism and market theory are even more alike, differing only in the level of their analysis: the former examines the market within cities, the latter the market between cities.

19. For a sampling of this literature, see Kenneth Newton, "American Urban Politics: Social Class, Political Structure and Public Goods," *Urban Affairs Quarterly* 2, no. 2 (Dec. 1975): 241–64; Harvey Molotch, "The City as Growth Machine: Toward a Political Economy of Place," *American Journal of Sociology* 82, no. 2 (Sept. 1976): 309–32; John R. Logan, "Growth, Politics and the Stratification of Places," *American Journal of Sociology* 84, no. 2 (Sept. 1976): 404–16; Lawrence D. Brown, "Mayors and Models: Notes on the Study of Urban Politics," in *American Politics and Public Policy*, ed. Walter Dean Burnham and Martha Wagner Weinberg (Cambridge, Mass.: MIT Press, 1978), 251–79; James O'Connor, *The Fiscal Crisis of the State* (New York: St. Martin's Press, 1973); and David Harvey, *Social Justice and the City* (Baltimore: Johns Hopkins University Press, 1973).

20. Dennis R. Judd, *The Politics of American Cities*, 2d ed. (Boston: Little, Brown, 1984).

21. To sample the debate on the new urban political economy, especially its structuralist varient, see Michael Peter Smith, ed., *Cities in Transformation*, vol. 26, Urban Affairs Annual Review (Beverly Hills, Calif.: Sage Publications, 1984).

22. Lindblom wrote with Dahl a still classic pluralist analysis of economic and political processes, *Politics, Economics and Welfare* (Chicago: University of Chicago Press, 1953). The 1976 edition contains a commendably self-critical preface that indicates how their thinking on pluralism has evolved. Lindblom also wrote a classic defense of pluralist decision making: "The Science of 'Muddling Through,' " *Public Administration Review*, Spring 1959: 79–88.

23. Charles Lindblom, *Politics and Markets* (New York: Basic Books, 1977), 154–55.

24. For explanations of urban decline that emphasize inevitable technological change, see Edward C. Banfield, *The Unheavenly City* (Boston: Little, Brown, 1968), chap. 2, "The Logic of Metropolitan Growth"; and George Steinlieb and James W. Hughes, eds., *Post-Industrial America: Metropolitan Decline and Inter-regional Job Shifts* (New Brunswick, N.J.: Center for Urban Policy Research, Rutgers, 1975).

25. David Gordon, "Capitalism and the Roots of the Urban Crisis," in *The Fiscal Crisis of American Cities*, ed. Roger Alcaly and David Mermelstein (New York: Vintage Books, 1977), 102–3.

26. A recent book on urban development takes this same approach *contra* Peterson: *Restructuring the City*, ed. Susan S. Fainstein and Norman I. Fainstein (New York: Longman, 1983). The last chapter, written by the Fainsteins, is an effort to construct a theory of growth politics that shares my method of tacking back and forth between structuralist and instrumentalist theories of the state.

27. O'Connor, 6.

28. See Donald Stillman, "The Devastating Impact of Plant Relocations," *Working Papers*, July–Aug. 1978, 40–53.

29. Harvey Molotch and John Logan analyze the central role of the rentier class in urban politics, calling those who attempt to manipulate land prices by influencing public policies "structural speculators." "Urban Fortunes: A Reconstruction of Urban Sociology," unpublished manuscript, 1984, chap. 1.

30. Those costs included windfall profits for unscrupulous promoters, overbuilding of railroads caused by intercity competition, and defaults by cities on railroad bonds during economic downturns. After the Panic of 1873, itself partly caused by the overbuilding of railroads, an estimated $100–150 million of municipal debt was involved in railroad bond defaults, an astounding one-fifth of all municipal debt. A. M. Hillhouse, *Municipal Bonds: A Century of Experience* (New York: Prentice-Hall, 1936). This book, written in 1936, is one of the best histories of urban growth politics in the United States, albeit from the limited perspective of municipal bond aid to private enterprise.

31. Robert Caro, *The Power Broker* (New York: Random House, 1974), 207–8.

32. *Plunkitt of Tammany Hall*, recorded by William L. Riordan (New York: E. P. Dutton, 1963), 3–6. See also Caro, 713.

33. For a general discussion of the problem of uneven development, including its relevance to state and local governments, see Stephen Hymer, "The Multi-National Corporation and the Law of Uneven Development," in *Economics and World Order*, ed. Jagdish Bhagwati (New York: World Law Fund, 1971), 128–29; and Barry Bluestone, "Economic Crisis and the Law of Uneven Development," *Politics and Society* 3, no. 1 (Fall 1972), 65–82.

34. There is considerable evidence that inequality between cities is increas-

ing. Using a number of different indices, James W. Fossett and Richard P. Nathan conclude that between 1960 and 1970 the rich cities got richer and the poor cities got poorer. "The Prospects for Urban Revival," in *Urban Government Finance*, ed. Roy Bahl (Beverly Hills, Calif.: Sage Publications, 1981). The 1980 census shows that in the past decade the gap between central cities and the suburbs and sunbelt cities and northern cities widened. See John Herbers, "Census Data Reveal 70's Legacy: Poorer Cities and Richer Suburbs" and "Cities Data Show Gap Between Sunbelt and North," *New York Times*, Feb. 27, 28, 1983.

35. Logan. Many statistical studies have shown that demographic factors, obvious indicators of the need for municipal expenditures, are not good predictors of actual expenditures. Income and wealth are. In other words, inequalities in private wealth between cities generate inequalities in city services, increasing class differences. O'Connor cites five studies corroborating this point (147, n. 28).

36. See Michael Danielson, *The Politics of Exclusion* (New York: Columbia University Press, 1976).

37. See James Sundquist, *Dispersing Population* (Washington, D.C.: Brookings Institution, 1975).

38. While the issue of the mobility of private investment began to enter political debate in the 1970s (largely because of the problems of uneven development), direct control still rests almost totally in private hands. Jeremy Rifkin and Randy Barker, for example, argue that workers have proprietary rights over their pension funds, but, until now, these funds have remained under the control of banks and insurance companies. *The North Will Rise Again* (Boston: Beacon Press, 1978). Staughton Lynd argues that unions have the right to bargain collectively with employers over plant location, but they gave up this right when they first negotiated no strike agreements during the Second World War. "Investment Decisions and the Quid Pro Quo Myth," *Case Western Reserve Law Review* 29 (1979): 396–427.

39. See Morton S. Baratz, "Corporate Giants and the Power Structure," *Western Political Quarterly* 9 (June 1956): 413–14. This is an early effort at a theory of growth politics at the national level.

40. See George E. Peterson, "Federal Tax Policy and Urban Development," in *Central City Economic Development*, ed. Benjamin Chinitz (Cambridge, Mass.: Abt Books, 1979), 67–78.

41. Probably the most comprehensive compilation of evidence is contained in a series of Rand Corporation studies, especially Roger J. Vaughan, *The Urban Impacts of Federal Policies*, vol. 2, *Economic Development* (Santa Monica, Calif.: Rand Corporation, June 1977). For further evidence, see Kirkpatrick Sale, *Power Shift: The Rise of the Southern Rim and Its Challenge to the Eastern Establishment* (New York: Random House, 1974); Seymour Melmen, "The Federal Rip-Off of New York's Money," in *The Fiscal Crisis of American Cities*, ed. Roger Alcaly and David Mermelstein (New York: Vintage Books, 1977), 181–88; "How Federal Politics Are Hurting the Cities," *Busi-*

ness Week, Dec. 19, 1977, 86–88; Norman I. Fainstein and Susan S. Fainstein, "Federal Policy and Spatial Inequality," in *Revitalizing the Northeast*, ed. George Steinlieb and James W. Hughes (New Brunswick, N.J.: Center for Urban Policy Research, Rutgers University, 1978), 205–28; H. V. Savitch, *Urban Policy and the Exterior City* (New York: Pergamon Press, 1979); and Norman Glickman, ed., *The Urban Impacts of Federal Policies* (Baltimore: Johns Hopkins University Press, 1980).

42. See Advisory Commission on Intergovernmental Relations, *Public Assistance: The Growth of a Federal Function* (Washington, D.C.: Government Printing Office, Aug. 1980). James Maxwell estimates that local governments carried 95 percent of the cost of general relief in 1929–1930. To give some idea of the low level of funding, expenditures for relief, welfare, and social security increased twenty-five times over the next decade. *The Fiscal Impact of Federalism in the United States* (Cambridge, Mass.: Harvard University Press, 1946), 135–36.

43. For example, in *Hammer v. Dagenhart* (1918), the Supreme Court struck down an attempt by Congress to regulate child labor. The Court reserved that power to the states while admitting that states would be dissuaded from exercising the power because of the "economic disadvantage" such regulation would involve. See the opinion of the Court delivered by Justice Day. *Hammer v. Dagenhart*, 247 U.S. 251, 38 S.Ct. 529, 62 L.Ed. 1101 (1918).

44. Caroline Bird, *The Invisible Scar* (New York: David McKay, 1966), 32–33.

45. A good example is unemployment insurance. Before the New Deal, only Wisconsin had a significant unemployment insurance program. After the Social Security Act of 1935 put into place a complicated system of incentives, every state established an unemployment compensation program.

46. A major bibliography on community power states, "One of the greatest gaps in literature on community power is the impact that extra-community forces—especially county, state and federal governments—have on local patterns of decision making." Willis D. Hawley and James H. Svara, *The Study of Community Power: A Bibliography* (Santa Barbara, Calif.: Cleo Press, 1972). G. William Domhoff in a critique of Dahl's *Who Governs?* asserts, "Dahl's most serious theoretical error was to consider decision making in New Haven as totally divorced from the national and state governmental contest." Domhoff, 45.

47. After examining theories of power, Steven Lukes concludes that "social life can only be properly understood as a dialectic of power and structure": *Essays in Social Theory* (London: Macmillan, 1977), 29. See also Anthony Giddens, *Central Problems in Social Theory* (Berkeley and Los Angeles: University of California Press, 1979), esp. 88–94. The theoretical perspective presented here is similar to that developed by John Mollenkopf. See "Community and Accumulation," in *Urbanization and Urban Planning in Capitalist Society*, ed. Michael Dear and Allen J. Scott (London: Methuen, 1981), 319–37.

Chapter 2

1. Morris Birkbeck, *Notes on a Journey in America from the Coast of Virginia to the Territory of Illinois,* 3d ed. (London, 1818), 69, quoted in John W. Reps, *The Making of Urban America* (Princeton, N.J.: Princeton University Press, 1965), 349.

2. For a perceptive discussion of the distinction between social and structural reformers, see Dennis R. Judd, *The Politics of American Cities,* 2d ed. (Boston: Little, Brown, 1984), chaps. 3 and 4.

3. Thomas F. Campbell, "City Nationalism," a talk delivered before the City Club Forum, Nov. 16, 1963, reproduced by the Citizens League of Cleveland.

4. The early history of Cleveland's iron industry can be found in Harlan Hatcher, *The Western Reserve* (Indianapolis: Bobbs-Merrill, 1949), chap. 19.

5. Quoted in Bayard Still, "Patterns of Mid-Nineteenth Century Urbanization in the Middle West," *Mississippi Valley Historical Review* 28 (Sept. 1941): 199.

6. Cleveland bought stock in three railroad companies with mixed results: two yielded healthy returns on the investment; one yielded no dividends and was eventually sold at a loss. Charles C. Williamson, *The Finances of Cleveland* (New York: Columbia University Press, 1907), 218–20. Because of the many failures of private railroad companies and subsequent loss of taxpayers' money, Ohio became one of the first states, in 1851, to prohibit state and local aid to private companies. See Ohio Constitution, Article 8, Section 6.

7. William Ganson Rose's indispensable history of Cleveland is a good example. Underwritten by Cleveland's industrial elite, it dwells on their successes with barely a nod in the direction of the daily struggles of working people. *Cleveland: The Making of a City* (Cleveland: World, 1950).

8. Williamson, 169–70.

9. Rose, 509.

10. *Cleveland Leader,* July 10, 1873, excerpted in *An Ohio Reader,* ed. Thomas H. Smith (Grand Rapids, Mich.: William B. Erdmans, 1975), 94.

11. Wilfred Henry Alburn and Miriam Russell Alburn, *This Cleveland of Ours,* vol. 1 (Chicago: S. S. Clarke, 1933), 356.

12. "*Annual Reports,*" 1884, xx, quoted in Charles C. Williamson, 149.

13. Quoted in Rose, 117.

14. Typhoid fever, caused by contaminated well water, continued to plague Cleveland as late as 1890, when 182 people died of the disease.

15. See Rose, 509.

16. This point is made by Campbell.

17. The Cleveland World, comp., "*The World's*" *History of Cleveland* (Cleveland: Cleveland World, 1896), 159–60.

18. The following section relies heavily on Edmund H. Chapman, *Cleveland: Village to Metropolis* (Cleveland: Western Reserve Historical Society and the Press of Western Reserve University, 1964). Chapman's study is a searching examination of the destructive effects of conservative growth politics on Cleveland's physical development.

19. *Cleveland Leader*, March 5, 1861, quoted in Chapman, 117.

20. See Rose, 457, 575, 597.

21. For a perceptive discussion of the relationship between industrialization, social order, and the rise of a professional police force, see Alan Dawley, *Class and Community: The Industrial Revolution in Lynn* (Cambridge, Mass.: Harvard University Press, 1976), esp. 104–10.

22. Henry B. Leonard, "Ethnic Cleavage and Industrial Conflict in Late Nineteenth Century America: The Cleveland Rolling Mill Company Strikes of 1882 and 1885," *Labor History* 20, no. 4 (Fall 1979): 528.

23. See James Beaumont Whipple, "Cleveland in Conflict: A Study in Urban Adolescence, 1876–1900," Ph.D. diss., Western Reserve University, 1951.

24. *Ibid.*, 162.

25. Annual report of Park Commissioners, *City Documents*, 1890, quoted in Williamson, 179.

26. Chapman, 112.

27. *Ibid.*, 104. In 1851 citizens lost their fight to preserve the lakefront for parks and docks. Rose, 240. The present land between the tracks and the lake was filled in later.

28. Quoted in Elroy M. Avery, "The Federal Plan of Municipal Government as Illustrated at Cleveland, Ohio," *Lehigh Quarterly* 2 (June 1892): 15.

29. Hanna secretly contributed $20,000 to McKisson's opponent in 1899. Frederic C. Howe, *The Confessions of a Reformer* (1925; reprint, Chicago: Quadrangle Books, 1967), 86.

30. See Thomas F. Campbell, "Background for Progressivism: Machine Politics in the Administration of Robert E. McKisson, Mayor of Cleveland 1895–1899," Ph.D. diss., Western Reserve University, 1960.

31. Henry George, *Progress and Poverty* (1879; reprint, New York: Robert Schalkenbach Foundation, 1933), 404–6.

32. Tom L. Johnson, *My Story*, ed. Elizabeth A. Hauser (Seattle: University of Washington Press, 1911), ix.

33. Johnson's dream of a city-owned transit system was not realized until 1942.

34. Lincoln Steffens, *The Struggle for Self-Government* (1906; reprint, New York: Johnson Reprint Corporation, 1968), 183.

35. Johnson, 125.

36. In *The Confessions of a Reformer*, Frederic C. Howe gives a vivid account of his conversion from moralistic reform to Johnson's philosophy and

the social ostracism he suffered from his upper class associates as a consequence.

37. Johnson, 112.

38. Samuel Haber, *Efficiency and Uplift* (Chicago: University of Chicago Press, 1964), chap. 6.

39. See Frederic C. Howe, *The City: The Hope of Democracy* (1905; reprint, Seattle: University of Washington Press, 1967).

40. Edward C. Banfield and James Q. Wilson, *City Politics* (New York: Vintage Books, 1966), 41. Banfield and Wilson have since adopted the less value-laden terms "unitary ethos" and "individualist ethos." See "Political Ethos Revisited," *American Political Science Review* 65 (Dec. 1971): 1049.

41. In the two sources cited above, as well as in a separate article, "Public-Regardingness as a Value Premises in Voting Behavior," *American Political Science Review* 58 (Dec 1964): 876–87, Banfield and Wilson present evidence supporting the hypothesized relationship between demographic variables and the two orientations toward politics. Empirical research relating these demographic variables to reformed institutions has produced mixed results. This research is summarized in Banfield and Wilson, "Political Ethos Revisited," 1048, n. 1.

42. The good government reform movement has been interpreted in almost complete isolation from the context of growth politics. Two exceptions to the rule that have greatly influenced the interpretation given here are Samuel P. Hays, "The Politics of Reform in Municipal Government in the Progressive Era," *Pacific Northwest Quarterly* 55, no. 4 (Oct. 1964): 157–69; and James Weinstein, *The Corporate Ideal in the Liberal State: 1900–1918* (Boston: Beacon Press, 1968), chap. 4.

43. In fairness, it should be pointed out that Banfield and Wilson do recognize certain undemocratic effects of reform. But they still maintain, "City government is vastly more honest, efficient, and democratic than it was a generation or two ago" because of "the steady diffusion in our culture of the political ideal of the Anglo-Saxon Protestant middle-class ethos." *City Politics*, 149–50.

44. See Charles R. Adrian, "Some General Characteristics of Nonpartisan Elections," *American Political Science Review* 46 (Sept. 1952): 766–76; and Oliver P. Williams and Charles R. Adrian, "The Insulation of Local Politics Under the Nonpartisan Ballot," *American Political Science Review* 53 (Dec. 1959): 1052–63.

45. Robert L. Lineberry and Edmund P. Fowler, "Reformism and Public Policies in American Cities," *American Political Science Review* 61 (Sept. 1967): 707; and Michael Aiken and Robert R. Alford, "Community Structure and Innovation: The Case of Public Housing," *American Political Science Review* 64 (Sept. 1970): 851–52. Lineberry and Fowler qualify their result for partisan and nonpartisan cities.

46. See Kenneth Newton, "Feeble Governments and Private Power: Urban

Politics and Policies in the United States," in *The New Urban Politics*, ed. Louis H. Masotti and Robert L. Lineberry (Cambridge, Mass.: Ballinger, 1976), 46–49.

47. Robert L. Briggs, "The Progressive Era in Cleveland, Ohio: Tom Johnson's Administration 1901–1909," Ph.D. diss., University of Chicago, 1961, 87.

48. There is no doubt that the pressure for reform in Cleveland came out of the upper class. In 1930, the Citizens League, which spearheaded the reform movement, had a membership that was 70.5 percent business or professional and only 1.8 percent tradesmen or laborers. Elmer Ernest Hilpert, "The Function of the Citizens League in the Government of the City of Cleveland and Cuyahoga County," master's thesis, University of Minnesota, 1931, 37.

49. The following account relies heavily on Thomas F. Campbell, *Daniel E. Morgan, 1877–1949: The Good Citizen in Politics* (Cleveland: Press of Western Reserve University, 1966), chap. 4.

50. Quoted in Leonard D. White, *The City Manager* (Chicago: University of Chicago Press, 1927), 13.

51. National Resources Committee, *The Structure of the American Economy*, part 1 (Washington, D.C.: 1939), app. 13; reprinted in Paul M. Sweezy, *The Present as History* (New York: Monthly Review Press, 1953), chap. 12.

52. David Rogers, *The Management of Big Cities* (Beverly Hills, Calif.: Sage Publications, 1971), 121. For evidence of big business support of Johnson over Goldwater, see Thomas R. Dye and L. Harmon Zeigler, *The Irony of Democracy* (Belmont, Calif.: Duxbury Press, 1971), 187–88.

53. Edie Black and Fred Goff, *The Hanna Industrial Complex* (New York: North American Congress on Latin America, 1969), 13.

54. Greater Cleveland Growth Association, *Cleveland: A New Generation* (Cleveland: Emerson Press, n.d. [circa 1978]), 26, 31.

55. *The Foundation Directory*, 6th ed. (1977), xiv.

56. Deena Mirow, "Local Foundation Librarian Aids Those Trapped in a Maze of Funding Options," Cleveland *Plain Dealer*, Feb. 9, 1980.

57. Robert Dahl describes how the "ex-plebs," or ethnic working class, displaced the entrepreneurs in New Haven city politics at an earlier period. *Who Governs?*, chaps. 3–4.

58. "The day after he [Lausche] was elected [mayor] they took him to the Union Club [elite businessmen's club], showed him the promised land and he became as fine a Republican as you could ask for" (Cleveland *Plain Dealer*, Dec. 28, 1975).

59. The analysis offered here of Cleveland politics is similar to Edward Greer's interpretation of ethnic machines in his study of Gary, Indiana. Greer views local politics as essentially a compromise between monopoly capital and competitive capital, whereby the basic conditions of capital accumulation are upheld in exchange for certain concessions, in the form of taxes, pollution controls, etc. Urban ethnic machines, Greer says, are basically "petit

bourgeois" in character; by distributing concessions, they serve to deflect challenges to control over capital accumulation. *Big Steel: Black Politics and Corporate Power in Gary, Indiana* (New York: Monthly Review Press, 1979), esp. 31–32.

60. Kenneth L. Kusmer, *A Ghetto Takes Shape: Black Cleveland, 1870–1930* (Urbana: University of Illinois Press, 1978), 145–46.

61. For a vivid account of machine politics among immigrant groups in Cleveland, see Wellington G. Fordyce, "Nationality Groups in Cleveland Politics," *Ohio State Archeological and Historical Quarterly* 66, no. 2 (April 1937): 109–27.

62. See Robert K. Merton, *Social Theory and Social Structure* (New York: Free Press, 1968), 125–36.

63. Whipple, 335.

64. Even though the merit system began in Cleveland in 1910, patronage practices remained. See Joseph Willard, "Municipal Personnel Administration in Cleveland," master's thesis, Western Reserve University, 1955.

65. From 1900 to 1910, the years before and after Johnson took office, city revenues almost doubled. *Annual Report of the Departments of the City of Cleveland for the Years 1900 and 1910* (Cleveland: Universe Publishing Company).

66. William E. Nelson and Philip J. Meranto, *Electing Black Mayors* (Columbus: Ohio University Press, 1977), 77.

Chapter 3

1. Factoring out the central city's population decline reveals that the suburban part of the Standard Metropolitan Statistical Area (SMSA) actually showed a population gain of 16,000 from 1970 to 1980. But this means that the period of tremendous population growth for the suburbs has ended.

2. For evidence on this point, see John H. Mollenkopf, "Paths Toward the Post Industrial Service City: The Northeast and Southwest," in *Cities Under Stress*, ed. Robert W. Burchell and David Listokin (Piscataway, N.J.: Rutgers University, Center for Urban Policy Research, 1981), esp. 83.

3. A recent report on the Cleveland area economy by the Rand Corporation, however, points out that certain Cleveland manufacturing industries actually increased their share of the U.S. market. Aaron S. Gurwitz and G. Thomas Kingsley, *The Cleveland Metropolitan Economy: An Initial Assessment*, Executive Summary (Santa Monica, Calif.: Rand Corporation, March 1982), 17–19.

4. Data originally compiled by the Community Development Improvement Program of the City of Cleveland. Cited in Cleveland City Planning Commission, *Jobs and Income*, vol. 1 (Cleveland: City Planning Commission, Dec. 1973), 79, 82.

5. "Understanding Central City Hardship," *Political Science Quarterly* 91, no. 1 (Spring 1976): 47–62.

6. On a series of five measures of "urban distress," Cleveland ranked consistently near the bottom. In fact, out of thirty cities, Cleveland's average ranking once again put it in second place, this time tied with St. Louis behind Newark. See Robert W. Burchell et al., "Measuring Urban Distress: A Summary of the Major Urban Hardship Indices and Resource Allocation Systems," in Burchell and Listokin, 219.

7. Suburban refers to all areas in the SMSA outside the city of Cleveland. Unless otherwise noted, all figures are from the 1980 Census.

8. Greater Cleveland Growth Association, *A Summary of Cleveland's Employment and Unemployment Trends*, Nov. 1981, 8.

9. Cleveland City Planning Commission, *Jobs and Income*, vol. 1 (Cleveland: City Planning Commission, Dec. 1973), 35.

10. Robert Wood, *Suburbia: Its People and Their Politics* (Boston: Houghton Mifflin, 1958).

11. Charles M. Tiebout, "A Pure Theory of Local Expenditures," *Journal of Political Economy* 64 (Oct. 1956): 416–24.

12. Paul Peterson, *City Limits* (Chicago: University of Chicago Press, 1981), 18–20.

13. See chap. 1, n. 39.

14. See Kusmer, *A Ghetto Takes Shape: Black Cleveland 1870–1930*, chap. 1.

15. This account of suburbanization in Cleveland relies heavily on Jon C. Teaford, *City and Suburb* (Baltimore: Johns Hopkins University Press, 1979).

16. *Ibid.*, 19–20.

17. R. B. Navin, *An Analysis of a Slum Area in Cleveland*, report of a study for the Cleveland Metropolitan Housing Authority in 1934 (Cleveland: Regional Association of Cleveland, Nov. 1939), 10.

18. Bruce E. Lynch, *Shaker Heights: The Ambient Vision of the Suburb* (Champaign-Urbana: University of Illinois, 1978).

19. *The Terminal Tower Complex* (Cleveland: Cleveland Landmarks Press, 1980), 10.

20. John A. Zangerle, *Cleveland and Its Suburbs in Perspective* (Cleveland: County Auditor's Office, 1922), 7.

21. Restrictive covenants continued to be used in the Cleveland area to prevent blacks from buying into white areas after 1948, even though the U.S. Supreme Court had ruled them judicially unenforceable that year. *United States v. City of Parma, Ohio*, 494 F. Supp. 1049 (1980), transcript, 938.

22. Using statistical methods, scholars have argued that only a small proportion of residential segregation by race can be explained by income differences. See Karl E. Taeuber and Alma F. Taeuber, *Negroes in Cities* (New York:

Atheneum, 1969), chap. 4, and the work of John Kain discussed in *United States v. City of Parma, Ohio.*

23. Racial zoning, for example, was outlawed by the U.S. Supreme Court in 1917. Michael Danielson, *The Politics of Exclusion* (New York: Columbia University Press, 1976), 13. On the other hand, a federal district court upheld the right of Cleveland suburbs to exclude public housing on economic grounds. In the words of the majority opinion: "Wealth, *per se*, is not a suspect classification in the context of the constitutional examination of a provision relating to housing assistance or welfare." *Mahaley v. Cuyahoga Metropolitan Housing Authority*, 355 F. Supp. 1245, 1249 (1973).

24. E. Branfman, B. Cohen, and D. Trubek, "Measuring the Invisible Wall: Land Use Controls and Residential Patterns of the Poor," in *Land Use Controls: Present Problems and Future Reform*, ed. D. Listokin (New Brunswick, N.J.: Rutgers University, Center for Urban Policy Research, 1974).

25. Capital intensive industrial investment and retail establishments bring in much more in local revenues than they consume in services. However, since the external costs of industrialism damage residential values, cities often zone out dirty industries. Regarding residential development, only the highest value homes and families without children provide more tax revenues than they take away in services.

26. *Hearing before the United States Commission of Civil Rights in Cleveland, Ohio, April 1–7, 1966* (Washington, D.C.: Government Printing Office, 1966), Exhibit no. 28, 727.

27. Regional Planning Commission, *Land Development Regulations* (Cleveland: Regional Planning Commission, Oct. 1974).

28. Danielson, 61.

29. *United States v. City of Parma, Ohio*, 627.

30. Interestingly, subsidies for conventional public housing require approval of the local government; no such approval is required for middle class subsidies, such as deduction of mortgage interest and taxes from income for federal taxes.

31. *Mahaley v. Cuyahoga Metropolitan Housing Authority*, 355 F. Supp. 1245 (1973).

32. Many of these programs, such as Section 8, were specifically designed to foster the mobility of low income households. Recent research on the Section 8 Existing Program for the Cleveland area, however, came to the following conclusion: "Section 8 rental assistance in Cleveland and its suburbs did not promote racial and economic integration, spatial deconcentration, or interjurisdictional mobility." Harry L. Margulis, "Housing Mobility in Cleveland and Its Suburbs, 1975–1980," *Geographical Review* 72, no. 1 (Jan. 1982): 48.

33. *United States v. City of Parma, Ohio*. Potentially, the court's ruling has far-reaching implications for suburban exclusion. For the first time, the Federal Fair Housing Act is applied to a municipality. Also, the decision relies on discriminatory effect, as well as intent, and strikes down local ordinances ostensibly aimed against low income residents, not minorities. The Sixth Circuit

Court of Appeals upheld the ruling but rejected some of the remedies. The U.S. Supreme Court refused Parma's request to review the case.

34. Karl and Alma Taeuber gave the city of Cleveland a segregation index rating of 91.3 in 1960. This means that 91.3 percent of all nonwhites would have to move from the block on which they lived in order to produce an integrated living pattern (32).

35. *Banks v. Perk*, 341 F. Supp. 1175 (1972). As a result of this decision, Cleveland was ordered to build all future public housing on the white West Side.

36. Norton Long, "Political Science and the City," in *Urban Affairs Annual Review*, vol. 1, ed. Leo F. Schnore and Henry Fagin (Beverly Hills, Calif.: Sage Publications, 1967), 257. For further analysis of the effects of suburban segregation, see Kenneth Newton, "American Urban Politics: Social Class, Political Structure and Public Goods," *Urban Affairs Quarterly*, no. 2, Dec. 1975: 241–64; and Lawrence D. Brown, "Mayors and Models: Notes on the Study of Urban Politics," in *American Politics and Public Policy*, ed. Walter Dean Burnham and Martha Wagner Weinberg (Cambridge, Mass.: M.I.T. Press, 1978), 251–79.

37. Governmental Research Institute, *Governmental Facts*, no. 330 (Feb. 14, 1978).

38. This point is emphasized in David Harvey's perceptive discussion of urban political economy, *Social Justice and the City* (Baltimore: Johns Hopkins University Press, 1973).

39. Roger J. Vaughan and Mary E. Vogel, *The Urban Impacts of Federal Policies*, vol. 4, *Population and Residential Location* (Santa Monica, Calif.: Rand Corporation, May 1979), 84.

40. Cleveland has the sixteenth highest auto insurance rates among 100 cities with populations over 100,000. Donald Sabath, "Premiums Up 84% for Auto Insurance Here in Last Five Years," Cleveland *Plain Dealer*, June 26, 1981.

41. Cleveland City Planning Commission, *Patterns of Commercial Activity in the Cleveland Area: 1950–1974*, prepared by June Lazarz (Cleveland: City Planning Commission, 1974), 4.

42. See *United States v. City of Parma, Ohio*.

43. See Cleveland City Planning Commission, *Transportation and Poverty* (Cleveland: City Planning Commission, July 1971).

44. Regional Planning Commission, *The Housing Stock*, prepared by Edward Waxman.

45. Northeast Ohio Areawide Coordinating Agency, *Residential Investment and Sales: Indicators of Change, Cuyahoga County, Ohio, 1977–1979* (Cleveland: NOACA, 1981), 33. The ratio of sales prices in Cleveland to average sales prices in the suburbs fell from 49 percent in 1977 to 44 percent in 1979.

46. "Indeed, controlling for income and other neighborhood characteristics, financial institutions are significantly less likely to finance title transfers with

conventional mortgages in black and racially mixed neighborhoods. This finding would constitute redlining under the definition used earlier." Robert B. Avery and Thomas M. Buynak, "Mortgage Redlining: Some New Evidence," *Federal Reserve Bank of Cleveland Economic Review*, Summer 1981: 31. See also a series of articles in the Cleveland *Plain Dealer* by Thomas S. Andrzejewski, reprinted as *Redlining in Greater Cleveland?* (Cleveland: Cleveland Plain Dealer, 1977).

47. The argument here draws heavily on the works of Ann Markusen, "The Economics of Social Class and Metropolitan Local Government," Ph. D. diss., Michigan State University, 1974; "Class and Urban Social Expenditures: A Local Theory of the State," *Kapitalistate* 4–5 (Summer 1976): 50–65.

48. Teaford, 180.

49. Victor Fuchs in an early seminal study, *The Service Economy* (New York: National Bureau of Economic Research, 1968), emphasized differential rates of productivity in explaining the rise of service employment. More recent evidence indicates that there has been a shift in final demand (toward health, regulatory, and educational services and services attached to products), as well as a very significant increase in intermediate producer services (management, planning, and innovation of corporate production). See Thomas M. Stanback *et al., Services: The New Economy* (Totowa, N.J.: Allanheld, Osmun, 1981).

50. Moreover, it is estimated that the percentage of office space located outside Cleveland's central business district increased from 3 percent to 36 percent between 1960 and 1972. Gerald Manners, "The Office in Metropolis: An Opportunity for Shaping Metropolitan America," *Economic Geography* 50, no. 2 (April 1974): 94.

51. Greater Cleveland Growth Association, *Downtown Cleveland Office and Retail Presentation* (Cleveland: Cleveland Area Development Corporation, Nov. 1980), 2–21.

52. Manners, "The Office in Metropolis," 100.

53. See Jean Gottman, "Urban Centrality and the Interweaving of Quaternary Activities," *Ekistics*, May 1970: 322–31; Manners, "The Office in Metropolis"; and Robert C. Cohen, "The Changing Transactions Economy and Its Spatial Implications," *Ekistics*, Jan.–Feb. 1979: 7–15.

54. Stephen Hymer, "The Multinational Corporation and the Law of Uneven Development," in *Economics and World Order*, ed. Jagdish Bhagwati (New York: World Law Fund, 1971), 113–40.

55. Robert B. Cohen, "Urban Effects of the Internationalization of Capital and Labor," unpublished manuscript, p. 15; and Robert C. Cohen, "Changing Transactions Economy," 14.

56. Mollenkopf, 98. All other data on downtown advanced services is from Greater Cleveland Growth Association, *Downtown Cleveland Office and Retail Presentation*.

57. Greater Cleveland Growth Association, 1-1.

58. According to Jean Gottman, "The skyscraper is an expression of the

social evolution of employment"—namely, the rise of white collar service functions. "Why the Skyscraper?" *Geographical Review* 56, no. 2 (April 1966): 190–212.

59. J. Thomas Black, *The Changing Economic Role of Central Cities* (Washington, D.C.: Urban Land Institute, 1978), 22. In the mid-1980s, however, there is evidence that demand has finally caught up with supply and some new office buildings are having trouble filling their space.

60. Richard Knight, *The Cleveland Economy in Transition—Implications for the Future* (Cleveland: Regional Development Program, College of Urban Affairs, Cleveland State University, July 1977), 40.

61. For a taste of post-industrial social theory, see Daniel Bell, *The End of Ideology* (New York: Free Press, 1960); *The Coming of Post-Industrial Society* (New York: Basic Books, 1973); John Kenneth Galbraith, *The Affluent Society* (New York: Mentor, 1958); Galbraith, *The New Industrial State* (New York: Mentor, 1967); and Ralf Dahrendorf, *Class and Class Conflict in Industrial Society* (Stanford, Calif.: Stanford University Press, 1959).

62. Knight exaggerates the salary difference between headquarters jobs and production jobs, ignoring the numbers of low paid clericals in headquarters jobs. According to a recent study of five corporate headquarters in Cleveland, the largest occupational category is clericals (37 percent). Cleveland Women Working, *White Collar Employment in Cleveland: A Study of Banking, Insurance, and Corporate Headquarters* (Cleveland: Cleveland Women Working, Dec. 1979), 11. Knight also essentially doublecounts advanced services jobs, overlooking that factories also buy local goods and services and that production jobs generate highly paid supervisory personnel. Knight's calculations, in short, seem more designed to prove a point than to objectively assess the facts.

63. U.S. Bureau of the Census, *Census of Manufacturing, 1977*, and *Census of Selected Services, 1977* (Washington, D.C.: Government Printing Office, 1979).

64. Stanback *et al.*, 82; and Emma Rothschild, "Reagan and the Real America," *New York Review of Books*, Feb. 5, 1981, 13.

65. Harry Braverman argues that office work is being drained of skill: "The progressive elimination of thought from the work of the office worker thus takes the form, at first, of reducing mental labor to repetitious performance of the same small set of functions. The work is still performed in the brain, but the brain is used as the equivalent of the hand of the detail worker in production, grasping and releasing a single piece of data over and over again": *Labor and Monopoly Capital* (New York: Monthly Review Press, 1974), 319.

66. Rothschild, 13.

67. See Saskia Sassen-Koob, "The New Labor Demand in Global Cities," in *Cities in Transformation*, ed. Michael Peter Smith (Beverly Hills, Calif.: Sage Publications, 1984), 139–71.

68. Although, it should be pointed out, because it is less capital intensive, service employment generates less property tax revenue than manufacturing.

69. Cleveland Women Working, 92.

70. Out of fourteen cities tested, Cleveland ranked third in percentage of professional and managerial jobs located in the city held by suburban commuters. Andrew J. Gold. *Economic Interdependence in the Greater Hartford Region—City and Suburbs* (Hartford, Conn.: Capital Region Council of Governments, Oct. 1976), 10.

71. A 1972 study of white collar employment in Cleveland found that only 10 percent of women in white collar jobs (and only 4 percent of minority women) held managerial or professional jobs. By contrast, over 40 percent of white males held such high level jobs. Reported in Cleveland Women Working, 96.

72. Greater Cleveland Growth Association, 5-1.

73. Cleveland City Planning Commission, *Patterns of Commercial Activity*, 16.

74. Black, 17.

Chapter 4

1. Quoted in Richard Murway, "Council Puts Slum Plan Up to Voters," Cleveland *Plain Dealer*, Sept. 3, 1952.

2. In Leonard I. Ruchelman, ed., *Big City Mayors* (Bloomington: Indiana University Press, 1969), 349–68. Originally published as "Urban Politics: The New Convergence of Power," *Journal of Politics* 26 (Nov. 1964): 775–97.

3. *Ibid.*, 357.

4. Senate Committee on Banking, Housing and Urban Affairs, Subcommittee on Housing and Urban Affairs, *The Central City Problem and Urban Renewal Policy*, prepared by the Congressional Research Service, Library of Congress (Washington, D.C.: Government Printing Office, 1973), 7.

5. For details on the unmet needs of Cleveland's infrastructure see Nancy Humphrey, George E. Peterson, and Peter Wilson, *The Future of Cleveland's Capital Plant* (Washington, D.C.: Urban Institute, 1979). For details on the unmet needs of Cleveland's indigent population, see Herman D. Stein, ed., *The Crisis in Welfare in Cleveland: Report of the Mayor's Commission* (Cleveland: Case Western Reserve University, 1969).

6. Richard F. Tompkins *et al.*, *All the Necessary Service the People Need and Deserve: Federal Grants in Cleveland during 1978*, a case study for the Brookings Institution (Cleveland: Cleveland Foundation, Oct. 1979), 11.

7. *The Central City Problem and Urban Renewal Policy*, 65.

8. In 1954, no urban renewal projects were completed; by 1966, 289 were completed. Roger Friedland, "Class Power and the Central City: The Contradictions of Urban Growth," Ph.D. diss., University of Wisconsin–Madison, 1977, 186. See also Friedland's *Power and Crisis in the City* (New York: Schocken, 1983), chap. 4.

9. G. William Domhoff, *Who Really Rules?* (Santa Monica, Calif.:

Goodyear, 1978), 74. Domhoff criticizes Dahl's *Who Governs?* for misinterpreting the impact of urban renewal on local power by overlooking the way the national legislation was shaped to benefit commercial interests over slum dwellers. Far from being a politician's program (Dahl's thesis), Domhoff says, urban renewal was basically pushed by businessmen who then used politicians to sell it to the public. While fundamentally agreeing with Domhoff, my account stresses the more impersonal pressures and contradictions of growth politics.

10. *The Central City Problem and Urban Renewal Policy*, 56.

11. Roger Friedland, "Corporate Control in the Central City: The Case of Urban Renewal," unpublished paper, University of Wisconsin, 1974, 14, quoted in Domhoff, 75.

12. John H. Mollenkopf, "The Postwar Politics of Urban Development," *Politics and Society*, 1975: 247–95. See also his recent book length treatment of these issues, *The Contested City* (Princeton: Princeton University Press, 1983).

13. Mollenkopf, "Postwar Politics," 256.

14. For a full catalog of the costs of urban renewal, see Mollenkopf, "Postwar Politics," 285.

15. Mike Royko, for example, discussed community opposition to urban renewal in Chicago, where almost 30,000 families were displaced and only 11,000 housing units built, mostly high rent. *Boss* (New York: E. P. Dutton, 1971), 121–24 and 202–3.

16. Quoted in Estelle Zannes, *Checkmate in Cleveland: The Rhetoric of Confrontation during the Stokes Years* (Cleveland: Press of Case Western Reserve University, 1972), 173.

17. Eugene Segal, "Pass 4 Measures on City Housing," Cleveland *Plain Dealer*, Sept. 3, 1982.

18. Eugene Segal, "Urban Program Showing Defects," Cleveland *Plain Dealer*, Jan. 1, 1959.

19. John C. Weicher concludes that, under the matching grant system, urban renewal was a "profitable investment" for cities, but if all money came essentially from local funds, e.g., using federal revenue sharing monies, it would not be a profitable investment. "The Fiscal Profitability of Urban Renewal under Matching Grants and Revenue Sharing," *Journal of Urban Economics* 3 (1976): 193–208.

20. Martin Anderson estimates that 50 percent of the urban renewal projects would have been built somewhere else in the city without the urban renewal program. *The Federal Bulldozer* (New York: McGraw-Hill, 1964), 167. More recently, Roger Friedland studied the relationship between the number of acres involved in urban renewal and aggregate investment in housing and industry, controlling for other factors likely to affect investment. His conclusion: "Urban renewal had no net additive effects on the level of new investment." Friedland, "Corporate Control," 230.

21. Karen Anderson-Bittenbender, Roldo Bartimole, *et al.*, *The Cleveland Papers* (Cleveland: West Side Community House, 1971–72), 39. This infor-

mally published work is the closest thing in existence to a full-scale community power study of Cleveland. It was written by a group calling itself, satirically, the Illuminating Company, "a radical Cleveland Research Group."

22. Quoted in Roldo Bartimole, "Neighborhoods Beware of Foundation Role," *Point of View* 11, no. 24 (June 23, 1979): 3.

23. *Cleveland Papers*, 40.

24. Cleveland *Plain Dealer*, Jan. 25, 1976.

25. For a detailed account of mismanagement in Cleveland's urban renewal program, see Comptroller General of the United States, *More Effective Federal Action Needed to Meet Urban Renewal Objectives in Cleveland, Ohio*, Report to the Congress, Jan. 9, 1968.

26. See the testimony of Charles Sheboy, commissioner of housing, and James Friedman, commissioner of slum clearance and blight control, in *Hearings before the United States Commission on Civil Rights*, Cleveland, Ohio April 1–7, 1966 (Washington, D.C.: Government Printing Office, 1966), 126–36 and 179–93. This is also discussed in Carl Stokes, *Promise of Power* (New York: Simon and Schuster, 1973), 121.

27. Cleveland Little Hoover Commission, *The Chapla Report on Urban Renewal, City of Cleveland*, Nov. 16, 1966, 34, 36.

28. Staff Report on Urban Renewal Relocation, in *Hearings before the United States Commission on Civil Rights*, 705. Overall, the city had no record of where or how 60 percent of those displaced by urban renewal in Cleveland were relocated. Earl Selby and Robert S. Strother, "Cleveland in Crisis: An Urban Renewal Tragedy," *Reader's Digest*, May 1968, 244.

29. Susan Olson, *Cleveland's Urban Renewal Experience* (Cleveland: City Planning Commission, Dec. 1973), 12.

30. George P. Rasanen, "Millions in Renewal Funds Hinge on U.S. Forgiveness," Cleveland *Plain Dealer*, Oct. 15, 1972.

31. "Erieview: An Urban Renewal Plan for Downtown Cleveland," prepared for the City of Cleveland, Ohio, by I. M. Pei and Associates (1961), 2.

32. Olson, 5.

33. See the critical account of Erieview in Philip W. Porter, *Cleveland: Confused City on a Seesaw* (Columbus: Ohio State University Press, 1976), 180–88.

34. Ada Louise Huxtable, "The Revitalization of Cleveland Is at a Turning Point," *New York Times*, Nov. 23, 1973.

35. Freeways were for the West Side what urban renewal was for the East Side. It is estimated that the interstate highway system displaced 19,000 Cleveland residents. Cleveland City Planning Commission, *Cleveland Policy Planning Report*, vol. 1 (1975), p. 34. Many of the existing freeways have spurs designed to connect with highways in the city that were never built because of community opposition. If a political history of highways in Cleveland were ever written, it would center on the powerful person of Albert Porter, Cleveland's

Robert Moses, who, for many years, combined the roles of County Democratic Chairman and County Engineer, dispensing federal highway funds and patronage.

36. Richard Hatcher was elected mayor of Gary, Indiana on the same day but did not assume office until after Stokes. Gary's population was about 180,000.

37. I am not suggesting that urban renewal was the only cause of the riots; it was, however, a crucial precipitating factor. By no means am I the first to draw this connection between urban renewal and the Hough riots. See Selby and Strother, 237–44; Porter, 186; *Cleveland Papers*, 41; and David A. Snow and Peter J. Leahy, "The Making of a Black Slum Ghetto: A Case Study of Neighborhood Transition," *Journal of Applied Behavioral Science* 16, no. 4 (1980): 469–71.

38. Carolyn Milter, *In Search of Community Federal Block Grants in Housing*, master's thesis, Urban Studies, Cleveland State University, 1976, 18.

39. Stokes, 96.

40. Roldo Bartimole, "Downtown," *Point of View*, Sept. 22, 1973, 2.

41. Roldo Bartimole, "History of Corporate Manipulation Reveals Attempts in 1960's to Elect Acceptable Mayor," *Point of View* 12, no. 2 (Aug. 18, 1979). See also: *Point of View* 1, no. 20, and vol. 2, no. 3.

42. *Cleveland Papers*, 10.

43. Cleveland Little Hoover Commission, *Dorward C. Witzke Wrap-Up Report*, project no. 29 (Nov. 3, 1967), 17.

44. The final recommendation of the *Wrap-Up Report* called for creating a "higher authority" to define the issues and their consequences for the voter and to establish priorities for the community. The report lamented the "lack of followership" in Cleveland, noting that present leadership was "functional," i.e., fragmented by issue area. Back in its Golden Age, Cleveland had been fortunate to have a small core of businessmen (about six) who could set priorities for the community. But in "mature cities" the situation was different, the writers said, and in Cleveland there was no one dominant business group, like the Mellons in Pittsburgh. In order to accomplish things such as "revitalizing the downtown area," a civic council was needed, representing the existing "power structure," notwithstanding its fragmented nature (twenty persons). The Little Hoover Commission showed clearly the tension between the imperatives of growth politics and democracy. See Cleveland Little Hoover Commission, 292–99.

45. The torch was passed from conservative business leaders like Gund and Humphrey. This was symbolized by the close friendship of Stokes and Cyrus Eaton, a self-made millionaire whose liberal views and opposition to the Cold War made him *persona non grata* in Cleveland's conservative business community. Eaton had long fought the conservative Cleveland business establishment centered on Cleveland Trust and CEI.

46. Stokes, 72.

47. Kenneth G. Weinberg, *Black Victory: Carl Stokes and the Winning of Cleveland* (Chicago: Quadrangle Books, 1968), 162. In the 1979 mayoral election, Stokes campaigned for Kucinich and opposed the sale of Muny Light.

48. Two main recommendations of Stoke's Commission of the Crisis in Welfare were: (1) raise welfare benefits; (2) institute a state income tax to help pay for this. Stein, 5–6.

49. Roldo Bartimole, "Buying Peace The Private Way," *Point of View* 1, no. 2 (June 26, 1968): 1–3.

50. "Business Now Backs Cleveland," *Business Week*, Sept. 21, 1968, 118–24.

51. Quoted in Roldo Bartimole, "Carl's Cop-Out-Thinking of One's Self," *Point of View* 3, no. 20 (April 19–24, 1971): 1.

52. Stokes, 130. The most thorough account of the shoot-out, which casts doubt on this guilty verdict, is Louis H. Masotti and Jerome R. Corsi, *Shoot-Out in Cleveland: A Report Submitted to the National Commission on the Causes and Prevention of Violence* (New York: Praeger, 1969).

53. Stokes, 244.

54. *Near Town News*, Jan. 1970, quoted in Zannes, 174.

55. *Ibid.*, 172.

56. *Ibid.*

57. Quoted in Thomas J. Brazaitas and George P. Rasanen, "Cleveland on the Brink," Cleveland *Plain Dealer*, Aug. 3, 1978.

58. Ralph Perk, a Republican in an overwhelmingly Democratic city, succeeded in getting a City Charter amendment passed in 1971 that made the mayor's race nonpartisan: all candidates run in the primary and the two top vote getters go on to the final election. This rule change did not apply until 1973. For an analysis of nonpartisan elections, including how they benefit Republicans, see the articles cited in chap. 2, n. 44.

59. Perk quoted in Joseph D. Rice and Joseph L. Wagner, "Time Changes Ralph Perk," Cleveland *Plain Dealer*, Sept. 25, 1977. Kucinich quoted in Estelle Zannes, *Checkmate in Cleveland* (Cleveland: Press of Case Western Reserve University, 1972), 250.

60. In 1975, this practice of the Perk administration was criticized by the Greater Cleveland Growth Association. Committee on Taxation, *Interim Report: City of Cleveland Finances*, Sept. 4, 1975.

61. Joseph L. Wagner, "U.S. Funds: Catch-22 for City Budgets," Cleveland *Plain Dealer*, April 18, 1976.

62. Greater Cleveland Growth Association.

63. Margaret Foster, quoted in "Neighborhoods Should Get Funds First, City Told," Cleveland *Plain Dealer*, July 17, 1976.

64. See Roldo Bartimole, "Arena Mortgage-Holder, Miller Kin Partners in Perk Deal with Neighborhoods' $1 Million," *Point of View* 9, no. 2 (Aug. 15, 1976): 1–4.

65. William Silverman & Co., *Cleveland Works!* A report prepared at the request of Mayor Perk, Feb. 1976, 8.

66. Charles Tracy, "Jetport Study Is Nation's Biggest, Most Expensive," Cleveland *Press*, July 26, 1973.

67. Edward R. Waxman was fired from the Regional Planning Commission for leaking information and testifying against the jetport at Kucinich's hearings. Waxman was later appointed city planning director by Kucinich.

68. Roldo Bartimole, "Downtown," *Point of View* 6, no. 5 (Sept. 22, 1973): 1.

69. Richard F. Tompkins *et al., All the Necessary Service the People Need and Deserve: Federal Grants in Cleveland During 1978,* a case study for the Brookings Institution (Cleveland: Cleveland Foundation, Oct. 1979), 58.

70. *Ibid.,* 61.

71. See Diana Tittle, "Is This Any Way to Move People?" *Cleveland Magazine*, April 1977, 74–81.

72. Dennis Kucinich, speech before the National Press Club, reprinted in the Cleveland *Press*, Oct. 3, 1978.

73. Terence Sheridan, "Dennis, the Menacing Mayor of Cleveland," *New Times*, May 1, 1978, 25.

74. Perk, in his first public attack on Kucinich, accused him of trying to stack the Board of Ethics and demanding that Bob Weissman, Kucinich ally and Perk-appointed member of the Civil Service Commission, be appointed secretary of the commission at a $12,000 raise. Kucinich denied the charges.

75. Roldo Bartimole, "Perk-Forbes Unity Being Sold by News Media as Political Dealing Hits Intolerable Level," *Point of View* 9, no. 12 (Jan. 1, 1977): 2.

76. William Carlson and David T. Abbott, "7 Incumbents on Council Ousted in Voter Revolt," Cleveland *Plain Dealer*, Nov. 9, 1977.

77. For a summary of the work of the Cleveland planners, as well as critical commentary by Herbert Gans, Francis Fox Piven, Norton Long, and Paul Davidoff, see *Journal of the American Institute of Planners* 41, no. 5 (Sept. 1975): 298–318. See also the recent retrospective on equity planning in Cleveland, *American Planning Association Journal*, Spring 1982, 163–83.

78. Cleveland City Planning Commission, *Cleveland Policy Planning Report*, vol. 1 (1975), 9.

79. *Ibid.,* 12.

80. John Rawls, *A Theory of Justice* (Cambridge, Mass.: Harvard University Press, 1971).

81. Norman Krumholz and Janice Cogger, "The Challenge of Contracting Municipalities," in *Revitalizing the Northeast,* ed. George Sternlieb and James W. Hughes (New Brunswick, N.J.: Center for Urban Policy Research, 1978), 371—77.

82. In the course of this battle, they succeeded in having the Northeast Ohio Areawide Coordinating Agency (NOACA) decertified by HUD as a regional planning and review agency. NOACA was later recertified.

83. See *Transportation and Poverty*, "General Plan—Transportation Paper no. 2" (Cleveland: City Planning Commission, July 1971).

84. See *Cleveland City Planning Commission Staff Report on the Ten-Year Transit Development Program* (Cleveland: City Planning Commission, July 1974).

Chapter 5

1. Interview with Dennis Kucinich by Robert Scheer, *Playboy*, June 1979, 116.

2. Quoted in Joseph L. Wagner, "Feighan, Kucinich: It's Promises, Promises," Cleveland *Plain Dealer*, Oct. 27, 1977.

3. Quoted in Harry Boyte, "A Democratic Awakening," *Social Policy*, Sept.–Oct. 1979, 13.

4. The most important force behind community organizing in Cleveland was the Catholic Commission on Community Action, led by Director Harry Fagan. While Fagan specifically rejected Alinsky's dictum that the end justifies the means in fighting for social justice, the Catholic Commission groups in Cleveland followed, in broad outline, the path forged by Alinsky. See Harry Fagan, *Empowerment: Skills for Parish Social Action* (New York: Paulist Press, 1979), 57.

5. Saul Alinsky, *Reveille for Radicals* (New York: Vintage Books, 1946), xiv.

6. Saul Alinsky, *Rules for Radicals* (New York: Vintage Books, 1971), 24.

7. Alinsky, *Reveille for Radicals*, 132.

8. Shel Trapp, *Dynamics of Organizing* (Chicago: National Training and Information Center, 1976), 4.

9. I am not the first to note this connection: "In his style and tactics he [Kucinich] brings to mind the late Saul Alinsky, the Chicago community organizer." Alexander Cockburn and James Ridgeway, "Is Dennis Kucinich as Mad as They Say?" *Village Voice*, Jan. 22, 1979.

10. *Ibid.*

11. Harry C. Boyte's excellent survey of the community organizing movement, *The Backyard Revolution: Understanding the New Citizen Movement* (Philadelphia: Temple University Press, 1980), discusses the need for going beyond the interest group methods of American politics and formulating a majoritarian electoral strategy. This case study suggests, however, that there are problematic anti-political tendencies within the community organizing movement itself.

12. Many community activists in Cleveland would object to this line of reasoning. How could Kucinich have been "like" the community groups when, as mayor, he had violent conflicts with them? In Chapter 8, however, I argue that it is precisely the similarities that help explain these conflicts. But wait,

other critics would say, the Kucinich administration was not an effort to apply the tactics of community organizing to electoral politics but simply an attempt, by certain aberrant personalities, to manipulate neighborhood sentiment for their own ambitions. After noting that community organizers themselves have frequently been accused of manipulation, the best reply to this is to argue that Kucinich promoted certain personality types ("abrasive" and "confrontational" are two of the most common adjectives) because they fit the political style and tactics of the administration, not vice versa. All this is not to deny that personalities played a major role or that Kucinich made serious errors in judgment. It *is* meant to deny that urban populism in Cleveland was a pure aberration.

13. E. E. Schattschneider, *The Semi-Sovereign People* (New York: Holt, Rinehart and Winston, 1960), 68.

14. Dennis Kucinich, speech at the Washington Press Club, reprinted in the Cleveland *Press*, Oct. 3, 1978, A9.

15. *Ibid.*

16. Economic democracy is, perhaps, most closely associated with Tom Hayden and his Campaign for Economic Democracy (CED) in California. The ideas have been fleshed out in a book by Martin Cranoy and Derek Shearer, *Economic Democracy: The Challenge of the 1980's* (White Plains, N.Y.: M. E. Sharpe, 1980).

17. Kucinich's views are similar to those of his predecessor Tom Johnson (1901–1909). In Johnson's autobiography, which Kucinich has called his bible, Johnson stated: "The Socialists, regarding competition as the source of evil, demand its destruction. We who hold that the evils arise from a denial of competition demand the abolition of law-made advantage, of governmental favor." *My Story*, ed. Elizabeth J. Hauser (Seattle: University of Washington Press, 1911), 151.

18. Statement by Mayor Dennis Kucinich, press release, September 18, 1978.

19. Walter Dean Burnham, "The Changing Shape of the American Political Universe," *American Political Review* 59 (March 1965): 10. Burnham's thesis has been the center of controversy in the political science profession, with critics arguing that the decline in voting turnout can be largely explained by certain rules changes, such as personal registration statutes. Burnham has argued that these rules changes cannot explain most of the change and, besides, "They were, in the main, devices by which a large and possibly dangerous mass electorate could be brought to heel and subjected to management and control within the political system appropriate to 'capitalist democracy.'" Walter Dean Burnham, *Critical Elections and the Mainsprings of American Politics* (New York: W. W. Norton, 1970), 90. For details of the controversy see Philip E. Converse, "Change in the American Electorate," in *The Human Meaning of Social Change*, ed. Angus Campbell and Philip E. Converse (New York: Russell Sage Foundation, 1972), esp. 263–301; Walter Dean Burnham, "Theory and Voting Research: Some Reflections on Converse's 'Change in the American

Electorate,'" *American Political Science Review* 68 (Sept. 1974): 1002–23, and the various comments and rejoinders that follow in the same issue.

20. This surge in voter participation in the 1930s and gradual decline since then parallels nationwide trends calculated by Burnham. See Burnham, "The Changing Shape of the American Political Universe," 11.

21. Figures from Walter Dean Burnham, "Political Immunization and Political Confessionalism: The United States and Weimar Germany," *Journal of Interdisciplinary History* 3 (Summer 1972): 26. In 1967, the Ford Foundation gave a special grant of $25,000 to the Congress on Racial Equality (CORE) for voter registration in Cleveland. More people voted in the 1967 primary election, in which Stokes upset Locher, than in any mayoral race in Cleveland's history. Estelle Zannes, *Checkmate in Cleveland* (Cleveland: Case Western Reserve University Press, 1972), 77.

22. Penn Kimball, *The Disconnected* (New York: Columbia University Press, 1972), 148.

23. M. Craig Brown, "Political Machine Documentation for the City of Cleveland," unpublished manuscript, 1983.

24. With the exception of the period 1958 to 1971, Cleveland has had nonpartisan mayoral elections since 1913. After the primary election, the two highest vote-getters move on to the final election. While there is no partisan identification on the ballot, this does not prevent the parties from exerting as much influence as possible.

25. William E. Nelson, Jr., and Philip J. Meranto, *Electing Black Mayors* (Columbus: Ohio State University Press, 1977), 75.

26. Maurice Duverger, *Political Parties*, tr. Barbara and Robert North, 2d Eng. ed. rev. (New York: John Wiley and Sons, 1959), book 1.

27. Quoted in Joseph Rice, "New Day Is Dawning for County Democratic Party," Cleveland *Plain Dealer*, Jan. 2, 1976.

28. This concept of political alienation relies heavily on David C. Schwartz, *Political Alienation and Political Behavior* (Chicago: Aldine, 1973).

29. Ada Finifter, "Dimensions of Political Alienation," *American Political Science Review* 64 (June 1970): 389. See also Arthur Miller, "Political Issues and Trust in Government," *American Political Science Review* 68 (Sept. 1974): 951–72. A critique and rejoinder follow this article.

30. As someone who has knocked on thousands of doors in political campaigns, I can attest to the high level of political alienation among Cleveland residents. Clearly, a large number regard politics as only a step above prostitution in honor as a profession.

31. Burnham, *Critical Elections and the Mainspring of American Politics*, 72–73, 95–97. The military analogy is taken from Richard Jenson, "American Election Campaigns: A Theoretical and Historical Typology," paper delivered at the 1968 convention of the Midwest Political Science Association.

32. This pattern seems to be increasingly common, even in national politics.

In Richard Nixon's 1972 re-election campaign, for example, the Committee to Re-Elect the President (CREEP) was run independently of the Republican National Committee. Jimmy Carter, of course, won the presidency in 1976 without the initial support of Democratic powerbrokers, including organized labor, and portrayed himself as the political outsider, running against Washington.

33. Quoted in Joseph L. Wagner, "Jesting Kucinich Jabs for Next Round," Cleveland *Plain Dealer*, Oct. 6, 1977.

34. For a discussion of the intriguing concept of "political immunization" see William McPhee and Jack Ferguson, "Political Immunization," in *Public Opinion and Congressional Elections*, ed. William McPhee and William Glaser (New York: Free Press, 1962), 155–79.

35. While Kucinich was constantly in the public eye, Weissman shunned all publicity. Weissman grew up in a middle class home, graduated from Temple University, and went to work in a factory to become a union organizer. A UAW leader in the Cleveland area, he was elected four times president of UAW Local 122 (about 4,000 members) and in 1970 president of the Community Action Program (CAP), UAW's political arm in the area. Weissman and Kucinich met in 1969 and established a close working relationship. Weissman was Kucinich's top political strategist and his behind the scenes comments serve as a valuable supplement to the public pronouncements of Kucinich.

36. In 1977, Feighan outspent Kucinich $247,127 to $110,000. In 1979, Voinovich raised $522,954 to Kucinich's $174,586.

37. Interview with Bob Weissman, November 28, 1979.

38. Cleveland *Plain Dealer*, Oct. 6, 1977.

39. Quoted in Wagner, "Jesting Kucinich Jabs for Next Round."

40. Kucinich's political analysis has sometimes been mistakenly labeled Marxist. Notwithstanding his emphasis on economic inequalities, Kucinich's political analysis was much closer to elite theory than Marxist class analysis. For a succinct discussion of the difference between the two, see Isaac Balbus, "Ruling Elite Theory vs. Marxist Class Analysis," *Monthly Review*, May 1971, 36–46.

Chapter 6

1. From an interview with Fred McGunagle in a series of articles written for the Cleveland *Press* in 1978. These articles are collected under the title "The Tax Cut War" and reprinted in *Tax Abatements: Resources for Public Officials and Activities*, ed. Ed Kelly and Lee Webb (Washington, D.C.: Conference on State and Local Policies, May 1979), 52–59.

2. "A Counterattack in the War Between the States," *Business Week*, June 21, 1976.

3. Bennett Harrison and Sandra Kanter, "The Great State Robbery," *Working Papers for a New Society*, Spring 1976, 62.

4. Jerry Jacobs, *Bidding for Business: Corporate Auctions and the 50 Disunited States* (Washington, D.C.: Public Interest Research Group, Aug. 1979), 4.

5. *Ibid.*, summary.

6. Quoted in Brent Larkin and Norman Mlachak, "Kucinich Firm on Tax Breaks," Cleveland *Press*, Nov. 9, 1977.

7. See Joseph Pechman and Benjamin Okner, *Who Bears the Tax Burden?* (Washington, D.C.: Brookings Institution, 1974), 62–64; Dick Netzer, *Economics of the Property Tax* (Washington, D.C.: Brookings Institution, 1966), 40. For a summary of the state of knowledge of property tax incidence, including the new theory that a major portion of it falls on capital and therefore is progressive, see Robert D. Ebel, "Research and Policy Developments: Major Types of State and Local Taxes," in *State and Local Government Finance and Financial Management: A Compendium of Current Research*, ed. John E. Peterson *et al.* (Washington, D.C.: Government Finance Research Center, Aug. 1978), 6.

8. Governmental Research Institute, *Governmental Facts*, nos. 305 and 330 (Jan. 5, 1977, and Feb. 14, 1978).

9. Betty Klaric, "Tax Burden Is Shifting to Homeowners," Cleveland *Press*, Oct. 10, 1978. The reasons for this shift were complex. Ironically, the main reason was a bill passed to prevent a Proposition 13 in Ohio by capping property tax increases caused by inflation. Since all millage reductions had to be uniform, and residential valuation was increasing more than twice as fast as industrial property, it had the unintended effect of giving a tax windfall to business. For a discussion of the nationwide shift in the property tax burden, including a discussion of Ohio, and the effect of all this on the tax revolt, see Robert Kuttner and David Kelston, *The Shifting Property Tax Burden: The Untold Cause of the Tax Revolt* (Washington, D.C.: Conference on Alternative State and Local Policies, Dec. 1979).

10. Quoted in McGunagle, 57.

11. While, in principle, there is no reason why tax abatements should be reserved for the largest corporations, in practice, it is the multistate, multinational corporations that can use their investment mobility and political clout to obtain abatements, Jacobs, 35–36.

12. See J. Richard Elliott, "Bankers of the Year: Claude Blair and Julien McCall of Cleveland's National City Corporation," *Finance Magazine*, Sept.–Oct. 1978, 17. National City Bank was not the developer for the building, but it benefited directly from the project.

13. "An Oil Giant's Dilemma," *Business Week*, Aug. 25, 1980.

14. Quoted in Daniel R. Biddle, "Tax Abatement: Mayor's Record," Cleveland *Plain Dealer*, Aug. 6, 1978.

15. One of the few examples of an argument that local tax subsidies increase

the efficiency of capital investment nationwide is a book by John E. Moes, *Local Subsidies for Industry* (Chapel Hill: University of North Carolina Press, 1962). Moes contends that wages are higher than the market ideal because of unions and minimum wage laws. Local subsidies to industry, in effect, lower social wages and therefore lead to a greater utilization of manpower and capital than would otherwise be the case. This argument has the virtue of boldly stating the regressive effect of local tax abatement. For a critical discussion of Moes' argument, see Benjamin Bridges, Jr., "State and Local Inducements for Industry: Part 2," in *Locational Analysis for Manufacturing*, ed. Gerald Karaska and David Bramhall (Cambridge, Mass.: MIT Press, 1969), 205–8.

16. This point is made by Joe Summers Floyd, Jr., *Effects of Taxation on Industrial Location* (Chapel Hill: University of North Carolina Press, 1952), 112–13.

17. *Industrial Mobility in Michigan* (Ann Arbor: University of Michigan Press, Dec. 1950).

18. "Plan Site Preferences of Industry and Factors of Selection," *Business Week Research Report*, 1958.

19. U.S. Department of Commerce, *Industrial Location Determinants* (Washington, D.C.: Government Printing Office, 1975).

20. Surveys of the literature based on responses from corporate executives can be found in John F. Due, "Studies of State-Local Tax Influences on Location of Industry," *National Tax Journal* 14 (1961): 164–65; Susan Olson, *An Evaluation of Tax Incentives as a Means to Encourage Redevelopment* (Cleveland: City Planning Commission, April 1978), 17–23; Harrison and Kanter, 61; and Bridges, 193–94.

21. Interviews of business executives in Massachusetts and Connecticut came to this conclusion. "Every single interview yielded the same result: the company took actions according to its own plans, then learned about the existence of the tax credits and applied for them." Harrison and Kanter, 61.

22. C. C. Bloom, *State and Local Tax Differentials* (Iowa City: Bureau of Business Research, State University of Iowa, 1955).

23. Advisory Commission on Intergovernmental Relations, *State-Local Taxation and Industrial Location* (Washington, D.C., April 1967), 66. For surveys of the literature using this methodology see Due, 163—164; Harrison and Kanter, 61—63; and Jacobs, 43-45.

24. Ohio Department of Taxation, "Business Taxes in Ohio: A Study of the Level of Business Taxation in Ohio Compared to Other States" (Aug. 1974).

25. Greater Cleveland Growth Association, Regional Economic Development Council, "Confidential Abstract of Fantus Report" (*circa* 1977). The release of this report to the newspapers was embarrassing to the Growth Association, which was lobbying for tax abatement.

26. Harrison and Kanter, 63. See also Due, 165–68, and Olson, 15–16.

27. Bridges, 177.

28. Robert Goodman, *The Last Entrepreneurs* (New York: Simon and Schuster, 1979), 43–44.

29. David Gordon points out that incentives like tax abatement assume that capital markets are flexible enough to make marginal adjustments to small changes in profitability, such as tax breaks. In reality, Gordon argues, there are substantial "structural rigidities" in the U.S. economy that prevent "continuous substitution at the margin." *The Working Poor: Towards a State Agenda* (Washington, D.C.: Council of State Planning Agencies, 1979).

30. One prominent exception is a book by Daniel L. Mandelker, Gary Feder, and Margaret P. Collins, *Reviving Cities with Tax Abatement* (New Brunswick, N.J.: Rutgers University, Center for Urban Policy Research, 1980). The authors give a very positive evaluation of tax abatement in St. Louis, asserting that it "leveraged" over $367 million in private investment over a sixteen-year period (27), and concluding, for a sample of ten projects, that it "generate[d] an estimated $72.6 million in excess of the total value of the revenue foregone to the city as a result of tax abatements" (45). The analysis even concludes that tax abatement had a progressive, not a regressive, impact on income distribution. This *entire* positive evaluation, however, rests on one crucial point: that the projects in St. Louis would not have occurred without tax abatement. The evidence on this point (30–41) is flimsy and contradictory. In short, the entire edifice of this informative book is constructed on a foundation of quicksand.

31. New York Office of the Comptroller, Bureau of Performance Analysis, *Performance Audit of the Industrial and Commercial Incentive Board* (New York: Office of the Controller, March 12, 1979). Quotation is from the official news release on the report (March 22, 1979).

32. Intradepartmental memorandum from Jerry Finch to Carol Bellamy, Sept. 29, 1981, 3, reported in Frank Domurad and Ruth Messinger, *Citizen Program to Eliminate the Gap* (New York: City Project, 1983), 26.

33. Susan Olson, *Impact of New Construction on the Market for Existing Downtown Office Space: Implications for the City's Revenue Base* (Cleveland: City Planning Commission, June 1974), 10.

34. Greggar Sletteland, "Economics of Highrise," in *The Ultimate Highrise*, ed. Bruce Brugmann *et al.* (San Francisco: San Francisco Bay Guardian Books, 1971), 35.

35. Roldo Bartimole, "Perk-Forbes Unity Being Sold by News Media as Political Dealing Hits Intolerable Level," *Point of View* 9, no. 12 (Jan. 1, 1977): 2.

36. At a City Council hearing on the Sohio building, a lawyer for Sohio stated that the corporation was not interested in tax abatement, land write-offs, or "other rip-offs." "Don't use the word rip-off," Forbes replied, "use subsidy. There are those of us who favor that approach." Quoted in Gary Clark, "Commitments Asked of Sohio by City for Deal on HQ," Cleveland *Plain Dealer*, April 16, 1981.

37. "Growth Association States Confidence in Indicted Officials," Cleve-

land *Press*, Oct. 31, 1978; Brent Larkin, "For Forbes the Trial is Topic A," Cleveland *Press*, June 18, 1979; and Jim Marino, "From Carnival Midway to Court," Cleveland *Press*, June 25, 1979.

38. Murray Edelman, *The Symbolic Uses of Politics* (Urbana: University of Illinois Press, 1964).

39. Forbes was well aware of the lack of positive alternatives, saying, "It [tax abatement] is a give away. If we don't give away what do we do? We can't continue to tear down without building up." Quoted in Andrew Juniewicz, "City Tax Abatement Plan Meets Resistance," Cleveland *Plain Dealer*, Oct. 28, 1976.

40. U.S. Bureau of the Census, *County and City Data Book*, 1977 (Washington, D.C.: Government Printing Office, 1978).

41. The Urban Institute, *The Struggle to Bring Technology to the Cities* (Washington, D.C.: Urban Institute, 1971).

42. Governmental Research Institute, *The Inconspicuous Governments: An Inventory of Special Governmental Agencies in Cuyahoga County* (Cleveland: Governmental Research Institute, Jan. 1976), 4–8.

43. This irrationality of tax abatement programs is perceptively examined in Michael J. Wolkoff, "The Nature of Property Tax Abatement Awards," *Journal of the American Planning Association*, Winter 1983, 77–84.

44. Office construction in Cleveland has gone through a number of cycles, determined by supply and demand. From the Depression until the late 1950s, office building was at a near standstill. Pent-up demand fueled a building boom throughout the 1960s and early 1970s. The 1974–1975 recession brought this to a halt. About the time Kucinich became mayor the building boom started again. See McGunagle, 55.

45. Geraldine M. Strozier, "National City Transfer Revives Rebate Debate," Cleveland *Plain Dealer*, Aug. 16, 1983.

46. See Ronald Alsop, "Property Tax Breaks for Firms Proliferate, but Need Is Disputed," *Wall Street Journal*, found in Kelly and Webb, 12–13; and "A Counterattack in the War between the States," *Business Week*, May 17, 1976.

47. Committee for Economic Development, Research and Policy Committee, *Public-Private Partnerships: An Opportunity for Urban Communities*, Feb. 11, 1982, 24, quoted in Domurad and Messinger.

48. Quoted in "Tax Abatement Draws Ire of Embattled Kucinich," Columbus *Citizen-Journal*, June 28, 1978.

49. Telephone interview with Dennis Kucinich, July 11, 1980.

50. Under the leadership of Jack Nicholl, Commissioner of Economic Development, attempts were made to develop an alternative program of economic development. Efforts focused on helping firms already in Cleveland, especially small firms, rather than attracting business away from other cities. As an example, the International Trade and Relations Office, designed to lure foreign business, was closed down. Only a few examples of the positive approach were

implemented, however, such as negotiating an agreement with a local savings and loan to invest $15 million in Cleveland's neighborhoods. For background on the Kucinich administration's efforts in economic development, see Fred McGunagle, "Commissioner Jack Nicholl: Bargaining for the Public," Cleveland *Press*, July 28, 1978; Biddle; Jack Nicholl, "Unabated: City Hall's Priorities for Economic Growth," Cleveland *Plain Dealer*, March 10, 1979; and *Report by the Division of Economic Development to Mayor Kucinich*, Oct. 5, 1979.

51. Michael Kelly, "Diamond Shamrock to Leave Area," Cleveland *Plain Dealer*, May 30, 1979.

52. "Shamrock's Move," editorial, Cleveland *Plain Dealer*, May 31, 1979.

53. For evidence on this, see articles from two disparate sources: Daniel J. Marschall, "Why Did Diamond Shamrock Go?" Cleveland *Plain Dealer*, June 16, 1979; and "Media Distorts Reason, Purely Economic," *Northern Ohio Business Journal*, June 11, 1979.

Chapter 7

1. Quoted in Julie Wiernik and Thomas Geidel, "Weir Warms to Rhodes' Plan for City," Cleveland *Plain Dealer*, Jan. 12, 1979.

2. Dennis Kucinich, letter to Representative Fernand St. Germain, Feb. 1, 1979, reprinted in *The Role of Commercial Banks in the Finances of the City of Cleveland*, staff study by the Subcommittee on Financial Institutions of the Committee on Banking, Finance and Urban Affairs of the U.S. House of Representatives (Washington, D.C.: Government Printing Office, 1979), 265. Hereafter cited as Congressional Study.

3. Milton Friedman, *Capitalism and Freedom* (Chicago: University of Chicago Press, 1962), 19–20.

4. Tom Johnson, *My Story* (Seattle: University of Washington Press, 1911), 192–94.

5. The following history of Muny Light relies heavily on articles in the Cleveland *Press* by Fred McGunagle and in the Cleveland *Plain Dealer* by David T. Abbott and Daniel R. Biddle in February 1979, as well as a history of Muny Light written by Elmer Lindseth, former president of CEI.

6. There was one last effort to expand Muny in 1942–1943, when legislation was introduced in council for the city to purchase CEI. The proposal lost in council by a vote of 19-13.

7. This price is deceptive since the agreement called for payments over thirty years without interest or inflation. An analysis for City Council in 1976 estimated that the true purchase price was about $88.1 million. David T. Abbott and Daniel R. Biddle, "Facts vs. Figures," Cleveland *Plain Dealer*, Feb. 12, 1979.

8. For detailed discussion of the efforts by CEI to sabotage the bond issue, as well as the taxpayer suits against Muny, see Roldo Bartimole, "So Much for Justice," *Point of View* 13, no. 7 (Nov. 1, 1980).

9. Cleveland's complaint was consolidated with a number of allegations by other small municipal utility systems against five large private utilities pooled together in the General Area Power Coordination Group (CAPCO). 5 NRC 133 (1977), cited in *Nuclear Regulatory Commission Issuances* (Jan. 1, 1977–March 31, 1977), vol. 5 (Washington, D.C.: Government Printing Office, 1977), 133–260.

10. 5 NRC 133 (1977) (168).

11. 5 NRC 133 (1977) (171).

12. 5 NRC 133 (1977) (176).

13. 5 NRC 133 (1977) (257).

14. *State, ex rel. Schulman, v. Tegreene* (1978), 55 Ohio St. 2nd 22.

15. Statement by Mayor Dennis Kucinich, press release, Sept. 18, 1978. Reprinted in *Role of Commercial Banks in the Financing of the Debt of the City of Cleveland*, Hearing Before the Subcommittee on Financial Institutions Supervision, Regulation and Insurance of the Committee on Banking, Finance and Urban Affairs, House of Representatives, 96th Cong., 1st Sess., July 10, 1979 (Washington, D.C.: Government Printing Office, 1980), 317–20. Hereafter cited as Congressional Hearing.

16. "Editorial: CEI Plays Scrooge," Cleveland *Press*, Dec. 14, 1978.

17. Quoted in Joseph Wagner and Frederick Freeman, "City Slides into Default," Cleveland *Plain Dealer*, Dec. 16, 1978.

18. Quoted in Congressional Study, 309.

19. According to a telephone poll reported in the *Plain Dealer* a little more than a month before the election, voters favored *selling* Muny 70-30 percent. Joseph Rice, "2 Issues Take Lead: Pollster Finds Sizable Margins for Tax Hike, Muny Light Sale," Cleveland *Plain Dealer*, Jan. 23, 1979.

20. A significant event of the campaign was an attempt by the Cleveland *Plain Dealer* to suppress information critical of CEI. Reporter Bob Holden was originally assigned to the story but was pulled off for alleged pro-Muny bias. In response, reporters picketed the *Plain Dealer* and organized a rare by-line strike. Eventually reporters Daniel Biddle and David Abbott were assigned to the story. They wrote a three-part series for the *Plain Dealer* (Feb. 12–13) that is one of the best treatments of the complex Muny issue and brought to light much embarrassing information concerning CEI's anticompetitive acts. For the full story, see Ellen S. Freilich, "Cleveland 'Plain Dealer' Pressured by Reporters, Prints a Story It Stifled," *Columbia Journalism Review*, May–June 1979, 49–57.

21. Congressional Study, 240.

22. *Ibid.*, 227.

23. Edward S. Herman, *Conflicts of Interest: Commercial Bank Trust Departments* (New York: Twentieth Century Fund, 1975), esp. chap. 2. Given major structural and legal impediments to complete separation, as well as the lack of any enforcement mechanism, Herman concludes that the Chinese Wall is rarely completely effective in practice.

24. Channel 8 read a retraction, exactly as dictated by lawyers for National City Bank, on the evening news for the following two days. The reporter who originated the story, Bob Franken, resigned in protest.

25. Congressional Study, 231.

26. Quoted in Mark Hopwood, "Why Saltzman Gave Up," Cleveland *Press*, Dec. 18, 1978.

27. This evidence is summarized in Congressional Study, 219–35.

28. In fact, on the day of default, an officer of Cleveland Trust even confirmed the newspaper reports linking Muny Light and default in conversation with Cleveland *Press* reporter Peter Phipps. See Peter Phipps, "Default Time Arrives as the Nation Watches," Cleveland *Press*, Dec. 15, 1978.

29. Copies of the letter and advertisement can be found in Congressional Study, 304–7.

30. As we have noted elsewhere, according to Ohio law, cities may borrow for capital projects using short term notes which may be renewed for up to eight successive one year periods. Cities are required to pay only interest for the first five years; after that they must begin to amortize the principal as well. At any time in the eight years, the city may convert the notes to long term bonds. This enables a city to time its entry into the bond market for the most advantageous interest rates. The Cleveland notes in question were still several years short of the five year limit.

31. Congressional Study, 235–36.

32. Mark Hopwood, "Assets of City Set at $1 Billion, Budget Balanced," Cleveland *Press*, May 12, 1981.

33. Ken Auletta, *The Streets Were Paved with Gold* (New York: Random House, 1975), 96. The official New York City figure was $3.5 billion but Auletta shows this excluded hidden expense items and unpaid pension contributions. The Cleveland estimate, by the Voinovich administration, was probably somewhat high. The state of Ohio estimated the long term deficit to be about $53 million in 1981.

34. See Ronald Berkman and Todd Swanstrom, "A Tale of Two Cities: Koch v. Kucinich," *Nation*, March 24, 1979, 297–99.

35. Committee on Taxation of the Greater Cleveland Growth Association, *Interim Report: City of Cleveland Finances*, Sept. 4, 1975. See also Edward P. Whelan, "Mayor Ralph J. Perk and the Politics of Decay," *Cleveland Magazine*, Sept. 1975.

36. Price Waterhouse declared the books unauditable in 1977. Cleveland

reportedly used a single-entry method of bookkeeping that predated Medici banking. In a massive study of Cleveland city finances, John F. Burke and Edric A. Weld compared the city's accounting system to a "magician's coat"—with so many pockets that no one knew where they all were. *Local Government Revenues and Expenditures: A Case Study of the City of Cleveland,* 1961–1971 (updated to 1974) (Cleveland: Cleveland Urban Observatory, 1974), 5.9.

37. This essentially involved halting the illegal use of Comprehensive Employment and Training Act (CETA) and Community Development Block Grant (CDBG) funds to subsidize the General Fund and using them instead for their federally mandated purposes, such as finding jobs for the long term unemployed and targeting improvements at low income neighborhoods.

38. The Kucinich administration was guilty of some fiscal sins, such as paying for bank notes out of city funds clearly intended for other purposes and failing to pay creditors on time. Compared to Perk administration lapses, however, these abuses were small.

39. Quoted in "Cleveland Trust Ready to Lend City More Cash," Cleveland *Daily Record,* May 3, 1979. Reprinted in Congressional Hearing, 35–36.

40. There is also evidence that the Kucinich administration was treated differently from the subsequent Voinovich administration. Shortly after the election, top bankers expressed willingness to help Voinovich, including raising bond money. Less than a year later the banks approved, without any major tax increase, a $36.2 million bond issue, at a highly favorable 8⅞ percent interest rate, that got city government out of default. See Mark Hopwood, "Business Is Ready to Aid Voinovich," Cleveland *Press,* Nov. 8, 1979; and Ronald Alsop, "Bankers in Cleveland Are Clearly Jubilant City Has New Mayor," *Wall Street Journal,* Dec. 8, 1979.

41. David Swiderski, "Kucinich to Seek Tax Reform Study," *The Sun,* March 20, 1975.

42. This was corroborated by an earlier study that concluded that local income taxes in Ohio are "slightly regressive." Seymour Sacks and William Hellmuth, Jr. *Financing Government in a Metropolitan Area: The Cleveland Experience* (New York: Free Press of Glencoe, 1961), 250. There are a number of reasons for this. There are no deductions for dependents, so a woman with five children pays the same tax on a $10,000 income as a single man. Those who itemize on their federal tax return—wealthier taxpayers—can deduct local income taxes. While corporate incomes are taxed, interest and dividend income, as well as capital gains, are not taxed. It is essentially a payroll tax. Also, state regulated corporations, such as banks and utilities, are not taxed at all. And corporations are able to shift a certain amount of their share to consumers.

43. Fred McGunagle, "Two Candidates Tax Each Other in Debate," Cleveland *Press,* Oct. 26, 1977.

44. Peter Phipps, "Only Last Weekend Did Kucinich Know," Cleveland *Press,* Dec. 15, 1978.

45. U.S. Bureau of the Census, *Journey to Work Census: Census of the Population 1960–70* (Washington, D.C.: Government Printing Office).

46. Between February 1979 and June 1980, suburban voters approved ten income tax increases. In March 1980 Cleveland retaliated by reducing its tax credit for Clevelanders working in the suburbs, creating a tax increase for them.

47. From 1974 to 1979, the vote for the income tax increase went up 111 percent in the wards Kucinich carried in 1977; it went up only 48 percent in the wards Kucinich lost.

48. David Abbott, "Mayor, Council Trade Barbs as Fiscal Drama Starts to Build," Cleveland *Plain Dealer*, Dec. 14, 1978.

49. Nancy Humphrey, George E. Peterson, and Peter Wilson, *The Future of Cleveland's Capital Plant* (Washington, D.C.: Urban Institute, 1979), 75.

50. John Judis, "Decline and Fall," *Progressive*, Jan. 1980, 38.

51. In order to free himself from dependence on the banks, Kucinich, at one point, contemplated marketing city notes in very small denominations to Cleveland residents. It soon became clear, however, that municipal bonds were attractive only to people in very high tax brackets. Alas, Kucinich, the populist, was beholden to the rich.

52. John Gelbach, Cleveland Bank Clearing House President, in a draft of a letter rejecting the city's request that the banks purchase $3.3 million in city notes, wrote: "This decision [to reject the notes] has been reached on an individual as well as on a collective basis." A subsequent private memorandum to clearing house members stated that the antitrust question had been addressed by indicating that the banks had reached their decision independently. In the final letter to Tegreene, the phrase "on a collective basis" was deleted. Congressional Study, 232.

53. *Control of Commercial Banks and Interlocks Among Financial Institutions*, staff report for the Subcommittee on Domestic Finance of the Committee on Banking and Currency, July 31, 1967, reprinted in *Commercial Banks and Their Trust Activities: Emerging Influence on the American Economy*, introduction by Adolf A. Berle (New York: Arno Press and the New York Times, 1969), 948–49.

54. *Commercial Banks and Their Trust Activities: Emerging Influence on the American Economy*, vol. I, Staff Report of the Subcommittee on Domestic Finance, Committee on Banking and Currency, July 8, 1968, reprinted in *Commercial Banks and Their Trust Activities*, 633. In his autobiography, Carl Stokes describes how Cleveland Trust successfully pressured the Ohio legislature, over the opposition of Cyrus Eaton, to allow banks to vote their own trust-held shares of stock. Stokes, 11–14.

55. Congressional Study, 196.

56. David Kotz has observed that the political consciousness of finance capital is often greater than that of other sectors, such as industrial capital, because, not being tied to any particular branch of production, it can better represent the long term interests of the entire capitalist system. *Bank Control of Large Corporations in the United States* (Berkeley and Los Angeles: University of California Press, 1978), 149.

57. Congressional Study, 195.

Chapter 8

1. Anthony Downs, "Using the Lessons of Experience to Allocate Resources in the Community Development Program," in *Housing Urban America*, ed. Jon Pynoos, Robert Schafer, and Chester Hartman (New York: Aldine, 1980), 522.

2. *United States v. Certain Lands in the City of Louisville, Jefferson County, Kentucky*, 78 Fed. 2nd 684, cited in Richard P. Nathan *et al.*, *Block Grants for Community Development* (Washington, D.C.: Department of Housing and Urban Development, Jan. 1977), 71.

3. Housing and Community Development Act of 1974, Sec. 104.

4. President Gerald R. Ford, Aug. 22, 1974.

5. Major studies of the benefits question were conducted by the Brookings Institution, the National Association of Housing and Redevelopment Officials, and HUD. For summaries of the benefits question, primarily focusing on the role of the regulations, see Dennis Keating and Richard LeGates, "Who Should Benefit from the Community Development Block Grant Program?" *The Urban Lawyer* 10, no. 4 (Fall 1978): 701, 736; Raymond A. Rosenfeld, "Who Benefits and Who Decides? The Uses of Community Development Block Grants," in *Urban Revitalization*, ed. Donald B. Rosenthal (Beverly Hills, Calif.: Sage, 1980), 211–36.

6. According to the Brookings studies, targeting to lower income persons increased during the first four years of the program but fell in the fifth. *Implementing Community Development* (prepared by Brookings Institution for HUD, n.d.), 100.

7. Office of Budget and Management, *Department of Community Development: O and M Survey No. 1* (Cleveland: Department of Community Development, April 29, 1966), 3.

8. Joseph Rice, "Allies Forbes, Kucinich Clash in Council over Public Housing," Cleveland *Plain Dealer*, Feb. 4, 1975.

9. Joseph Rice, "Race Still Political Force Here," Cleveland *Plain Dealer*, Feb. 9, 1975.

10. Neighborhood conservation was, indeed, the dominant strategy of most cities. *Implementing Community Development*, 81–87.

11. Paul R. Dommel *et al.*, *Decentralizing Community Development* (Washington, D.C.: Department of Housing and Urban Development, June 2, 1978), 198.

12. Housing and Community Development Act of 1974, Sect. 101 (c).

13. The number of persons per dwelling unit fell from 3.0 to 2.4 percent from 1960 to 1970. Cleveland City Planning Commission, *Housing for Low- and Moderate-Income Families* (Cleveland: City Planning Commission, Jan. 1972), 2.

14. The figure was based on a survey of 3,740 households in Cleveland in 1969 and 1970, with the results extrapolated to the entire city. Cleveland City Planning Commission, *Two Percent Household Survey* (1972).

15. See Cleveland City Planning Commission, *Housing Abandonment in Cleveland* (Oct. 1972) and *Cleveland Abandonment Problem in 1973: Survey Results and Policy Issues* (May 1974).

16. Housing codes in inner cities are rarely enforced. See Comptroller General, Report to the Congress by the Comptroller General of the United States, *Enforcement of Housing Codes: How It Can Help to Achieve Nation's Housing Goals*, B. 118754 (1972); Richard Carlton, Richard Landfield, and James Token, "Enforcement of Municipal Housing Codes," *Harvard Law Review* 78 (1964–1965): 801–60; and Edward Greer, *Big Steel* (New York: Monthly Review Press, 1979), 152–60. For a discussion of the weaknesses of the legal approach to housing code enforcement in Cleveland during the Stokes administration, see Department of Community Development, Community Development and Improvement Program, *Management Study of Housing and Building Code Enforcement*, Final Report, vol. 2 (March 1970), app. A, "Legal Remedies in Code Enforcement: Problems and Alternatives."

17. Roger S. Ahlbrandt, Jr., *Flexible Code Enforcement* (Washington, D.C.: National Association of Housing and Redevelopment Officials, 1976), 23.

18. There are, of course, absentee landlords who milk ghetto properties and often housing codes can be effective against them.

19. See Chester W. Hartman, Robert P. Kessler, and Richard T. Legates, "Municipal Housing Code Enforcement and Low Income Tenants," in Pynoos, Schafer, and Hartman, 560–73.

20. A series of reports by the Cleveland City Planning Commission in the early 1970s analyzed Cleveland's housing problem along these lines. See *Housing for Low- and Moderate-Income Families*, previously cited; Cleveland City Planning Commission, *Housing Summary and Recommended Policy Statement* (June 1970); and Cleveland City Planning Commission, *Poverty and Substandard Housing: An Analysis of Residential Deterioration in Cleveland*, prepared by John Linner (March 1973).

21. Units were deemed unsuitable for rehab if they had several defects or such severe defects that the cost of the needed repairs would probably exceed the dwelling's post-rehabilitation market value. *Two Percent Household Survey* (1971).

22. The other program was the relatively small Section 312 Loan Fund.

23. *Family Housing and Characteristics for 1977* (Cleveland: Real Property Inventory for Metropolitan Cleveland, 1979).

24. A Study for the Federal Reserve Bank of Cleveland, which carefully controlled for demand and risk factors, concluded that redlining of black and racially mixed neighborhoods existed in Cleveland. Robert B. Avery and Thomas M. Buynak, "Mortgage Redlining: Some New Evidence," *Federal Reserve Bank of Cleveland: Economic Review*, Summer 1981, 18–32.

25. Interview with Norman Krumholz, Dec. 19, 1979.

26. Downs, 530. For evidence of the dispersion effects, see Donald F. Kettl, *Managing Community Development in the New Federalism* (New York: Praeger, 1980); and Jack Fyock, "The Housing and Community Development Act

of 1974: A Study of Policy Formulation, Administration, and Impact," paper delivered at the 1978 Annual Meeting of the American Political Association, New York, Aug. 31–Sept. 3, 1978.

27. A Krumholz-initiated evaluation of the 3 Percent Program demonstrated its tendency to spread the benefits: in 93 percent of the wards covered, less than 1 percent of the owner-occupied housing units were improved.

28. Cleveland's neighborhoods are classified into five stages of deterioration, including one called "incipient decline," in Susan Olson and M. Leanne Lachman, *Tax Delinquency in the Inner City* (Lexington, Mass.: Lexington Books, 1976), chap. 4.

29. In 1977, amendments to the act added a second allocation formula intended to target physical development needs as well as poverty, including new factors such as age of housing and growth lag with the suburbs. The net effect was to steer more benefits to the older distressed cities of the Northeast, like Cleveland. See Paul Dommel, chap. 2.

30. For a basic description of increased targeting of CDBG expenditures under the Kucinich administration, see the third Brookings report: Paul R. Dommel *et al.*, *Targeting Community Development* (Washington, D.C.: Government Printing Office, Jan. 1980), 144.

31. Working as a planner for the Department of Community Development, I co-authored an evaluation of the program: *The Division of Housing: An Evaluation of Block Grant–Funded Activities* (Cleveland: Community Development, Monitoring and Evaluation, July 7, 1980).

32. Figures calculated from the beginning of CASH through November 1980 indicated an even lower leverage ratio, with only about 12 cents of private funds generated for each dollar of public funds.

33. U.S. Department of Housing and Urban Development, Community Planning and Development, Office of Evaluation, *Community Development Block Grant Program*, Second Annual Report (Washington, D.C.: HUD, Dec. 1976), 51. For further discussion of leveraging, that reported a median leverage ratio of 2.5 to 1, see Richard P. Nathan *et al.*, *Block Grants for Community Development* (Washington, D.C.: Government Printing Office, Jan. 1977), 333–62.

34. *Residential Investment and Sales: Indicators of Change, Cuyahoga County, Ohio, 1977–1979* (Cleveland: Northeast Ohio Areawide Coordinating Agency, Jan. 1981), figure D.

35. *The Housing Market in Cuyahoga County, Ohio: Sales, Price Appreciation, Market Potential* (Cleveland: Northeast Ohio Areawide Coordinating Agency, Feb. 1982), 20.

36. Calculated using data supplied by Tom Bier, Northeast Ohio Areawide Coordinating Agency.

37. That is, in fact, the solution that the Voinovich administration has pursued with CASH. Thomas S. Andrzejewski, "City Lures Middle Class Homeowners," Cleveland *Plain Dealer*, Jan. 16, 1983.

38. In fairness, it should be pointed out that the private loans were given at a 12 percent interest rate, below market rate. Nevertheless, the foregone interest represented only a few hundred dollars per lender per year.

39. For HUD regulations on lump sum drawdowns, see *Federal Register* 44, no. 68 (April 6, 1979): 20996–97. For the CRA regulation, see 12 USC 2901 (Sec. 804).

40. In exchange for withdrawing its CRA protest, the Kucinich administration got the First Federal Savings and Loan Administration to sign an "Urban Revitalization Agreement" in May 1979, pledging increased inner city lending.

41. The HUD on-site Monitoring Review, issued January 15, 1980, contained the following statement: "The City needs to develop the management and administrative capacity of the housing rehab programs commensurate with rehabilitation's position of importance in the City's Block Grant Program." Similar problems existed in the 3 Percent Loan Program, where processing of loans from start to finish took two to three years. A confidential memo written in September 1979 called the 3 Percent Loan Program, particularly at the Central Office, "a scandal waiting to be reported," pointing to "serious and unacceptable operational problems," including a backlog of cases going back to 1976, "primitive" accounting methods, and closed out cases "despite shoddy or incomplete work."

42. According to the HUD Monitoring Report, released in January 1979, after the first of the year of the Kucinich administration, the city's 50 percent drawdown rate ranked it thirteenth out of the twenty cities in the country with a population between 400,000 and 800,000.

43. It should also be pointed out that about this time the Carter administration began enforcing CDBG regulations to pressure cities to target their expenditures.

44. Interview with Betty Grdina, Dec. 17, 1979. Grdina claimed that not only was St. Clair–Superior getting more money than ever before but that she and Kucinich had helped build the organization up in the first place.

45. Krumholz was "kicked upstairs"—back to City Planning Director, a position of much prestige but little power, especially during the Kucinich years. The Grdina name, parenthetically, was well-known on Cleveland's East Side. Anton Grdina, known as the "little father of the Slovenes," was honored by the pope and the king of Yugoslavia for his work with Slovenian immigrants. The Grdina sisters, Betty, age 23, and Tonia, age 21 (who was appointed Assistant Safety Director), with their youthfulness, strong-arm methods, and unswerving loyalty to Kucinich, became lightning rods for attacks on the Kucinich administration.

46. Peter Phipps, "Kucinich Will Shake Money Tree," Cleveland *Press*, Sept. 2, 1978.

47. Betty Grdina, "City Official Praises Its Neighborhood Achievements," Cleveland *Plain Dealer*, May 26, 1979.

48. "Expected strength" was calculated by multiplying the percentage for Kucinich at the recall times the total vote for mayor in November 1979.

49. Grdina.

50. Grdina established no direct links between the corporate elite, foundations, and the actual behavior of community groups, other than funding. If funding is the criterion of manipulability, then, clearly, the Kucinich administration was also being manipulated. See Roldo Bartimole, "'Other' Kucinich Remains Disturbing," *Point of View* 11, no. 23 (June 9, 1979). This is not to deny that foundations exert powerful constraints through their control over funding.

51. Thomas Andrzejewski, "Community Groups Fight for Home Turf," Cleveland *Plain Dealer*, Feb. 18, 1979.

52. In the *Playboy* interview (June 1979) Kucinich remarked: "The last time we had any domestic programs in this country that had a favorable impact was during Roosevelt's WPA" (108).

53. Nathan *et al.*, 410.

54. This practice was criticized by HUD as "an obstacle to the timely implementation of the City's Block Grant Program." HUD, "Monitoring Review of Cleveland's Block Grant" (Jan. 1980).

55. CDBG was not primarily designed to fund social services. In fact, the original Senate version of the bill had a provision limiting expenditures on social services (software) to 20 percent of the grant—a general guideline that HUD continued to use.

56. Grdina charged that there was an important difference: Forbes and his allies benefited personally from corrupt social service contracts. There is evidence to support her charge. In one case, Black Unity House, the director, General Shabazz, held three jobs at once funded by the federal government. Shabazz stated that Forbes gave Black Unity $1,300 in cash between 1975 and 1978.

57. The preference of the poor and minorities for social services over public works is confirmed in the literature. Bernard J. Friedan, "Urban Aid Comes Full Cycle," *Civil Rights Digest*, Spring 1977, 17; Fyock, 18; and Donald Kettl, "Capacity and Vision: The Local Role in the Federal Systems," paper delivered at the 1978 Annual Meeting of the American Political Science Association.

58. Pluralists argue that politics and administration are not, in fact, separate; legislators and interest groups have direct links to the bureaucracy to influence administration. Two influential pluralist studies of this phenomenon at the national level are Harold Seidman, *Politics, Position and Power* (New York: Oxford University Press, 1970); and Richard E. Neustadt, *Presidential Power* (New York: John Wiley and Sons, 1960).

59. It should be pointed out that in Cleveland, although the block grant was broadly redistributive, there was a tendency for the pluralist process to spread the benefits instead of concentrating them on the poor.

60. Cleveland voters approved four year terms for mayor and council on November 4, 1980.

61. The tendency for the block grant to become the object of unstructured

bargaining among narrow interests is well established in the literature. See Kettl, "Capacity and Vision" and *Managing Community Developments*; Dommel, *Decentralizing Urban Policy*, esp. 240–41; and Fyock.

62. For the tendency of the block grant to mobilize neighborhood groups, see Victor Bach, "The New Federalism in Community Development," *Social Policy* (Jan.-Feb. 1977), 37; Kettl, *Managing Community Development*, 17; Nathan, 462–64; and Kettl, *Implementing Community Development*, 56–57.

Chapter 9

1. Quoted in Edward Schumaker, "Mayor Kucinich Himself Is Issue in Upcoming Cleveland Primary," *New York Times*, Aug. 26, 1979.

2. Quoted in Walt Bogdanich, "Mayor Accuses Rival on Funding," Cleveland *Press*, Sept. 21, 1979.

3. Kucinich denied that the leaflets were written by his top aides and later even denied knowledge of the leaflets altogether. I, however, saw the leaflets originate from Kucinich campaign headquarters.

4. Estelle Zannes, *Checkmate in Cleveland* (Cleveland: Case Western Reserve University Press, 1972), 45; see also 203–5.

5. Interview with Dennis Kucinich from the *CED News*, Feb. 1979, reprinted in *The Battle of Cleveland*, ed. Dan Marschall (Washington, D.C.: Conference on Alternative State and Local Public Policies, 1979), 40.

6. For a succinct account of the U.S. role in destabilizing the Allende regime, see North American Congress on Latin America, "U.S. Counter Revolutionary Apparatus: The Chilean Offensive," *Latin America and Empire Report* 8, no .6 (July–Aug. 1974).

7. Dennis Kucinich, "Stokes-Stanton Feud: A Study of Reportorial Notes in the Escalation of Urban Political Conflict," master's thesis, Department of Speech Communications, Case Western Reserve University, Aug. 1973.

8. Interview with Bob Weissman, Nov. 29, 1979.

9. Earlier, Voinovich had switched his own home from Muny Light to CEI and he had failed to take a stand on the Muny Light referendum the previous February.

10. Speech by Voinovich at Cleveland State University, Oct. 31, 1979.

11. Quoted in Joseph Wagner, "Mayor's Foes Plot His Defeat," Cleveland *Plain Dealer*, Sept. 15, 1979.

12. Dennis Kucinich, speech on urban populism, reprinted in Cleveland *Press*, Oct. 3, 1978.

13. Wards over 75 percent black were classified black; wards over 75 percent white were classified white. The fact that thirty-one of thirty-three wards fell in the segregated ends of the spectrum gives the reader an idea of the pattern of residential segregation in Cleveland.

14. Further evidence of the shift was that the correlation of the percentage of the vote for Kucinich and average home value by ward went from +.214 in 1977, indicating a mild positive relationship, to −.581, indicating a stronger negative relationship—as home values went down, support for Kucinich went up.

15. The ten wards with the highest average housing values were classified middle income; those with the lowest average home values were considered low income. The middle income wards all bordered on the suburbs; none of the low income wards did.

16. Walter Dean Burnham uses auto-correlations to examine the phenomenon of critical realignment. *Critical Elections and the Mainsprings of American Politics* (New York: W. W. Norton, 1970). Of course, caution must be exercised in drawing inferences about individual behavior from area voting statistics. For a helpful discussion of this problem, see William S. Robinson, "Ecological Correlations and the Behavior of Individuals," *American Sociological Review* 40 (1950): 351–57.

Chapter 10

1. A representative sample of the popular literature on the "new urban renaissance" would include: Horace Sutton, "America Falls in Love with Its Cities—Again," *Saturday Review*, Aug. 1978, 16–21; T. D. Allman, "The Urban Crisis Leaves Town (and Moves to the Suburbs)," *Harpers*, Dec. 1978, 41–56; "A City Revival?," *Newsweek*, Jan. 15, 1979, 28–35; Frederick C. Dlein, "Big Old Cities of East, Midwest Are Reviving after Years of Decline," *Wall Street Journal*, May 17, 1980; and "The North Fights Back," *U.S. News and World Report*, June 15, 1981, 27–30.

2. Recent scholarly work debunks the myth of an "urban renaissance." See George Sternlieb and Kristina Ford, "The Future of the Return-to-the-City Movement," in *Revitalizing Cities*, ed. Herrington J. Bryce (Lexington, Mass.: D.C. Heath, 1979), 77–104; Larry H. Long and Donald C. Dahmann, "The City-Suburb Income Gap: Is It Being Narrowed by a Back-to-the-City Movement?" *Bureau of the Census*, March 1980; James W. Fossett and Richard P. Nathan, "The Prospects for Urban Revival," in *Urban Government Finances in the 1980's*, ed. Roy Bahl (Beverly Hills, Calif.: Sage Publications, 1981); Katherine L. Bradbury, Anthony Downs, and Kenneth A. Small, *Urban Decline and the Future of American Cities* (Washington, D.C.: Brookings Institution, 1982).

3. See the article by Chicago's new commissioner of economic development, Robert Mier, "Job Generation as a Road to Recovery," in *Rebuilding America's Cities: Roads to Recovery*, ed. Paul R. Porter and David C. Sweet (New Brunswick, N.J.: Rutgers University, Center for Urban Policy Research, 1984), 160–72.

4. Robert Dahl, *Who Governs?* (New Haven, Conn.: Yale University Press, 1961), 311.

5. Katherine L. Bradbury, Anthony Downs, and Kenneth A. Small, *Urban Decline and the Future of American Cities* (Washington, D.C.: Brookings Institution, 1982), 237.

6. *Role of Commercial Banks in the Financing of the Debt of the City of Cleveland*, hearing before the Subcommittee on Financial Institutions Supervision, Regulation and Insurance of the Committee on Banking, Finance and Urban Affairs, House of Representatives, 96th Cong., 1st Sess., July 10, 1979 (Washington, D.C.: Government Printing Office, 1980); and *The Role of Commercial Banks in the Finances of the City of Cleveland*, staff study by the Subcommittee on Financial Institutions of the Committee on Banking, Finance and Urban Affairs, U.S. House of Representatives (Washington, D.C.: Government Printing Office, 1979).

7. For structural accounts of the fiscal crisis see William J. Baumol, "Macroeconomics of Unbalanced Growth: The Anatomy of Urban Crisis," *American Economic Review* 77, no. 3 (June 1967): 415–26; James O'Connor, *The Fiscal Crisis of the State* (New York: St. Martin's Press, 1973); and George E. Peterson, "Finance," in *The Urban Predicament*, ed. William Gorham and Nathan Glazer (Washington, D.C.: Urban Institute, 1976), 35–118

8. John Logan, "Growth, Politics and the Stratification of Places," *American Journal of Sociology* 84 (1976): 404–16.

9. For an analysis of the European experience, see James L. Sundquist, *Dispersing Population: What America Can Learn from Europe* (Washington, D.C.: Brookings Institution, 1975).

10. Thomas H. Boast, "A Political Economy of Urban Capital Finance in the United States," Ph.D. diss., Cornell University, 1977, 114.

11. International Union of Local Authorities, *Municipal Credit Banks* (The Hague, Netherlands: International Union of Local Authorities, 1963); G. W. Jones, "Local Government Finance in Great Britain," in *Local Government in Britain and France*, ed. Jacques Lagroye and Vincent Wright (London: George Allen and Unwin, 1979), 172; Arnold J. Heidenheimer, Hugh Heclo, and Carolyn Teich Adams, *Comparative Public Policy*, 2d ed. (New York: St. Martin's Press, 1983), 290–91; and Alberta Sbragia, "Cities, Capital, and Banks: The Politics of Debt in the United States, United Kingdom, and France," in *Urban Political Economy*, ed. Kenneth Newton (London: Frances Pinter, 1981), 200–20.

12. See "Special Report: State and Local Governments in Trouble," *Business Week*, Oct. 26, 1981; James W. Fossett and Richard P. Nathan, "The Prospect for Urban Revival," in *Urban Government Finance*, ed. Roy Bahl (Beverly Hills, Calif.: Sage Publications, 1981); United States Congress, *Trends in the Fiscal Condition of Cities: 1981–1983*, staff study prepared for the use of the Joint Economic Committee (Washington, D.C.: Government Printing Office, 1983).

13. The National City abatement of approximately $9 million supposedly leveraged a $59 million office tower, a leverage ratio of 6.6 to 1. However, the "present value" of the abatement was considerably less, and hence the leverage ratio was even higher, since the subsidy was paid out over a twenty year period.

14. Industrial Revenue Bonds (IRBs), as another example, enable local agencies to hand out tax free borrowing privileges to private developers. Since the subsidy comes from the federal government, there is little motivation to scrutinize the projects carefully. While there is no firm evidence that the reduced interest rates bring about economic activity that would not otherwise have occurred, they continue to be used for such dubious forms of economic development as racquetball clubs and fast food chains. Congress has cut back on the program but has not yet seen fit to kill it.

15. *Code of Federal Regulations*, Title 24, chap. V (Washington, D.C.: Government Printing Office, April 1978), 570.457.

16. David Cordish, "Overview of UDAG," *The Urban Development Action Grant Program*, ed. Richard P. Nathan and Jerry A. Webman (Princeton, N.J.: Princeton Urban and Regional Research Center, 1980), 9. In order to make it appear that neighborhoods were getting their fair share of the funds, the category "neighborhood projects" had to be stretched to the point of absurdity in reports to Congress.

17. Mier, 168.

18. The general policy direction recommended here is similar to sensible recommendations made by Rolf Goetze for dealing with the problems of gentrification, an offshoot of the expanding service sector. Among other things, Goetze recommends spreading housing demand around to weaker neighborhoods and taxing windfalls in housing appreciation. *Understanding Neighborhood Change* (Cambridge, Mass.: Ballinger, 1979).

19. Joel Werth, "Tapping Developers," *Planning*, Jan. 1984, 22.

20. For discussions of Hartford under Carbone, see Harry C. Boyte, *The Backyard Revolution: Understanding the New Citizen Movement* (Philadelphia: Temple University Press, 1980), chap. 6; Eva Bach, Nicholas R. Carbone, and Pierre Clavel, "Running the City for the People," *Social Policy* 12, no. 3 (Winter 1982): 15–23. I also benefited from reading a manuscript by Pierre Clavel, "Progressive Planning: The Experience of Berkeley, Cleveland, and Hartford in the 1970s," Cornell University, 1982.

21. Jane Jacobs, *The Death and Life of Great American Cities* (New York: Vintage, 1961), 14.

22. This view was reflected in the social science literature on the economic requisites of democracy in the 1950s and 1960s. Perhaps the best known statement is Seymour Martin Lipset's "Economic Development and Democracy" in *Political Man* (New York: Anchor, 1959), 27–63.

23. Samuel P. Huntington, *Political Order in Changing Societies* (New Haven, Conn.: Yale University Press, 1968), 20–21.

24. Hadley Arkes, *The Philosopher in the City* (Princeton, N.J.: Princeton University Press, 1981), 282–83. Arkes's analysis of urban power structures is penetrating, but his preoccupation with the political power of unions in the governmental market, true as it is, completely overlooks the much greater power of corporations.

Afterword

1. Leon Harris, "Cleveland's Come-Around," *Town and Country*, Oct. 1981, 240.

2. "City needs Forbes as Head of Council," editorial, Cleveland *Press*, Nov. 13, 1981.

3. "Fatter City: Cleveland Makes a Comeback," *Time*, Dec. 29, 1980. See also Eugene H. Methvin, "Cleveland Comes Back," *Reader's Digest* (March 1983).

4. *City of Cleveland Operations Improvement Task Force Final Report*, July 1980, as reported in Stuart M. Klein, "The Business of City Management: Cleveland, 1981," *Gamut* no. 2 (Winter 1981), 3–12. Klein's article is an unusually perceptive analysis of the limits of external management reviews.

5. Katherine L. Bradbury, Anthony Downs, and Kenneth A. Small, *Urban Decline and the Future of American Cities* (Washington, D.C.: Brookings Institution, 1982), 248. For a more detailed account of the Cleveland case, see the book by the same authors, *Futures for a Declining City* (New York: Academic Press, 1981).

6. From a study by Case Western Reserve University, commissioned by the Greater Cleveland Roundtable, as reported in the *Wall Street Journal*, June 22, 1984.

7. Mayor Voinovich, as quoted in Randolph Smith, "Kucinich's Anti-Bar-Mill Moves Anger Mayor," Akron *Beacon Journal*, Feb. 7, 1984.

8. George Voinovich, quoted in Roldo Bartimole, "No & No, Tax & Dome," *Point of View* 6, no. 16 (March 3, 1984): 1.

9. Quoted in Roldo Bartimole, "Voinovich Hit by Sohio," *Point of View* 15, no. 13 (Jan. 15, 1983).

10. Quoted in Gary R. Clark, "CEI Fighting Muny Legislation, Mayor Charges," Cleveland *Plain Dealer*, Feb. 26, 1982.

11. James Lawless, "Voinovich Kills Deal with CEI," Cleveland *Plain Dealer*, August 4, 1984.

12. Thomas W. Gerdel, "Shamrock Trims Offices," Cleveland *Plain Dealer*, Jan. 6, 1984.

13. Gary R. Clark, "Mayor Blames Kucinich for City's Credit Rating," Cleveland *Plain Dealer*, July 16, 1983; Editorial, *Crain's Cleveland Business*, July 4, 1983.

14. "Empty Threats," editorial, Cleveland *Plain Dealer*, Feb. 14, 1984.

15. Quoted in Gary R. Clark, "Despite Vote, Mill Uncertain," Cleveland *Plain Dealer*, Feb. 9, 1984.

Index